PARTICULAR
Places

PARTICULAR *Places*

A Traveler's Guide to Ohio's Best Road Trips

AN ORANGE FRAZER ROADBOOK

Edited by Jane Ware

ISBN 978-1933197-449
Copyright © 2008
by Orange Frazer Press, Inc.
All Rights reserved

Published by
Orange Frazer Press, Inc.
PO Box 214
Wilmington, OH 45177
www.orangefrazer.com

Library of Congress Cataloging-in-Publication Data

Ware, Jane.
  Particular places : a traveler's guide to Ohio's best road trips / by Jane Ware.
      p. cm.
  Includes index.
  ISBN 978-1-933197-44-9 (alk. paper)
  1. Ohio--Guidebooks. 2. Automobile travel--Ohio--Guidebooks. 3. Ohio--History, Local. I. Title.
  F489.3.W37 2008
  917.7104'44--dc22

                                        2008006684

Contents

Introduction

This book is a guide to fifteen places in Ohio, all of them smaller towns and scenic areas. They appeared in the original two volumes of *Particular Places*, published in 1990 and 1993. They were the work of six different writers, (not including this editor.) Each had a particular style, which accounts for some of the variations and charms, I believe, of the book.

For each place, we have looked for truly distinctive and locally particular places to stay, eat and see, along with good local characters to hear about and sometimes meet. To me, the biggest change since 1990 is the dispersal of trained chefs, who are running restaurant kitchens in out-of-the-way or otherwise unlikely places. For the traveler, traveling has become more rewarding than ever in the gastronomical dimension.

Rates cited for bed and breakfasts are rooms for two including breakfast. All rates—including places to stay, admission charges and restaurants—are in 2007 dollars.

This editor had help from several writers: Adrienne Bosworth did one chapter; Sherry Beck Paprocki, with help from Liz Sommer, did another; and Suzanne Hartford did two. My profound thanks to them.

Many others, not mentioned in the text, helped with particular chapters. Special thanks to Rick Byron, Judy Lewis, and Marilyn Ortt. And thanks to my husband, Brendan, who walked with me in Adams County, at Fort Ancient, and along the banks of the Maumee.

What a person can see and do in just fifteen Ohio places is astounding. It's possible to eat raccoon and to make your own golf club; to meet a horse rescuer and to see the country's biggest horse-and-carriage parade; to see a Stealth bomber and the world's only perambulator museum. You can go to a washboard music festival or a sternwheeler festival; you can eat a Gold Rush apple grown by a retired rocket scientist or meet a retired doctor who's been elected mayor. You can see hundreds of historic lunchboxes, the world's largest Doric column, and the world's only floating cranberry bog. You can meet a baker who was once a Parisian fashion model, or a Sicilian chef who converted a Dairy Queen into a Italian restaurant.

Thanks to these people, these events and phenomena. They are making Ohio a better place to travel.

—Jane Ware

PARTICULAR
Places

Granville

The Lafayette Hotel

Marietta

Marietta wears the garments of its heritage very well, thank you. The first town in the Northwest Territory is a *living* town, livelier than most, in fact, given its size and geographic isolation.

Ironically Marietta has been preserved by the very factors that kept it from being the next Paris (or New York or London or Edinburgh). First, it was hard to reach except via flatboat (a notoriously rugged method of travel) and the Northwest Territory was both huge and comprehensive: no one ever had to go through Marietta to get somewhere else: he just crossed an imaginary line somewhere upstream. So Marietta is a tiny town at the confluence of the Muskingum and Ohio Rivers that celebrated its boom years with dignity and grace, and now celebrates its past in much the same way.

Take, for example, the architecture, always a good key to understanding a town. The houses that line the streets between the Campus Martius Museum and the downtown are stately and some are textbook

Steamboat Gothic, which one might expect in a river town: the grandest residences look as though they're about to toot a whistle and cast off lines at any moment. That they exist today and serve largely as *homes* suggests something profound about a town that bears its history comfortably. Marietta looks like a place where people enjoy living, and all of its accoutrements (and many of its entrepreneurs) support this fact. It is a clever little place that very quickly begins to feel like home.

"No colony in America was ever settled under such favorable auspices as that which has just commenced at the Muskingum. I know many of the settlers personally . . . If I was a young man, just preparing to begin the world, or if advanced in life and had a family to make a provision for, I know of no country where I should rather fix my habitation . . ."
—*George Washington, 1788*

THE LAFAYETTE HOTEL—The records of this famous establishment relate how, in 1918, S. Durward Hoag helped his dad unpack the furniture that came upriver from Cincinnati and move it into a hotel built on the landing site of, and named for, a French hero of the American Revolution. After all that time, one of the last grand riverboat-era hotels still maintains a busy trade at the town's active and lovely portside. Many of its 77 rooms have a view of the Ohio, the Muskingum, or both. The ground floor has a mixture of Victorian and nautical décor that blends well with a mother–hen staff that treats you like family. They've even been known to detect a weary traveler and suggest a cool drink and a nap before heading out to see the town. The Lafayette is busiest during the Sternwheeler Festival in September; people spend 15 to 20 years on the waiting list for a room.
101 Front Street; 740/373-5522; www.lafayettehotel.com Rooms range from $55 to $180.

THE GUN ROOM is the hotel's restaurant, designed to look like a riverboat, with tablecloths and Colonial décor. They serve three meals a day, starting with a really good breakfast.
Address, phone and web site same as the hotel's. Mon-Sat 6:30-2, Sun 7:30 am-9 pm, Mon-Thur 5-9, Fri-Sat 5-10. Dinner entrées range from $14 to $27.

THE COTTAGE ON WASHINGTON STREET—Charlotte Furbee moved from Columbus back to her hometown of Marietta in 2002, and she soon became a Trolley guide and opened a B&B. The latter is small but very convenient and very attractive, both inside and out. She rents as a unit two rooms and a bath on the second floor of her house—the two rooms are a bedroom and a sitting room with a convertible, suitable for a single person, so altogether three can sleep comfortably. Also, guests may use a private enclosed garage.
406 Washington Street; 740/374-4439; www.mariettaohio.org and click on bed and breakfasts. Suite is $80, including full breakfast. Cash or check only.

HOUSE ON HARMAR HILL—This splendid Victorian

has a glorious site overlooking Marietta. The house has exceptional architectural detailing, and it would be hard to surpass the careful restoration that owners Doug and Judy Grize have undertaken. The B&B has four spacious bedrooms; if the house is full, the two baths at the back and the full bath on the first floor may have to be shared, but the Grizes provide robes so that everyone can scoot about properly garbed. There's a full breakfast too. One of the treats of the House on Harmar Hill is Doug Grize giving a tour, for furnishings are trophies of the Grizes' world travels while he was in the Air Force. You'll see an Edison phonograph, a Chinese medicine chest, and Indonesian dolls. The Grizes occupy the vast, high-ceilinged third floor, fully paneled with tongue-and-groove poplar.

300 Bellevue Street; 866/374-5451 or 740/374-5451; www.mariettaohio.org and click on bed and breakfasts. Rates for two: $95 king; $90 queen; $85 double. Singles less.

LEVEE HOUSE CAFÉ—This carefully restored and meticulously

decorated restaurant occupies the only surviving Ohio River riverfront structure in Marietta. When Harley Noland bought the building, it was in a dramatic state of disrepair, lacking, among other things, ceilings, floors and roof. He stared up at the stars for a moment (he was in the cellar at the time) and then got to work. What he wrought is one of the prettiest places to dine on the river. The front diningroom (once an auto repair shop) has floor-to-ceiling windows looking out on the Ohio River. In the yard he planted an herb garden; on the porch he installed tables for dining in the evening air; and in the kitchen he installed a chef who changes the menu seasonally and who cooks every single dish (from Russian chicken to pasta puttenesca) to order herself. Desserts and breads are baked daily here as well.

127 Ohio Street; 740/374-2233. Weekdays 11:30-9:30; Sat 11:30-10. Lunches are less than $6, dinners $10-20.

BETSEY MILLS CLUB—Betsey Mills, the woman, led her sewing

club into the thickets of social work, and Betsey Mills, the club, is the result: Betsey and her cohorts sought to provide a "healthy" place for young women, an alternative to the old boarding houses of riverboat-wild Marietta, where a young girl might fall in with the wrong sort of people—that is, men from the riverboats. The Betsey Mills is *still* a place where single women who are living alone and are over 18 may occupy one of 15 rooms (sharing baths, kitchen and living areas.) The "newer" parts of the club were built in the 1920s by Betsey's husband as a memorial to her; the older parts of the complex include the birthplace of Charles Dawes, Coolidge's Vice President and a Nobel laureate (he negotiated the war debts plan after World War I.) The main business of the building today is day care and preschool serving 100 families.

300 Fourth Street at Putnam; 740/373-4981; www.betseymills.org

Betsey Mills Club

BLACKSMITH BARBECUE—The restaurant at Betsey Mills, Blacksmith Barbecue, started out by winning the top prize for ribs in the all-Ohio Smoked Food tourney; its brisket came in third. Proprietor and chef Kevin Black is a Culinary Institute of America graduate who spent 15 years in some of Columbus's better restaurant kitchens; he's returned to Marietta because he grew up near here, in Beverly. Dinners include a half rack of ribs with sides for $15 and grills, such as steak or salmon. Among sandwiches is slow-smoked brisket with sauces on the side for $8; smoked wings are an appetizer for $8. No license but patrons can bring their own.
300 Fourth Street; 740/236-1561; www.blacksmithbarbecue.com Mon-Tue 11:30-3; Wed-Sat 11:30-8. Outdoor patio in warm weather.

MARIETTA RESTAURANTS—Since 2001 **Austyn's** has been offering an eclectic menu including not only salmon and New York strip, but also Thai dishes and Mongolian beef tossed in a wok with vegetables and hoisin soy sauce. *130 Front Street; 740/374-8188; www.austyns.com Mon-Thurs 11-9:30; Fri-Sat 11-10; Sun 11-9. Dinner $12-21.* **Tampico** is a Mexican restaurant with, one Mariettan says, "lightning service and delicious margaritas." Favorite dishes include fajita-style chimichangas and spinach quesadilla. *221 Second Street; 740/374-8623. Mon-Thur 11-10; Fri 11-10:30; Sat 11:30-10:30; Sun 11:30-9. Dinners $7-$15.* **Brighter Day Restaurant** specializes in natural foods with a good vegetarian selection (Mayan pita, with more vegetables than you can count, $6), signature salads (Greek, Rice, Tabouli, $2.50 or $9 by the pound), hot roast beef with salad and roll, $8.75. There are daily entrée specials (ham loaf on Wednesday) and bakery specials (blackberry pie on Tuesday). *211 Second Street; 740/374-2429. Lunch Mon-Sat 11-3; dinner Tue–Sat from 5.* The interior of **Marietta Brewing Company** is wonderful: the high brick walls have been painted with oversized posters, one depicting in black and white, a group of long-ago brewers. The pale ale and raspberry wheat beers have won prizes; the scotch ale took a best of show. If beer isn't your thing, they brew root beer too. Full menu for lunch (Texas club, $8, pepper-jack burger, $8) and dinner (beef tips or beer-battered shrimp, $11) and live entertainment Wed-Sat 10-2. *167 Front Street; 740/373-2739; www.mariettabrewingcompany.com Open daily 11; dinner until 10.*

ASIDE—When the Marquis de Lafayette made his triumphant tour of the U.S. in 1825, he visited Marietta. Actually the aging French hero of the American Revolution stopped overnight, probably to see his old comrades from the battles of Brandywine and Yorktown. The founders of this town were no rude trappers or rough pioneers, but educated, eminently civilized New Englanders. They were Revolutionary War veterans and friends of Washington, men rich with the ideals of liberty who went home to find their postwar prospects poor. When the Northwest Ordinance of 1787 opened up settlement in the land beyond the Alleghenies, they traded their Continental Army IOUs for 1.5 million acres of Ohio wilderness and headed down the Ohio River on a flatboat to the mouth of the Muskingum River, where they stayed. Like good soldiers they initially left their women and children safe at home (their dependents joined them, but four months later), while they faced the uncertainties of Indians and dark forests. As a nod to the part France played in the Revolution's success, they named their settlement for its Queen, Marie Antoinette. Though squatters and soldiers had gone into Ohio earlier, Marietta was the first permanent *American* settlement in the Northwest Territory; what happened in Marietta would set an example for all the Northwest Territory.

MARIETTA COLLEGE—This picture-postcard college was started in 1835 and has a marvelous and complicated history, but to the casual visitor it is most noteworthy that the campus is such a pleasurable place to walk. It is built on a human scale, with a minimum of parking lots and a plethora of footpaths and sidewalks; its corners are marked with inviting gates; and the red-brick, white-trimmed buildings are New England incarnate. Since it is a small college (enrollment hovers around 1300) visitors are often surprised with greetings, offers of a tour, offers of lunch, offers to see the original territorial grants and charters of the Ohio Company, which the college owns and displays intermittently (the library, where the papers repose, is being rebuilt and won't be finished before 2009.) And then there is the crew—not the cleanup crew or the wrecking crew, but the Harvard/Yale/Princeton type *crew*: healthy young men and women in pencil-thin racing shells, sculling up the Muskingum. Aficionados of crew know that the Marietta oarsmen are among the best in the nation; visitors know that they are lovely to watch. *215 Fifth Street; 740/376-7896; www.marietta.edu*

ACCESS—For a lasting perspective on Marietta go to Harmar Hill's Look Out Point, which offers the best view in town, geographically and historically. The vista, which sweeps broadly across both rivers and the town, is accompanied by an area map on a plaque—a map so detailed that even from afar you can pick out every point of interest in one of Ohio's most interesting towns.

TROLLEY TOURS INCORPORATED—Almost half the folks on this one-hour trolley tour are Mariettans with out-of-town relatives; almost the other half are the out-of-town relatives. Tourists with no familial connection get, then, two tours for the price of one: the official tour, historically interesting and downright patriotic, and the commentary from the locals in the next seat. When you pass Schafer's Leather Store (same family and location, at 140 Front Street, since the Civil War) you'll also hear that some Mariettans on the trolley are wearing Schafer's boots.

127 Ohio Street; 740/374-2233. July-Sept, daily except Mon, 10:30 and 12:30; check for more limited schedule April, May, June, Oct. Reservations strongly advised. Adults $7.50, seniors $7, 5-12 $5.

SCHAFER'S LEATHER STORE—This store has been here since 1867, but you'll find the merchandise up-to-date and attractive. There are handsome leather bags, western boots, jewelry, Tilley hats.
140-142 Front Street; 740/373-5101.

TOURING ON YOUR OWN—Do take the Trolley Tour, especially if you're pressed for time. But for a more leisurely approach, the Marietta Convention and Visitors Bureau (121 Putnam Street, Suite 110, 740/373-5178; www.mariettaohio.org), has material to help you find things on your own in city and county. Start with the CVB's principal multi-page Visitors Guide, which has a "Historic Marietta Tour" listing 58 sites in both Marietta and Harmar, the neighborhood across the Muskingum. Note that Marietta streets paralleling the Muskingum River are numbered; but the streets that parallel the Ohio bear the names of Revolutionary War generals or Marietta's Founding Fathers.

INDIAN MOUNDS—The first American arrivals found some spectacular mounds at Marietta, and left them intact. Most impressive originally was Sacra Via, two parallel embankments perpendicular to the Muskingum, probably built for ceremonial purposes. Up to 17 feet high, they were 231 feet apart and 360 feet in length, and led away from the river, sloping upward to a large rectangular mound the settlers called Quadranou. Alas, in the 1830s the Sacra Via embankments were dismantled to use the clay for bricks. Today only two streets named Sacra Via mark the site; they're off Third Street. The remains of Quadranou, also called Turtle Mound, are in a green on the other side of Third. Like many other important Ohio mounds, Marietta's were built around 2000 years ago. Sacra Via was from the earlier Hopewell Culture, while an example of a slightly later Adena mound is Conus, which is largely intact and named for its conical shape. It's in the middle of Mound Cemetery and there are stairs to its 30-foot-high summit— stairs added because climbers were wrecking the mound. Mound Cemetery, at 400 Fifth Street, has the graves of more Revolutionary War officers than any other site.

ARCHITECTURAL TOURS—The Castle (listed later in this guide) sponsors free architectural tours of its interesting neighborhood June-Aug on Saturdays at 10:30. They last one or two hours, depending, a docent says, on how many questions people ask.

COVERED BRIDGES—Much of rural Washington County feels very wild and remote. If you're not up to back-country hiking, one of the best ways to see back country from your car is to take the Covered Bridge tour. The county has nine of these bridges, mostly original. The CVB has a flyer listing them, with pictures of some and the locations of all, and the Visitors Guide has a map.

ASIDE— "The official line is that Marietta was the first organized settlement in the Northwest Territory. This takes some squinting at the facts to blot out the Americans at Fort Harmar, the British at Detroit, the French at Vincennes, and the many Indian towns dotting the territory. If you narrow the claim to Marietta's being the first permanent white American settlement organized in the Northwest Territory, you come closer to the mark. If they weren't leaping ashore into uncharted wilderness, Rufus Putnam and his followers did accomplish something historic. They brought ordinary life to the West. Marietta was the first test of the Ordinance of 1787 that set out the legal and civic structure of all the new territories to come. The Marietta pioneers brought lawsuits, taxes, politics, and schools to the heartland." —John Fleischman

BLENNERHASSETT ISLAND—Harman Blennerhassett will

forever be linked with the fortunes and deeds of Aaron Burr, but to what degree is something that historians still cudgel each other over: was it treason? Was Harman a participant or a dupe in what may or may not have been Burr's plan to separate the states of the Northwest Territory from the rest of the country? In its day Blennerhassett Island was a place where the rich and famous of the day stopped for a bit of culture in a harsh wilderness, but the Blennerhassetts left in 1806 and in 1811 the house burned down (some say accidentally, some say "mysteriously"). A nice reconstruction of the manse has been built on the island. Except for three maintenance vehicles there are no cars on the 500-acre island, but there are guided house tours, bicycles, a two-mile foot trail, and a horse-and-wagon tour. Blennerhassett, a West Virginia State Park, is accessible by a sternwheeler that leaves Parkersburg's Point Park hourly all day in summer; the trip takes 20 minutes. A museum is two blocks from where the boat leaves.

137 Juliana Street, Parkersburg; 304/428-1130, 800/CALL WVA; www. blennerhassettislandstatepark.com Boats June-Labor Day Tue-Fri 11-5:30, Sun noon-5:30. Less frequent times May and Sept-Oct. Island closed Nov to mid-March; museum open some hours all year. Museum adults $2, 3-12 $1; boat trip adults $8, 3-12 $7; mansion adults $3, 3-12 $2; wagon ride adults $5, 3-12 $3.

ASIDE Marietta's lively riverfront life centers around the levee on the Ohio River, and activity there peaks in September on the weekend after Labor Day, when 30 or so sternwheeler riverboats—and a hundred thousand people—come to town for the annual Sternwheeler Festival. The boats, all shiny paint, tall stacks and white gingerbread trim, waltz down the Ohio like the stately ladies that they are and moor at Marietta, tooting their own horns and announcing themselves with bright bursts of calliope music. For a few glorious days all of Marietta assumes the finest fettle, paying homage to the guest flotilla with entertainment and fireworks on Saturday night. On Sunday morning, they even accommodate the crowd with church services on the levee, a prelude to the afternoon's main event: high-spirited sternwheeler races down the Ohio, which acknowledge the importance of both time and the river in Marietta.

BIRD WATCHER'S DIGEST—In the 1970s Elsa and Bill

Thompson had a shop selling bird books and the merchandise of birding. Then it occurred to them that there was a market for a bird-watchers' magazine, so in September 1978 they launched one that has become the ornithological bible, *Bird Watcher's Digest*. Before long it displaced the shop, and in the mid 1990s Elsa and Bill themselves moved aside for their sons, Bill III, who is editor, and Andy, publisher. (Word has it that Elsa still shows up for work, but Bill is *retired*.) The editorial toilers are happy to see bird enthusiasts drop in.

149 Acme Street; 800/879-2473 or 740/373-5285; www.birdwatchersdigest.com Mon-Fri 8-5.

MARIETTA NATURAL HISTORY SOCIETY—Partly

because of the *Bird Watcher's Digest's* presence, partly because of the college, and partly because of a critical mass of environmentally aware citizens, Marietta has its own natural history society. Founded in the early 1990s, the society publishes quarterly newsletters and offers free monthly programs (sample topics: bluebirds, predators in nature, fireflies), sponsors bird and nature walks, and provides information on local flora and fauna.

For information check the website: www.marietta.edu/~biol/mnhs/mnhs.html

MARIETTA FABRICATORS:

ROSSI PASTA—Mike and John Rossi started this business in an Athens basement in 1981; volume necessitated the move to Marietta, where they now occupy a brick and stucco building not far from the river. Their product, made from a custom-milled flour, has been featured everywhere that pasta might be featured, and plenty of places where it often might not—Neiman Marcus, for example. The core of the business are pastas flavored with peppers and olives, herbs and spices, vegetables from tomato to zucchini.

106 Front Street; 800/227-6774; www.rossipasta.com Mon-Fri 9-7 (closing at 6 in winter); Sat 9-7; Sun 11-5.

SEWAH STUDIOS—Since its founding in 1927 this small company has produced close to a hundred thousand cast aluminum historical markers, with examples found now in every state. Today the company makes 70 percent of all those produced in America, and ships to an average of 35 different states a year. Signs are cast, letters and all, in a special sand mold—the pouring of molten aluminum is an exciting thing to watch.

190 Millcreek Road; 888/557-3924 or 740/373-2087; www.sewahstudios.com Free tours available but call ahead to schedule.

FENTON ART GLASS/WILLIAMSTOWN, WEST

VIRGINIA—Fenton is one of the last factories in the nation making hand-blown and painted glass. These artisans produce richly detailed designs, and you can not only see them at work, but also purchase both current and retired items, as well as "preferred seconds" at the gift shop.

420 Caroline Avenue, Williamstown, WV; 304/375-7772; www.fentonartglass.com Take I-77 south from Marietta to the first West Virginia exit, 185, and follow the signs. Sales outlet Mon-Fri 8-5; factory tours, Mon-Fri 8:15-2:30.

THE CASTLE—Built in 1855, the Castle is a fine and imposing Gothic Revival house set up on a hill. It's brick and stone, has a crenellated octagonal tower, stone topped turrets, and, luckily for us, tours. Furnishings are appropriately Victorian, and the woodwork is very interesting.

418 Fourth Street, 740/373-4180; www.mariettacastle.org One-hour tours on the hour, June-Aug 10-4 weekdays, 1-4 weekends. Apr-May and Sept-Dec Mon, Thur, Fri 10-4, weekends 1-4. Jan-March by appointment. Adults $6, seniors $5.50, 6-17 $3.

VALLEY GEM STERNWHEELER—In 1973 Jim Sands built the first *Valley Gem,* conceived on paper napkins. Sixteen years later the second *Valley Gem* came along, an improved version that still carries up to 296 passengers and has been called "the nicest and fastest sternwheeler on the river." The pilot is Jim's youngest son, Jason ("J. J.") Sands, who was a little boy when the first boat was built. Sometimes he hears people say that what he does must be boring, but to him the river is different every day. "Just today," he says, "I was piloting a lunch cruise, and I saw a deer swimming. Then when I got closer I saw it was a person, a woman." He kept an eye on her as she did a back stroke all the way to the bank, where she climbed out. He was surprised to see she was wearing jeans and boots and a red safety vest. It turned out she'd been working on the bridge overhead, and had fallen into the water.

Valley Gem boards at 601 Front Street near the Ohio River Museum. Charters year round, public tours April-October, fall foliage tours up the Muskingum. Ticket and tour information 740/373-7862; www.valleygemsternwheeler.com A 90-minute afternoon sightseeing trip is $10 for adults, $9 for seniors, 3-12 $5.

GRIMM'S GREENACRES—A friend in Marietta claimed that an orchard there was producing the best apples she'd ever tasted, and sent us a bagful for testing. She was right. Grimm's Gold Rush is not a big or handsome apple—it's brownish yellow with a pink blush—but it's very crisp and very good eating. Kate and Andy Grimm have made this orchard their "retirement" project—he was an Air Force rocket scientist and a teacher; she, a nurse with an ultimately relevant major in horticulture. They started this project in 1998 with a mission in mind, as Kate says: "We wanted people to get excited about apples again." Over seven years, they planted 1000 trees a year in 20 varieties, using high-density planting techniques developed in New Zealand and Australia. The trees are all dwarfs, which means only 10-12 feet tall, and have to be supported on wire trellises that the Grimms rigged up (explains Andy, "A two-inch trunk can't support 50 to 60 pounds of apples.") In 2007 spring frosts destroyed their crop, but as such a frost was reputed to be a "once-in-a-lifetime" event, the Grimms had high hopes for 2008 and beyond. "People," Kate says, "are amazed by the taste."

5680 State Route 26 (5.6 miles east of the Marietta city line); call to check harvest times, 740/376-9170. Apple orchard; cider; you-pick or buy pre-picked.

OUTDOOR BYWAYS: WAYNE NATIONAL FOREST—

Hikers are a varied lot, and therefore one man's vista is another man's vacancy. Thus the folks that oversee the 64,600 acres of the forest's

Marietta unit (Wayne National is in three separate parcels) provide varied trails. Archers Fork Loop is one that's long (nine-and-a-half miles) and offers maximum panorama and adversity, climbing from valley bottoms to 1,200-foot ridge lines. There's a cave and a natural bridge along the way, and you won't run into a lot of company.
The ranger office is three-and-a-half miles upriver from Marietta on State Route 7, across from the State Highway Patrol Office. 740/373-9055; www.fs.fed.us/r9/ wayne Mon-Fri 8-4:30, year round.

KRISMAR WOODS—The City of Marietta owns this 23-acre mature woodland which offers a mile-long trail and tall trees. There is a small parking area at trailhead at 213 Hillcrest Drive.

KROGER WETLAND—Kroger Wetland is still under development, so sponsors describe it has a "young floodplain forest community." At 21 acres in late 2007, Kroger Wetland has a flat half-mile trail, and another is planned.
80 Acme Street. A kiosk in the parking area has information on wildlife at the site.

CAMPUS MARTIUS MUSEUM—Whatever possessed 50-year-old Rufus Putnam to leave the civilized delights of Massachusetts and go to a howling Ohio wilderness ultimately rendered him the Founding Father of Marietta, a distinction that in 1888 inspired a successful grassroots campaign to preserve, protect, and defend his home from the wrecking ball. Today the Rufus Putnam House and another Marietta original, the Ohio Company Land Office, are the featured attractions at this museum built on the site of the Campus Martius, which was a fortified complex of attached houses that Putnam designed to preserve, protect and defend the first Mariettans from the Indians. A millwright by trade, Putnam got a crash course in military engineering during the Revolution when Washington buttonholed him to defend Boston's Dorchester Heights. Borrowing a French book on fortifications, Putnam learned how to build a barrier of felled and pointed trees, a technique he remembered when he got to Ohio. The old boy knew what he was doing; the Indians never attacked Campus Martius, which is a primary reason why the museum today can boast such a fine collection of the settlers' furnishings and tools.
601 Second Street (at Washington Street); 740/373-3750; www.ohiohistory. org/places/campus Open March-Oct Wed-Sat 9:30-5; Sun and holidays, noon-5. Closed Nov-Feb (except by appointment).

DIRECTOR'S FAVORITES

1. Rufus Putnam House, the only structure remaining from the original Campus Martius.
2. Ohio Company Land Office, 1788, the oldest frame building west of the Alleghenys, moved to this site
3. The land model depicting Marietta in the 1780s, as seen by the first settlers.
4. A silver spoon made by Paul Revere.
5. Artifacts belonging to the Blennerhassett family, especially Har man, who was not the best of investors and truly lost a fortune.—Andy Verhoff, Campus Martius Museum

OHIO RIVER MUSEUM—The Ohio River Museum is three buildings anchored on piers next to the Muskingum River. That's a big improvement for the Sons & Daughters of the Pioneer Rivermen, who began this museum in 1941 in a landlocked basement corner of the Campus Martius Museum. As their collection of riverboat memorabilia grew, so did the exhibit's concept, evolving into the award-winning architecture of today's museum, opened in 1974. Dedicated to preserving the nation's river and steamboat heritage, the Sons & Daughters have provided much of this collection, including the 22-foot model of a circa 1900 steamboat that's authentic down to the doorknobs. Children especially like the "hands-on" exhibits, but the real crowd-pleaser is the school of carp that takes up summer residence beside the towboat *W.P. Snyder, Jr.,* in order to feed on bread that visitors cast on the waters. Museum director Andy Verhoff says the carp—like the swallows at Capistrano or the buzzards of Hinkley, Ohio—are so fond of the locale that every April 15, they faithfully return.
601 Front Street; 740/373-3717; www.ohiohistory.org/places/ohriver Open weekends Memorial Day through October, Sat 9:30-5, Sun noon-5; open holidays. Self-guided; continuous guided tours of the W.P. Snyder. *Closed Nov-May; tours by appointment.*

DIRECTOR'S FAVORITES:

1. *W. P. Snyder, Jr.,* the museum's jewel, is the nation's last remaining pool-type steam-powered sternwheeler towboat.
2. The model of the 1900-era steamboat, which was painstakingly built by George Schotten of Hubbard, Ohio.
3. The Portland skiff, a fine two-seat rowboat built near Pomeroy, Ohio, in 1885.
4. The 1880s pilothouse from the steamboat *Tell City*, rescued from being used as someone's summer house.
5. The model collection, which illustrates the great variety of craft on the rivers a century ago.—Andy Verhoff

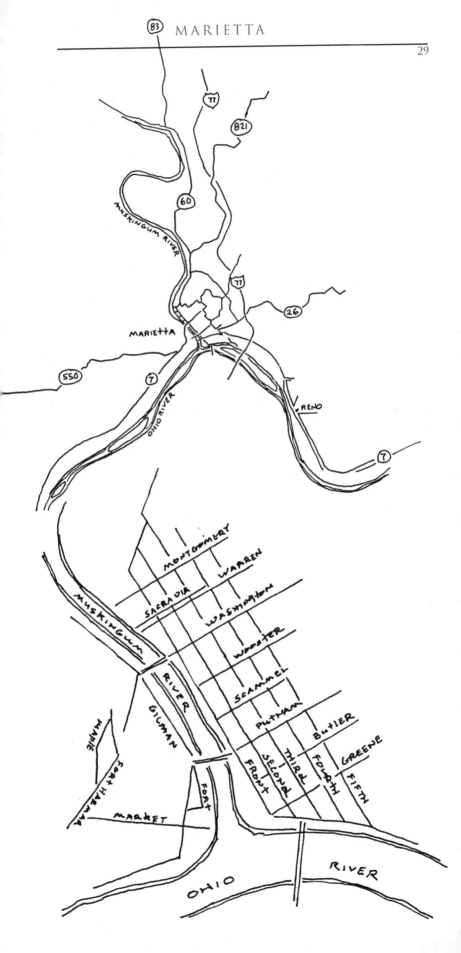

Athens

A thens, Ohio, is two places, really: there is the
Athens of Appalachia, of coal country and hills
and hollows—Gateway to West Virginia, local wags
call it, explaining the terrain and the smoke from
woodstoves and the pickup trucks with mud splashes
halfway up the windows and the blue grass music.
Then there is the Athens of Ohio University, the
first institution of higher learning in the Northwest
Territory, carved out by forward-thinkers in 1804,
who saw it, well, as the next *Athens*: the OU campus
looks like a post card from New England. On crisp
fall days, visitors feel smarter just walking around the
College Green.

There are places where the two Athens mix very
well, and places where the two don't mix at all, and
places where the two butt up against each other,
the irresistible force of 20,000 students and their
mentors ramming against the immovable object of
the Last Frontier. There is no interstate highway
serving Athens, but there is the Appalachian Highway,

winding in on its way through the county; there are places to buy harness for draft horses and places to eat sushi; there are garage mechanics who service an antique Allis Chalmers tractor in one bay and a professor's antique Morris Minor in another.

As for the *hippies*, who lingered in Athens long after the Sixties passed, they have faded away. The communes are gone, and today at the worker-owned restaurant, some of the workers are just employees. As one Athenian observes, "Now Yellow Springs is more Athens-like than Athens." But Athens is a distinctive place; in fact it's unique. In the 2004 elections, Athens was the only county in the state to reject Issue One, the constitutional amendment framed to ban legalized same-sex marriages or even partnerships in Ohio. And it was one of only a few rural counties to vote for Kerry—as it did by an almost two-to-one margin.

What are strong today in Athens are environment-alism and a back-to-the-land ethos alongside the culture and amenities of a large university. Sensitive to where they are, former college-linked Athenians restore and inhabit historic coal towns. They grow exotic plants or vegetables that make the Farmers Market such a big event on Saturdays. As they bridge the two Athens, they make Athens a worthy destination.

THE OHIO UNIVERSITY INN—This is Athens's only full-service hotel—though for a town of 21,800 even one is impressive. The OU Inn has evolved into a very nice hotel: lots of windows in the dining room look out into a flagstone-decked swimming pool. As the "nice" place in town to stay, the Inn is where OU puts up its visitors—professors in town for conferences or lectures, the Board of Trustees, dignitaries of every stripe. The advantages of this to the rest of the visitors include the dining room, Cutler's, which is open every night of the week, including holidays, a comfortable and quiet bar where you can have a drink among adults (it's a common escape for college professors for this very reason), and the sort of small amenities that become crucial in a tiny town: large rooms with nice windows, plenty of towels, excellent morning coffee.
331 Richland Avenue; 740/593-6661; www.ouinn.com Lunch buffet, $9.95; dinners $18-30; rooms $109-169.

COPPERTOP INN/SHADE—Two Athenians, Liz and Jan Schwarze, have taken the house his grandparents bought for their retirement in the 1960s, and turned it into a bed and breakfast. They live on the ground floor, and on the second and third floors they've installed fresh new guest rooms with private baths. The top floor unit has a sitting area on one side, two beds on the other, and views in four directions. Jan, whose mother had a B&B in Athens when he was growing up, makes the breakfast; and it always includes bacon, because he likes the aroma. This is really a rural place, ideal for soaking up fall colors. *1355 King Road, near Shade (Guysville post office); 740/594-2867; www.thecoppertopinn.com Rooms $125-$200.*

Seven Sauces

SEVEN SAUCES—Long an Athens institution, Seven Sauces started in a tiny store front with only six tables which meant plenty of waiting. They soon decamped to a restaurant-size space behind a bright multi-colored facade, but you still need a reservation on the weekends. Attractions include the shrimp and artichoke linguine ($18), baked mussels ($9), the popular Indonesian peanut chicken ($16.95), Vietnamese salad rolls with marinated tofu ($6). Owners Jean Walunis and Janne Wernet are around every day, and Jean has taken over the kitchen; she's making everything, even bread and salad dressing. *66 North Court Street; 740/592-5555; www.sevensauces.com Dinner only, Sun-Thur 5-9, till 10 Fri and Sat.*

COURT STREET DINER—The lines make it clear that this sparkling diner is an Athens favorite. Founded in 1997 it met a need, as co-owner Eric Moss explains: "Previously, there was nowhere in Athens to get a good fried egg sandwich." There is now. This mostly from-scratch diner serves all the usual items, plus breakfast anytime. But the real strengths are the spinach frittata ($7.49) at breakfast, the chicken salad quesadilla ($8) and baked-potato soup ($2.50) at lunch, and meat loaf ($8.49) and three-cheese macaroni and cheese ($7) in the evening. *18 North Court Street; 740/594-8700. Daily 7 am-10 pm.*

CABIN AT CHIMNEY LAKE—For their home, B&B and erstwhile bakery, Matt Rapposelli and Robin Dewey wanted a location that was historic and architecturally interesting. They settled on Canaanville, once a deep-mine coal company town, which Rapposelli claims is Ohio's most intact mining village. You'll pass through it on your way up the road to the B&B, an attractive 1970s log cabin complete with woods, an old reservoir, a front porch; inside it has a lounge, kitchen, three bedrooms (two upstairs with a shared bath, one down with a private bath) available for one, two or three parties. For breakfast they stock the kitchen with breakfast options and let you prepare your own.
8776 Mine Road; 740/592-4147; www.bigchimney.com Rooms are $80-115; whole house $300 or $950 a week.

ZOE/THE PLAINS—Scott Bradley came to Athens to major in English at OU, and afterwards stayed around ultimately to become proprietor of a chef-owned restaurant that's now among the best places to eat in the area. He also has located his business in an old coal community, Eclipse Company Town, where a dozen four-room houses for 1920s mining families are being renovated. His restaurant occupies two houses at the end of the street. There, wearing a navy blue baker's hat, Bradley is in the kitchen afternoons preparing entrées like chicken and apple crepes with sage sour cream and gruyere or pan-seared tuna with wasabi mirin slaw and toasted cashews. Besides entrées (at least two meat, two fish, one vegetarian), the menu includes hors d'oeuvres, soups and salads, and desserts. Zoe is in a dry precinct; bring your own wine. (Because people do bring their own, Bradley says, tables don't turn over; it's yours for the evening.)
11310 Jackson Drive, The Plains; reservations required, 740/797-4443; www.zoefinedining.com Dinner Tue-Sat 5-9. Entrées $14-25.

MILLER'S CHICKEN—They've been selling chicken at Miller's for four generations, and the chickens' loss is the chicken-lovers' gain. Poultriphiles can get just about any part of a chicken here, from the standard wings (60 cents), legs ($1), thighs and breasts ($2.39), to the more esoteric parts, like gizzards, hearts and livers ($5.50 a pound). It's all fresh, and it's available from 7 a.m. (the mind boggles at this) to 7 p.m. six days a week, and almost all is sold deep-fried, to eat here or to go, though uncooked chicken is available for those who want to cook at home. One might think that a deep-fried chicken heart is something of an oddity, but how do you explain that Miller's sometimes *runs out?* Clearly the chicken-lovers of Athens know something that the world at large does not. Located in a one-story brick building a couple blocks from downtown, Miller's also has seafood and sides, including deep-fried zucchini or jalapeno poppers.
235 West State Street; 740/593-6544; also listed on www.campusmenus.com

ACCESS—Stop at the log cabin (the county's first courthouse) on Richland Avenue and South Shafer, just north of the Hocking River and State Route 682, for a walking tour map of OU's beautiful Campus Green. The three oldest buildings there, forming a group at the top of the green, include Cutler Hall, 1818, the first college building in the Northwest Territory. Down the hill and across Union Street you'll find an old red-brick house with a white porch: Trisolini Gallery, which exhibits faculty art work year round, 10-4 daily except Sunday; free.

KENNEDY MUSEUM OF ART—In the 1990s Ohio University acquired The Ridges—a hilltop collection of two dozen or so red brick buildings that used to be the Athens Lunatic Asylum. Take a look around here: roads take you past the buildings to the north and encircle the central complex. The grounds are pretty and the buildings are handsome and seem in fine condition. The Ridges are a preservation coup; the only nineteenth-century hospital complex in Ohio that's still standing. Of most interest to the public is the Kennedy Museum of Art, in Lin Hall, built in 1874 as the hospital Administration Building. It's an imposing building, with two towers and setback residential wings alongside; original length was 853 feet. The imposing central section has become the museum; its hall, with marble floors and tall round-arched doors, is lined by galleries on both sides. The permanent collection's crown jewel is the Kennedy Southwest Native American Collection of weavings and jewels brought together by two OU alumni, the late Edwin L. and Ruth E. Kennedy. In 1954 they bought their first piece, a blanket on sale at a Navajo trading post, because of its beauty; today some part of the Kennedy collection is always on exhibit. A temporary show was work by photojournalist James Karales, OU 1955, whose subjects included Martin Luther King and civil rights marches. *Lin Hall, The Ridges, 740/593-1304, www.ohio.edu/museum/ Tue, Wed, Fri noon-5; Thur noon-8; Sat-Sun 1-5. Free.*

ASIDE—When the Corps of Engineers rerouted the Hocking River around the OU campus, they had in mind simply preventing the floods that swamped campus more than once a year. Unfortunately, the rerouted river took out the fabulous gardens of the asylum up on the hill: the arboretum, man-made lakes and islands. The loss was ultimately redeemed at least in part by what's become the Hockhocking Adena Bikeway, which follows the river from the park on East State Street to the ballfields on West State—about four miles. If your stamina is really good you can continue all the way to Hocking College in Nelsonville, a route of 16.4 miles. The path is quiet, level, well-maintained, and an excellent way to get around if you thought ahead and brought your bicycle. On a cool summer Saturday, you might be inclined to *buy* a bicycle.

ATHENS CYCLE PATH BICYCLE SHOP—In spite of the hills (or, for some, *because* of the hills), Athens is a big town for bicycling. One of the local bicycle providers is Athens Cycle Path, which sells everything from children's bikes to professional racers, mountain and road; and they *teach* bicycle maintenance. They'll customize your bicycle to fit—or they'll adapt it for fishing or camping. Their website describes the area's most challenging hills for cyclists; one of those in town climbs 200 feet in a quarter mile. *104 West Union; 740/593-8482; www.athenscyclepath.com Mon-Sat 10-5:30.*

ATHENS BICYCLE—Cycle Path has no bicycles for rent, but if you arrive in Athens, look at the bicycle path and want to start pushing pedals forthwith, Athens Bicycle does rent them.
14 West Stimson Avenue; 740/594-9944; www.athensbicycle.com Mon-Fri 10-6, Sat 10-5.

ASIDE—At 5:30 on a winter morning, an Ohio University policeman found a bike parked on campus, with a sticker reading, This Bike is a Pipe Bomb. Immediately four buildings were shut down and a bomb squad rushed down from Columbus. After spraying the bike with water, the squad tore it apart with a hydraulic device. There was no bomb, and after three hours the buildings were reopened. When the student owner of the bike turned up he explained that This Bike Is a Pipe Bomb is a band from Pensacola; even so, he was charged on a misdemeanor count of inducing panic. Four days later the university dropped the charges, but the student was still out his bike. University officials all backed the police, and other students mostly backed the student, though one of those interviewed by an inquiring photographer for *The News* observed that putting the sticker on a bicycle "probably wasn't a good idea." Anyway, the incident illustrated the chasm between town and gown, and the disconnect between generations.

Athens County Courthouse

ATHENS COUNTY COURTHOUSE—Red brick and sandstone rise in a flourish of dormers, louvers, peaks and statues: the creation of a construction crew that planned never to mow lawn. Building meets sidewalk in the heart of town, making this one of the very few county seats on a summer-long tour of Ohio's small towns that looks like somebody pulled the grass out from under it. Wings sprout in all directions from a center hall lined with a bicentennial gallery of portraits and biographies of early Athenians, and if you want to know something about local history-makers, start here. In the summer the courthouse steps are *the* place for sitting in Athens and gather some national-class sitters; everybody in town practices here at one time or another. Overhead, the four clocks on the tower all show slightly different times, so if you're running a couple minutes late you can find an excuse.
15 Court Street at Church Street

COURT STREET COLLECTION—Yes, this is truly an exceptional shop. It's exhilarating to find a place with nothing but the finest in handmade *contemporary* crafts, the sort you're unlikely to see offered anywhere else. You'll find distinctive porcelain tableware, custom jewelry, blown and stained glass, fabric bags, metal sculptures and, among dozens of other gift and self-indulgent choices, a rotating show of photographs and paintings. Some items are signed, one-of-a-kind pieces, making them, we suppose, rather distinguished purchases. *64 North Court Street; 740/593-8261. Tue-Sat noon-6.*

BLUE EAGLE MUSIC—The bench outside Blue Eagle Music serves two purposes; it's a terrific place to watch Athens go by on a sunny afternoon, and, if the weather's warm enough for the door to be open, it's a terrific place to listen to the music that wafts out. This guitar, banjo and fiddle shop offers sales, service, lessons and repair for virtually any type of string instrument: they can restring a ukulele or a harp, and if perchance the bangles on your tambourine need refitting, they can do that too. When they're not fixing something, the proprietors, staff and hangers-out are playing something: probably a guitar but sometimes an accordion, a hammer dulcimer, an autoharp. This is not the place, by the way, to play Stump the Band: someone in Blue Eagle knows every song ever written, and someone can play it too, on snare drum or tuba, steel guitar, or steel drum. *40 North Court Street; 740/592-5332; www.blueeaglemusic.com Mon-Thur 10-7, Fri 10-6, Sat 10-5, Sun Noon-5.*

The Dairy Barn

DAIRY BARN ARTS CENTER—The Dairy Barn started in 1977 with a barn rescue. Built in 1914 as part of the Athens Asylum, the barn was part of the hospital's regimen; patients milked cows as therapy. For over fifty years, the patient-dairymen regularly won prizes for their herd and its products, but when the Asylum got out of the milking business, the barn was abandoned. Then a group of civic-minded types shoveled the place out; local artists, builders and designers donated their time; and the result is a true community arts center. The Dairy Barn is famous especially for juried international summertime shows: the Bead

International, held in even years and now shown at the same time as Beyond Basketry, a juried basket exhibit; and in odd years, the Quilt National. In 2007 the quilt show exhibited 83 works and drew 7000 visitors from all 50 states and 19 foreign countries.

8000 Dairy Lane; 740/592-4981; www.dairybarn.org/ Tue-Sat noon-5; Thur noon-8, Sun 1-5. Closed Mon and between shows. Adults $3.50, students and seniors, $2.50.

LITTLE PROFESSOR BOOK CENTER---A *chain* bookstore,
you say? Really a franchise, independently-owned, explains Rich Purdy, co-owner with his brother-in-law, Curt Holsapple. Situated in a town of readers, this store caters to its particular clientele, like the professor who came in one morning for a copy of the newly-announced winner of the Man-Booker prize, so he could read it that night on his plane to Japan. Sure enough, Purdy found it for him. Then there was the graduate student who wanted an illustrated book on Ohio architecture. She wanted to send it to her parents in Colombia, so they'd know what Ohio *looks* like. Of course local authors, including Jack Matthews, are on the shelves here; there's a great rack of magazines and one of comics too. Sure enough, Purdy and Holsapple got into this business because they like to read. Now, though, Rich admits what he's reading are "mostly small blurbs about a million books."

65 South Court Street; 740/592-4418; www.littleprofessor.com/ athens Mon-Fri 9-7; Sat 9-5; Sun 9:30-4:30.

THE FARMERS MARKET—Since 1972 the enterprising
farmers of southeast Ohio—especially those in Athens, Meigs and Morgan counties—have been trucking their best and their most exotic produce to the Athens Farmer's Market, which planned to move to the Community Center parking lot in 2008. The Market has all the basics in season (corn, potatoes, tomatoes, apples, zucchini) plus many of the frills—Belgian endive, baby eggplant, a dozen varieties of lettuce. You'll find the likes of homemade pasta, brown eggs laid by free-range chickens, dried flowers, herbs and spices and Amish molasses cookies. In the fall, the local apple farmers sound like wine snobs as they search for the vocabulary to describe the often subtle differences in texture and taste between their eleven varieties of apples. One was once heard to say, "This apple here tastes like a Northern Spy—with an attitude." Vendors here are all producers, and you'll find, say, bakers and delis as well as growers. Though originally founded by a county extension agent, the market now is an independent non-profit. In 2008 Sarah Conley was expected to succeed David Gutknecht as manager.

East State Street; 740/593-6763 for Sarah Conley; www.athensfarmersmarket.org Check hours, which may change in 2008, but were previously Sat year-round and Wed in season, 9-1.

LAST CHANCE CORRAL—What's going on here is rescuing
horses. This place is 2.65 acres of corrals and barns with a house in the middle; Victoria Goss explains, "We take in abused, neglected, unwanted equine, put them back together and find them adoptive homes." The Last Chance Corral has been at this location since Goss founded it in the late 1980s. Athens reminds Goss of her original home,

New England, as it used to be. On any given day, 15-25 horses will be in residence. From January to June a succession of up to 200 foals arrive from Kentucky—foals born so that their mothers would be able to nurse thoroughbred foals whose own mothers would be bred again. Last Chance buys as many as it can, then feeds them a mixture of milk and yogurt from a baby bottle. It also takes in grown horses that are no longer wanted; some have been mistreated and need to be coaxed back to good behavior. And some animals that come in are sick, requiring round-the-clock attention, which is why one of the barns connects to Goss's house. When animals are ready for permanent homes, they're offered for sale on the Corral's website. Most of the people working here are employees, but some are volunteers, whose help Goss treasures. "The quality of mercy is not cheap," she says. If you visit you'll see not only fine animals, but also Victoria Goss, a whirlwind of energy who's received national recognition for her humane work.

5350 Pomeroy Road (old U.S. 33); 740/594-4336; www.lastchancecorral.org Sunday open house year round 10-4; at other times call first.

UNITARIAN FELLOWSHIP—In 1971 Athens Unitarians built themselves a new hall, a rectangular box to save money. But then, to their everlasting credit, they hired an Athens artist named John Spofforth to lay the brick. Spofforth had spent 11 years working as a bricklayer and mason, and by 1971 he'd also spent seven studying fine arts at OU: thus what he gave the Unitarian Fellowship was brick laid both professionally and artistically. The brick is laid in waves and bulges; at the chimney it seems to cascade like molten wax. The result is wonderful, and no one but Spofforth could have done it. Other artists were members of the Fellowship, and they did paintings, elegant doors, and windows in the mode of Le Corbusier.

184 Longview Heights Road; 740/592-2083; www.uuathens.org

GLASSHOUSE WORKS/STEWART—Tom Winn and Ken Frieling, former English professors, migrated just east of Athens when a hobby literally grew out of town and into a one-time hotel, greenhouses and acreage in the small town of Stewart, where their Glasshouse Works has long since become *the* destination. It offers an enchanting display garden of ponds and narrow winding paths amidst abounding foliage, a small conservatory, a houseful of garden art and sales areas. This is one of the few spots in Ohio where you can buy orchids, along with succulents, ferns, bromeliads, bizarre perennials, original hybrids, and more variegated plants than in any one place in the U.S. Collectors come thousands of miles to make their selections in a place where frogs jump between the lilies in outdoor pools and Scottish thistles look like trees.

8950 State Route 144, just off SR 329; 740/662-2142; www.glasshouseworks. com Fri-Sat 10-6 year-round.

ASIDE—The last day of October was once reserved for children: dress the little monsters up as monsters, the angels as angels and so on, and turn them loose on the neighborhood to ring doorbells and get sick on chocolate. For two or three decades now, however, Athens has been the scene of a political and social drama centered on what was originally a holiday for witches. Don't say "Halloween" in Athens County unless you know what you're in for. The origins of the Court Street debauch that masquerades as Halloween in Athens rest in Ohio's once-lowered age of majority for the consumption of alcohol and Ohio University's accident of the calendar that made the last weekend of October part of a fall hiatus of classes: what better place to celebrate demon rum than a town with a lot of college bars, particularly when there are no classes in session? As the crowds grew, so did the reputation; with the reputation came the crowds. Now, ten thousand-plus revelers gather in Athens to celebrate the weekend before Halloween. It's a night when adults and children do best to stay at home. Depending on your point of view there is plenty of blame or credit to go around. The drinking age went back up to 21 years ago, and OU has given up the fall break, but the reputation still draws, egged on by a covey of bar owners and beer vendors who do the goblin's portion of their business this one weekend. Banning liquor sales for the weekend smacks of totalitarianism (drinkers and sellers agree on *this*, at least), but turning over the town to outside agitators smacks of revolution. Attempts to have a "sanctioned" party at, say, the fairgrounds, have pleased no one—the bars, remember, are on Court Street. Attempts to sanction what borders on a riot is too tough for the town to swallow. So every year, the party goes on. Many people come in costume; the whole thing seems like mardi gras; and city fathers grumble about the extra expense for safety. The weekend before Halloween is (also, of course, depending on your point of view) a terrific weekend to go to Athens, or a terrific weekend to stay away.

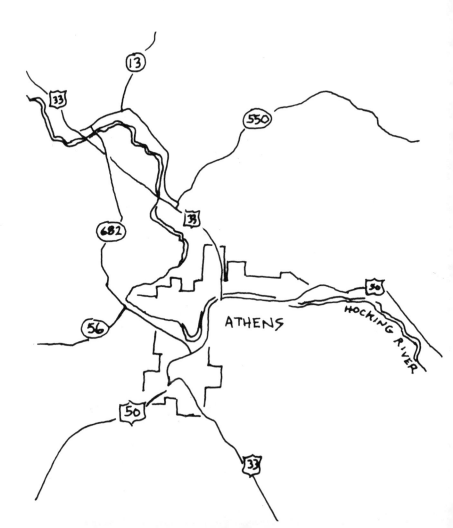

The Inn at Cedar Falls

Logan

L ogan is an authentic place, a town in rural Ohio
untainted and untouched by the imported
erudition of a university, like Athens, or the weight
of national history, like Marietta. What Logan has, of
course, is *location*, which to a large degree determined
its history and wisdom. As industries—coal, timber,
canals, railroads, clay—have boomed and faded, so
has Logan. It remains the seat of Hocking County,
where the Hocking Hills State Park is. Tourism is in
the ascendant; the park and the Hocking Hills pulse
with opportunities. Lured by the wild outdoors, by
the beauty of a forest road with a ravine alongside,
young people and retirees and some in between visit
repeatedly and then move in. They're drawn by a
neighborhood with 200-foot-deep gorges and 90-
foot waterfalls and ten-mile views and caves, each
with a smuggler or hermit story. They're drawn by
chances to kayak and canoe, or hike, or simply admire
the landscape, so they stay. In Nelsonville, just south
of Logan, a flock of artisans and artists have been
arriving and settling down; they like working amid
natural beauty and each other. Sometimes people who
want to live close to nature, start businesses here, and
become so busy they hardly have time anymore for

what lured them in the first place. But for the visitor, all these incomers are bringing better restaurant meals than southeast Ohio ever dreamed of; they're bringing art galleries, and a theater with live programs 100 nights a year; they're teaching skills they love, like rock climbing or ceramics. They're keeping the pretty old towns of Logan and Nelsonville much as they were. They are changing the Hocking Hills from a byway into a destination.

Will their numbers change the Hocking Hills from a peaceful and beautiful place, into an urban kind of place? So far, there's still plenty of room; and excepting mostly brilliant fall days, there are still tranquil days in the Hocking Hills.

THE INN AT CEDAR FALLS—In 1987 this inn became a Hocking Hills treasure: a really nice place to stay and to eat, without giving up proximity to park trails—on three sides the inn is surrounded by park property and it's just down the road from Cedar Falls. Now the inn has a dozen cottages for two people, and five cabins with kitchens and some whirlpools for two to four, but it also has rooms, which are becoming less common around here. The nine rooms occupy a barn up the hill; all have private baths, antique beds and rocking chairs. There are no telephones or television, so all your time can be quality time; but they do offer wireless internet everywhere, so you can keep up if you have to. From the beginning, the inn has paid a lot of attention to food. Everyone, whether inn guests (spared a drive after dinner, a nice detail), or those staying elsewhere, needs a reservation for dinner; one winter night there were two couples at dinner, and the chef ended up waiting table and chatting; but 50 were expected the next night. There's a bar and a wine list. Breakfasts are for guests only; brown bags and lunches are available, (lunch from 11:30 to 1:30.) The dining room is in an 1840s log cabin; in summer there's outdoor seating too.
21190 State Route 374; 740/385-7489; www.innatcedarfalls.com Dinner entrées range from $28 to $34. Accommodations in 2007 ranged from $109 (midweek off season) to $269 (peak-season weekend cabin with whirlpool.)

GROUSE NEST RESTAURANT AND HOCKING HILLS RESORT/SOUTH BLOOMINGVILLE—To find this place

you take a turn across from Ash Cave, then drop to first gear and go slowly uphill on the gravel road—slowly so that you can also see the woods and ravine alongside. It's also beautiful at the top of the hill, where there's a lawn next to the restaurant. And the menu here doesn't sound like the outback; it's up-to-date, adventuresome, often offering venison. There's a bar and wine list also. Grouse Nest will take dinners to people anywhere in the area—you could have a catered dinner in your cabin. Dinner entrées range from $14 to $32. Hocking Hills

Resort, the parent company, has cabins in the woods, including small ones called Love Bugs, 20 feet square, cunningly designed and including an open back porch. Breakfast is not included; a basket breakfast is $12 to $16. The Love Bugs are $100 in winter; an October (most expensive) weekend rate in a cabin three times as big and sleeping ten is $360.
25780 Liberty Hill Road, South Bloomingville; restaurant, 740/-332-4501; resort, 800/222-4655 or 740/332-1902; restaurant, www.grousenest.com; resort, www.hockinghillsresort.net

OTHER PLACES TO STAY IN THE HOCKING HILLS—
More park visitors and more places to stay have grown in a symbiotic relationship: the Hocking County tourist office now lists 600 cabins operated by 200 different businesses. It tries to help you sort them out with an accommodations web site that you can search by amenity and availability: *www.1800hocking.com*

BEAR RUN INN: CABINS & COTTAGES—This is a 550-
acre place with relatively new cottages scattered around, some in the woods. They accommodate from two to 12 (that one has five bedrooms, three baths); all have kitchens and most have hot tubs; some are on ponds stocked for fishing, and the owners can give you maps for hiking or provide hayrides. Some bed and breakfast rooms are available in the house. Rates range from $95 for a B&B off season to $240 for the biggest cottage in October.
8260 Bear Run Road; 800/369-2937; www.bearrun.com

GLENLAUREL INN/ROCKBRIDGE—Glenlaurel is the
third of the fine-dining plus accommodation resorts in this area; it has a Scottish country theme. The prettiest spot is the dining terrace in summer; there are a few rooms in the main house, but most guests stay in the stucco cottages or crofts (smaller ones) along a circular road up on the hill.
14940 Mount Olive Road; 800/809-7378; www.glenlaurel.com Dinners (five courses) are $49 plus tax and tip, or $59 (seven courses) on Sat; overnight stays (same rates all year) range from $119 to $319; higher in October.

INN AT HOCKING COLLEGE/NELSONVILLE—Hocking
College has taken over and redone a former chain motel with a restaurant.
15770 State Route 691; 740/753-3531; www.hocking.edu/theinn A double room is $85 Fri-Sat, $75 Sun-Thur.

RHAPSODY/NELSONVILLE—Nelsonville has not only a
theater and a monthly arts festival, but since May 2005 it's also had a fine restaurant. Besides being a good place to eat, it's a "learning lab," says the chef, Doug Weber. He himself teaches culinary arts at Hocking College; the people serving you in the dining room are hotel and hospitality students; and those in the kitchen are students of culinary arts. Broiled grouper with tequila and lime butter is a popular specialty.
18 Public Square; 740/753-5740. Wed-Thur 5-9; Fri-Sat 5-10. Reservations recommended on weekends. Entrée prices range from $16.95 to $34 (for two deep-fried lobster tails.)

ETTA'S LUNCHBOX CAFÉ/STARR—This place is a media darling. When I was there one July day, I was the third writer that day. LaDora Ousley, co-proprietor with her husband, Timothy Seewer, was especially impressed with a phone call from London, England: a television station there had arranged to come in early August. Etta's Café deserves the attention; it's worth a detour for the lunchboxes and the proprietors. The official name is Etta's General Store and Lunchbox Café, for the sprawling cinder block building had been a general store before LaDora and Tim arrived from Columbus, and local residents couldn't bear to lose it. LaDora has been collecting lunchboxes for years, and the first thing she did here was put 650 of them on display (some hang from the ceiling, others are on shelves in the cooking area) because she'd never before seen them all together. They almost all have pictures on their metal sides: a record of the late twentieth-century Roy Rogers-superhero side of American culture. Because of them, none of the food offered here is fried—LaDora doesn't want grease on her collection. One is the oldest lunchbox made with a picture on it: Space Cadet, from 1952. As for Tim, he's an artist (that's why the chairs here are bright with painted flowers) as well as cook (how he's usually supported himself.) Off the store there's a room that shows his art, along with Fisher Price toys, which are another of LaDora's collections. The menu (yes, you can *eat* in this café too) includes pizza and subs as well as soup, sandwiches and hamburgers; prices are low and the food is good. They make their own pie crusts, sauces and soups. Outside there's a large garden on one side, and llamas, acquired originally for fertilizer, on the other. The couple moved into the building in 2000, but the café opened only in 2002, after septic and electrical upgrades. They're open every day except Christmas, when LaDora and Tim drive around Ohio to visit their families. Maybe when their major loans are paid off they'll be able to visit the Smithsonian, to see the lunchbox exhibit. And as for who's Etta, she was LaDora's grandmother. There's a picture of her on the wall and on the café web site.

35960 State Route 56 at the junction of State Route 328, New Plymouth post office; 740/380-0736; www.ettaslunchboxcafe.com Mon-Sat 10-8, Sun 11-6. Pizza $20, Sub $4.55, twelve-inch sub, $7.55.

FULLBROOKS CAFÉ/NELSONVILLE—This coffee and sandwich shop occupies a corner of the old Dew Hotel, and it is one of the handsomest renovations you'll ever see. It has a few tables, and, in summer, a few more outside under the trees.

6 Public Square; 740/753-3391. Mon-Fri 8 to 5, Sat 8 to 4, Sun 10 to 4. Sandwiches $5.

HOCKING COUNTY HISTORICAL SOCIETY—A complex of buildings, not all of them old, make up the Hocking County Historical Society's museum; and, especially if your guide is Sam Sloan, a fifth-generation resident, it's a good place to start finding out about Logan. You'll learn, for instance, that Thomas Worthington laid out the town and named it for Chief Logan, whom he admired. You'll hear about the canal coming to town; about the steam washing machine made here—it looks like a little copper trunk with a crank at the end; and about the brick plant, built by Niles Kachelmacher, a Norwegian, who left all his money to Logan for varicose-vein treatment. To this day,

Sloan says, there's a clinic for free treatment of varicose veins. On one side of the 1976 red brick museum building there's the Schempp House Museum, which has a portrait of the lady from Logan who founded Ohio Poetry Day. On the other side, in a separate building, is the Historical Society's prize exhibit, the Logan-built Henry Lutz steam car, made in 1898 and the only steam car in the world. Sloan says that Lutz drank, and one time he drove this car into the canal. Sloan's dad helped pull him out. It used to be that this extraordinary car was on display in Cleveland, but according to Lutz's will, it was to return to Logan if the community got a museum by a certain date. That's why Logan has the big red-brick museum, and why Logan is where you have to go to see the Lutz car.

64 North Culver; 740/385-6026; www.hockingcountyhistoricalsociety.com Tue-Sat 1-4 May-Oct or call for appointment. Donation box.

COLUMBUS WASHBOARD COMPANY—Logan not only has the world's only steam car, it has the only U.S. washboard factory. Washboards are indeed still made; the surprise is that 25 to 30 percent are used for washing clothes. Even some American troops in Iraq are washing clothes with them—the company has sent over thousands of washboard-and-pail sets. Columbus Washboard started in Columbus in 1895, but in 1999 new owners brought it to Logan, where the factory occupies part of an old three-story brick factory building with an oversized washboard (the world's largest) hanging on its outside wall. Five or six people make the washboards, using traditional machines. They make a hundred a day, with wooden frames enclosing a corrugated and crimped metal surface that will help jostle dirt out of clothes. That's the traditional washboard, with galvanized metal. Now washboards also come with mirrors, chalk boards and cork. Or the metal can be brass for toughness. Glass washboards go to the Bahamas because they won't corrode in salt water. Production, which peaked at over a million boards during World War II, now runs 30-40,000 a year. All this we learned on a factory tour. "I don't think we've had anyone come in who wasn't impressed," says Betty Ellinger, floor supervisor, who gives some of the tours. Once Columbus Washboard had moved to Logan, it took only a couple years to cook up the Washboard Music Festival, which began in 2001. Some musicians really do play washboards, though they prefer ones that haven't been nailed; they're more musical. The three-day festival has its own web site: *www.washboardmusicfestival.com*

14 Gallagher Avenue; 800/343-7967, 740/380-3828; www.columbuswashboard.com Mon-Fri 9-3; tours anytime if a staffer has time or, weekends by appointment.

LOGAN ART GALLERY—This gallery shows Ohio artists; everything is handmade and original. They also offer pottery classes for children and adults; a one-hour class including firing is $12. This art gallery is just one of the Main Street, Logan, enterprises set up by two investors, one from Worthington and one from Hide-Away Hills. Their other ventures include Hocking River Emporium across the street, which sells clothes, home items, and Minnetonka moccasins; Sandstone, Logan's white tablecloth restaurant, which has a summer barbecue at the back, and Spotted Owl Café, which features panini and soup.

65 West Main; 740/385-9455.

MIDWEST GLASSWARE OUTLET—This is an unusually interesting outlet store, It has a terrific selection of glassware—barware, cake plates, Fiestaware, bakeware, everyday glasses—and prices are low. The company started out by buying out a warehouseful of Fostoria glassware, which is no longer made. Another feature: products on offer here are 99 percent American-made, which you won't find in most stores.
12811 State Route 664 South; 740/380-9400. Mon-Sat 10-8; Sun 11-6; Jan-April 10-6, Sun 11-6.

HOCKING HOUSE—Hocking House is a log cabin filled with extraordinary ceramics. It's the home shop of artist Jean Magdich, who has her own distinctive style and a national following. There's a good display here of the colorful porcelain she makes in a studio at the other end of the property: fruit bowls, flowers, plates. Magdich also works regularly in town at Logan Clay, where she makes and fires an array of gardenware produced in high-density clay that becomes vitreous in firing. Logan Clay makes durable sewer pipes from this clay, which also works well for Jean Magdich's collection of similarly enduring lawn ornaments, including winsome figures, planters, and a snail. She makes patio floor tiles and stepping-stone tiles, all on sale at Hocking House. She and Logan Clay were also responsible for the heads and flowers on the former parking meter posts downtown. Magdich did some; artists from out of town and out of state did the others.
29580 Big Pine Road at State Route 664 South; 740/385-4166; www.hockinghouse.com June-Aug Tue-Sun noon-5. Rest of year, weekends 10-3.

HOCKING HILLS STATE PARK—Among parks, this one is Ohio's greatest treasure. Mostly, it is an in-state treasure, though when the newspaper in Honolulu writes about hidden wonders on the mainland, they praise the Hocking Hills. These are the wooded cliffs and rugged gorges of Hocking County. When the glaciers to the north melted, the running water eroded the hills to the south. Weak, crumbly areas of sandstone washed away. Left behind was a water-resistant stratum known as Black Hand Sandstone, a true Rock of Ages, which forms every craggy dip and peak in today's park landscape. Because the pre-glacial, long-gone Teays River brought in seeds of southern plant species, and then the ice brought in northern flora, hemlocks, Canada yew and teaberry grow in the cool, damp valleys of the Hocking Hills, while Southern tulip trees and mountain laurel flourish in the high places. As one park naturalist puts it, "The Hocking Hills are Canada in the valleys and Carolina and Tennessee on the ridges." The park has 2000 acres in often separate areas rather than one continuous place: it is six parks, all different, all of interest for rock formations and/or water falls, and all with well defined trails. The greatest boost to park improvements came in the 1930s, when the Works Progress Administration did a wonderful job in laying out trails, bridges, stone steps, roads and tunnels. Some of those were damaged in the flood of January 1998, though the park says all have since been repaired or replaced. The Hocking Hills State Park drew 2.3 million visitors in 2005; that was up by nearly half a million from 2002. If you'd prefer to avoid crowds, go on weekdays and choose less crowded parks, like Cantwell Cliffs and Rock House. Fall tends to be busiest, but winter is gorgeous, and so too is spring. Parks are listed here in order of descending popularity.

Park office, 19852 State Route 664 South, near Old Man's Cave; 740/385-6841; www.hockinghillspark.com Park has cabins and campsites for rent; park lodge is for dining only.

OLD MAN'S CAVE—In 1939 the old travel writer, Claude Shafer, said, "Here you climb ladders, cross bridges, and drop into weird nooks and shadowy crannies, go into ecstasies at the ferns and moss, admire the pretty creek and waterfall, and shout to hear the echo. Your mind wanders and you get an eerie feeling in the semi-darkness and you sort of wish you were home in bed with the covers over your head." Which is mostly how it is at Old Man's Cave, except that the ladders really are stairways, and many of the ferns and moss have long since vanished. This is the busiest site in the Hocking Hills; park headquarters are nearby, rest rooms have flush toilets, and there is a gift shop and an ice cream stand. At least, this park has an unforgettable name. Of course there really was once an old man, and his name was Richard Rowe. He came to Ohio about 1796 and before long reached the Hocking Hills. Eventually he came to the large recess cave here and found it happily commodious: 200 feet long, 50 feet high and 75 feet deep. A hermit by inclination, Rowe settled in and lived out his life in this shelter. He was buried nearby. Besides the Old Man's Cave, this park has an upper falls and a lower falls, a 150-foot gorge, and the Devil's Bathtub, a narrow section of swirling, churning water. The big cave where Rowe lived is just above the lower falls.
State Route 664

CEDAR FALLS—One thing you won't see at Cedar Falls is cedars; early settlers made a mistake identifying the hemlocks. Do bring your camera to Cedar Falls. Everyone else does. Voted most photogenic by most everyone, this waterfall has more water falling than anywhere else in the Hocking region. In January it's a mass of ice, in spring it's a torrent, in summer it practically disappears. It's possible to sample the Buckeye Trail by walking the 2.5 miles from Old Man's Cave to Cedar Falls. The trail follows the valley of Queer Creek—a "remote and primitive chasm laden with hemlock and bound by steep rock walls," as one writer put it.
State Route 374 between State Routes 664 and 56

ASH CAVE—This is the *crème de la crème* waterfall spot for small boys, not as it happens for the waterfall, which at 90 feet, gives an intermittent show, depending on the amount of recent rainfall, but because of the cave behind and alongside it—this cave is bigger than the Old Man's. But this cave was named not for a hermit but for ashes the Indians left here. The valley trail, which has been paved to make it wheelchair-accessible, leads to the pool at the bottom of the waterfall. The best time to visit is in the early spring, during the week, say, of Easter break. Here, young boys' eyes glaze over with imaginative possibilities, not the least of which is to stand on a rock next to the falls and, with great splendor and panache, create one of their own.
State Route 56 just east of State Route 374.

CONKLES HOLLOW—This is a wonderful gorge—200 feet deep, so deep that in places little or no sunlight reaches the ground; it's a state nature preserve. As for Conkle, we don't know who he was, where he came from, or what became of him. We only know that he made himself immortal in the Hocking Hills by stopping long enough to carve his name and the date in the gorge, "W.J. Conkle 1797". Perhaps, like some latter-day conquistador planting a flag on a rich discovery, Conkle was trying to claim the view, for many folks believe it is the best in the county. And the best place to take in that view is from the observation platform in the middle of Rim Trail, a two-and-a-half mile trail that winds along the edges of some of Ohio's highest cliffs. *State Route 374, south of SR 678.*

ROCK HOUSE—This cave in the middle of a 150-foot cliff is a house of ill-repute. According to stories the locals tell, the Indians who once lived here were succeeded by a slew of undesirables—horse thieves, robbers, murderers and bootleggers. In fact, today Rock House—and the trail to it—is a natural wonder built ages ago by water, a major project considering that the main chamber is 200 feet long. The "windows" consist of cracks in the Black Hand sandstone, while the interior decoration comes from deposits of iron compounds, which created patterns of red and brown on the walls. In fall you might get to taste a "Buck Run banana," the fruit from a papaw tree. If you look very closely, you might be able to make out the letters: I T F B R B A R I T F F A W M T A W over the entrance to Rock House. According to another legend, that hoary inscription means, "In the fall, Buck Run bananas are ripe; in the frosty fall, a wise man takes a wife." *State Route 374, southeast of SR 180.*

CANTWELL CLIFFS—Though this park has a 150-foot high palisade, it has the fewest visitors, probably because it's 17 miles from Old Man's Cave; but it's well worth visiting, both for itself and for there being fewer people. Your only problem may be a Hobson's choice of approaches. If visitors follow the valley trail, they face a long hike and hundreds of steps, but they are rewarded with the view and the advantage of gravity on the return trip. Those who approach from above have the view without effort, but as they descend the stairs into the gorge, they must remember that he who goes down must come back up. *State Route 374, north of SR 180*

ACCESS—For pure view, travel State Route 664, one of the most popular scenic drives in Ohio. Or cut across the hollows by taking Big Pine Road (from U.S. 33 take the State Route 664 exit south to West Big Pine Road) where the colors change all year round. The hillsides turn white in May when the dogwood blooms, while October brings precious gold to the trees. But January claims a special beauty. Hemlocks keep these U-shaped valleys verdant on the grimmest days, and wherever there is water winter turns it into spectacular ice sculptures.

HOCKING HILLS WINTER HIKE—The trail that winds its way from Old Man's Cave to Ash Cave in Hocking County is distinctive in that it is one of the few places in Ohio that doesn't look like Ohio. There are vast quantities of rock. There are caves. There are dizzying heights and dramatic depths. Waterfalls. Heavy wood. And it is well well *well* off the beaten path, unless your beaten path tends to include the Hocking Hills State Park.

On the third Saturday each January, it seems as though everyone's beaten path includes Hocking Hills State Park. Along twisty, windy State Route 664, signs sprout on homeowners' lawns that say, "Keep Going." The signs are not meant to be inhospitable, but encouraging. They are encouraging some 3,000 people who are driving the unfamiliar road to the park and the annual Winter Hike.

Since 1965, hikers amateur and professional, but mostly amateur, have been converging on the park from points as diverse as Buffalo, New York and Goshen, Indiana. The professional hikers are easy to recognize: for one thing, they've arrived early, and for another, they're dressed appropriately for the weather, which over the years has ranged from temperatures in the 60s to temperatures in the single digits. The amateurs are the ones who show up in light jackets and gym shoes. Or with a poodle on a leash. The amateurs are also the ones who show up around nine o'clock, which is when the Hike is supposed to *officially* start, and find out that they are about two-thousandth in line.

The annual Winter Hike is so perfectly American. Three hundred sixty-four days a year, this geographically and geologically fascinating stretch, with streams like Buck Run and Queer Creek, is relatively quiet; even on lovely fall days, gorgeous spring mornings, and balmy summer afternoons, it is possible to feel, and be, alone on a trail. It is possible to park at the trail's beginning, middle or end, and simply saunter awhile. But at the Winter Hike, there is no sauntering—and no turning back. It is the Long March of winter activities, folks strung out in a line, two by two in some places, single file in others, over the course of the whole trail. This is a *group* nature experience, the outdoors-activity equivalent of having a block party.

Much of the distance is measured in ups and downs. There are long and steep flights of stairs cut into the cliff sides; there is an astonishingly steep climb at the end—"Heart Attack Hill," people jokingly call it, when it is still in the distance. When they are climbing it, they call it nothing, because they are breathing too hard. So when one of the rangers says that Cedar Falls—and the bean soup—is a quarter mile away, just put your head back down and hike. The black kettles, the assemblage of which must have denuded productions of *Macbeth* across the entire Midwest, sit atop real wood fires, and gurgle like city plumbing. The recipe includes beans, onions, piglet-size chunks of ham, and black pepper. In short order each hiker is given a bowl of soup, a cup of hot chocolate and a corn muffin.

This midpoint is a good place to take stock, to catch a breath, to contemplate the rest of the Hike. It is also a good spot to catch a shuttle bus back to one's car, which about one third of the hikers decide to do.

A bonus of sorts occurs in the stretch from Cedar Falls to Ash Cave. Lunch and shuttle buses have caused the ranks to disintegrate and string out; it is possible to walk more slowly, to stop and look, without causing 2000 people to stumble into you from behind. Perhaps because of this, the full pleasure of this gorge becomes apparent. It was cut by glacial runoff after the last ice age; Black Hand sandstone forms the cliffs and walls of the gorge. Where the sandstone is exposed to wind, rain, or stream, it has been weathered and worn away: there are piles of sand along the trail in many places.

By the time the hikers get to Ash Cave, most are ready for four things. The first would be a chair. The second, indoor plumbing. The third would be another bowl of bean and onion soup. Alas, none of these are forthcoming. The Fourth? Hands down, it's the most important: a shuttle bus. One pulls up every few minutes, and the drivers, who have been hauling people around the forest at this point for more than six hours, have cauldron-size reserves of good cheer. On the ride back to Old Man's Cave, the talk is of next year.

Park office, 740/385-6841. A winter hike is scheduled for January 17, 2009.

EARTH-WATER-ROCK: OUTDOOR ADVENTURES

LTD.—Another thing to do in the Hocking Hills is to hook up with Dylan Crawford, who teaches rock climbing, canoeing or kayaking. He'll even take people hiking or backpacking. The most demand is in rock climbing, which is in the Hocking State Forest Climbing and Rappelling Area off State Route 374 near Conkles Hollow. Boating will be on the Hocking River, Clear Creek or Lake Hope. In the winters Crawford is a teacher at Athens Middle School, though he does take people out on autumn weekends. In fact he likes his summer job so much he'd really like to do it all the time.
740/664-5220; www.ewroutdoors.com

ACCESS—U.S. 33, running southeast out of Columbus, goes to Lancaster, Logan and Athens on its way to the Ohio River. It has bypasses for all three, but then when it arrives in Nelsonville, it goes right through town.

NELSONVILLE—An Ohio place that has changed a lot in this new century is Nelsonville: the handsome downtown square has become a destination for its monthly art fairs. And the theater is back in business. Lots and lots of people are visiting Nelsonville. During its annual season, which now includes all the year except January to March, the Hocking Valley Scenic Railway draws over 25,000 people, mostly for weekend excursions to Haydenville and Logan. Rocky Boots, whose old three-story brick factory looms over U.S. 33, has moved its own manufacturing offshore, but has reoccupied the factory building with a boot and clothing store, plus a restaurant. The store is popular; it sees one- to two-thousand people every weekend, about 53,000 in a year. Coal mining enabled Nelsonville to build its handsome central square just east of U.S. 33; the collapse of coal meant the square kept its nineteenth-century postcard look intact, complete with a wonderful opera house and hotel (now restored into apartments) looking across the square and its fountain. The streetlights are the old cast iron type, and the streets themselves are paved in the locally-made "star" pattern bricks.

HAYDENVILLE—A few miles north of Nelsonville and just off U.S. 33 is Haydenville, a tiny community that is one of the most distinctive Appalachian company towns. In the 1870s Peter Hayden, a wealthy Columbus businessman, started a clay products factory and then built this self-contained community. The town was nothing like the usual clapboard company towns; it built itself out of the factory's tile and brick, enhanced by decoration and craft. These elements are still visible today, particularly in the Haydenville United Methodist Church, built with eight different kinds of brick and tile.

County Road 25 parallels U.S. 33 for a couple miles; all of Haydenville is along it, or a block away.

HOCKING VALLEY SCENIC RAILWAY/

NELSONVILLE—Trains made up of 1927 passenger cars and two 1952 diesel engines leave from Nelsonville and head northwest toward Logan through the Wayne National Forest. (The railway does own a coal-fired steam engine, but that's in the shop and, we hear, whether it'll run again is anybody's guess.) The ride compresses the history of the Hocking Valley, with remnants of the old canal, for example, and old brick kilns and old coal mines. At Logan, passengers stand up and flip their seatbacks for the reverse ride back to Nelsonville: same track, different scenery, if you can find someone to swap sides of the train with you. On summer weekends, you'll go two miles beyond Nelsonville to the new-old village of Robbins Crossing, an interpretive history project staffed by faculty and students of Hocking College. You can watch bread being baked, candles dipped, shingles split and logs sawn in the manner of the 1850s. With the locomotive huffing and puffing behind you, it will all become a most pleasantly disorienting experience. The railway has one full-time employee and three part-time for its shop, ticket sales and general maintenance; otherwise it's all run by volunteers, including railroad retirees and railroad wannabes.

U.S. 33 at Hocking Parkway Drive; 800/967-7834, or, on weekends only, 740/753-9531; www.hockingvalleytrain.com Weekends from mid-April to early November, plus four Santa Claus trains; some weekday specials, caboose and train robbery specials. Trains to Haydenville leave at noon, return 1:45; Logan trains leave 2:30, return 4:45. No toilets on trains. Adult rates from $11 to $18. Reservations recommended for foliage and Santa trips.

STARBRICK CLAY/NELSONVILLE—One of the best storefronts in the Nelsonville square area is that of Starbrick Clay, where Ann Judy, a ceramic artist, manages a cooperative gallery for 12 artists in clay. Ann Judy does more than that, for she's been the principal mover and shaker in launching Nelsonville's arts community. She went to Ohio University and married a painter, Aaron Smith, who had a home in Nelsonville. "I told him that if I was going to stay in Nelsonville, this was going to become the kind of town I wanted to live in," she says. It was 2000, and she and her husband became involved with Foothills School of American Crafts, which had just moved onto the square. Judy opened her gallery in 2001, and early the next year her husband, then director of Foothills, came up with the idea for a gallery hop; they called the monthly event Final Friday, and it draws up to 1000 people. Not surprisingly, other artists came, and Final Friday extended

exhibits into ordinarily non-gallery spaces, like the theater lobby or an insurance office. Before Judy arrived the square was virtually lifeless. That is not true now, and Judy has even found that people are wanting to move to Nelsonville. She says, "Towns are calling us for ideas on how to get art festivals going."
21 West Columbus Street, 740/753-1011; www.starbrick.com/ Wed-Sat 11-6, Sun noon-5.

PAPER CIRCLE/NELSONVILLE—At Paper Circle, you can see paper being made (using fibers ranging from flax to banana peel), or see paper artifacts, including bowls and waste paper baskets, or even take classes and learn how to do it all yourself.
35 West Columbus Street; 740/753-3374; www.papercircle.org Thur-Sat 1-5.

SPINNING TURTLE YARNS & GIFTS/ NELSONVILLE—Yarns here come in all hues and fibers and range in price from $2 to $30 a skein. They come, for example, from Italy, from one of the few remaining American mills, from a women's co-op in Uruguay and a dyer in Athens. Classes are available, and hand-knitted goods are sold on consignment.
25 Public Square; 740/753-3885; www.spinningturtle.com Wed-Sun open at 11; close 8 Thur, 5 Sun, 6 Wed, Fri, Sat.

STUART'S OPERA HOUSE/NELSONVILLE—Stuart's Opera House has not only reopened, but since 2002 it's had Tim Peacock as impresario—or, according to his card, executive director. He brings in music, all kinds, he says, and lists folk, country, world, some classical, and some blues. In a year he schedules 100 events, and he expects 100 to 395 people for each show. Performers like the acoustics here; audiences like the auditorium's intimacy. A handsome feature of the Public Square streetscape, Stuart's Opera House opened in 1879—ten years after the railroad had arrived—and stayed in George Stuart's family until it closed in 1924, and then stayed closed. It did reopen in 1979, but a fire the next year shut it down again, and for want of funding, rebuilding was a slow process. But ultimately, the roof was rebuilt, and the interior and exterior, restored in accord with old photographs. Sprinklers, fire doors and exit signs were among the added safety features. In March, 1997, the Stuart reopened again, with Mark Twain impersonator Jack Spell on stage.
52 Public Square; 740/753-1924; www.stuartsoperahouse.org The web site lists upcoming events. Ticket prices depend on the event, and range from $5 to $33.

Stuart's Opera House

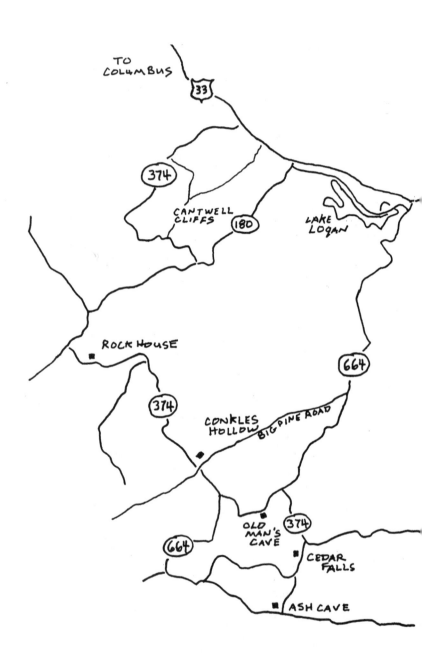

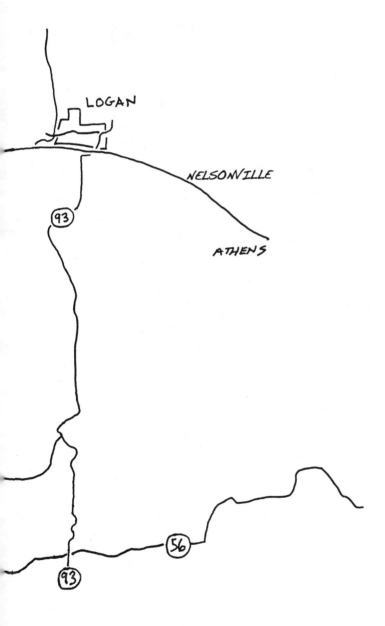

LOGAN

NELSONVILLE

93

ATHENS

56

93

Adams County Courthouse

Adams County

Though not really far away, Adams County seems very remote. For some people, including a New Jersey suburbanite or even an Amish man escaping the bustle of Holmes County, a remote place is where they want to be. For others, remote is where to go for escape—for country quiet and starry nights, back roads and, perhaps, some of that Amish blackberry jam cake. Adams County has no interstates, but it does have the pristine and scenic Appalachian Highway, designed to lure travelers.

Adams is one of Ohio's poorest counties, so there's no denying tired-looking trailers and yards full of junk cars. But it's rich in some things—plant species for one: it has more different ones than any county but Lucas. It has history, for in Ohio it's a relatively old county, named for John Adams, then president, and first settled in 1797. It has what is probably the state's oldest log cabin, Treber Inn, and West Union's Olde Wayside Inn, which has been serving lunch since 1804. That's not to say that Adams County has nothing modern, for it has an ultra-up-to-date facility where General Electric tests jet engines. It has no town with so many as 3,000 people but, perhaps because it's only an hour from Cincinnati, it has a place to stay that the National Geographic Traveler called one of the country's 54 great inns. It has the Edge of Appalachia Preserve; five state nature preserves, including one where you can see a geologic fault traversing a stream bed; and acres and acres for hunting and fishing and riding horses.

Adams County has one of Ohio's most singular landmarks, the mysterious Serpent Mound. It has resourceful natives who stay to write stories about local history or specialize in producing scented geraniums. It has an ever-growing Amish community, with many abandoning farm drudgery for the world of commerce, in which they are selling furniture, shoes, motion clocks and baked goods. And Adams County is beautiful. Especially noticeable when the leaves are down, the dark green of red cedars etches roadsides. Set on the Ohio River, it's very hilly, with creeks that nestle between hills and yield ribbons of steam when the morning sun comes on.

MURPHIN RIDGE INN/WEST UNION—If you're thinking of running away, run here. Listed as one of the top country inns in America, this venture is Ohio's best kept hideaway. The ten guest rooms, some with fireplaces, are in a striking contemporary guest house that overlooks the Appalachian uplift to the east. Cathedral ceilings and handmade furniture by Ohio artisan David T. Smith fill the rooms. A full breakfast is included and dinners, which feature local produce and are open to the public by reservation, are served in the 1828 Virginia-style brick farmhouse next door. Plan on spending two hours at a table. Upstairs there's a gift shop that exhibits and sells the work of Adams County artists. Owners Sherry and Darryl McKenney came from Dayton in 1997 when they bought the inn from its founders, Bob and Mary Crosset. The McKenneys added nine log cabins, all with hot tubs; and there's a swimming pool for summer use.

750 Murphin Ridge Road; 937/544-2263 and 877/687-7446; www.murphinridgeinn.com Open all year except for first two weeks of Jan; lower rates Jan-March 15. Rooms in 2007 were $124-$240. Restaurant dinners by reservation any night for inn guests; for others, Tue-Sat 5:30-8. Dinners $18-$32 per person; beer, wine and limited bar with no mixed drinks.

murphin ridge inn

UNITY WOODS/WEST UNION—Unity Woods offers
three Amish-style cottages, which means they have no electricity
and no television, but that does not mean they lack in amenities: the
refrigerators operate on propane, there's heat, and lanterns that will
enable you to read at night. The cottages accommodate from two
to six people, have porches and quiet settings, and are comfortable
and pleasing to the eye. A state nature preserve adjoins the property;
between that and Unity Woods' 175 acres, five-and-a-half miles of trails
are immediately available. The owners are Cindy and Jeff Cates, who
used to live and work in Cincinnati, where Jeff pined for the rustic way
of life they saw on vacations in Adams County.
*1095 Marjorie Johnson Road; 937/544-6908; www.unitywooods.org Open all
year. Rates range from $80-$100; lower rates and also senior discounts apply
weekdays. Pets all right weekdays.*

RIVERHAVEN/MANCHESTER—Judy Peterson redid the
house next door and opened a B&B overlooking the Ohio River. She
has six second-floor rooms, including a single, and promises a river view
for each one. Baths are in the hall, and she offers a full breakfast. On
the river side of the house there's a guest sitting room and a porch for
watching the river roll by. Some of her customers arrive by boat. Moyer
Vineyards is just up the road.
*407 West Front Street; 937/549-1999; www.ohioriverhaven.com Rates range
from $70 to $90; winter rates discounted; second nights half price on weekdays.
Senior rate.*

MOYER VINEYARDS WINERY & RESTAURANT/
MANCHESTER—Along with Murphin Ridge, Moyer's is one of
two notable restaurants in Adams County; it's a famous stop on U.S. 52,
where it overlooks the Ohio River. Though Moyer's owns 60 acres along
the river, only 12 of those are vineyards. That's enough for manager
Cindy Gilkison to promise that "there's a little bit of Moyer" in each
of the 60,000 bottles the winery produces every year, even though they
buy most of their grape stock. Gilkison and her husband, Robert, are
among the nine co-owners of Moyer. A group of retired teachers and a
judge, the owners are Adams County people who bought the business
from founders Ken and Mary Moyer. The Moyers still live next door
and show up often. Menu items include wild mushroom cabernet ribeye
($24), walnut feta chicken ($14), sandwiches and hamburgers, soups,
salads and desserts such as raw apple walnut cake and peanut butter pie.
And of course, Moyer wines are available.
*3859 U.S. 52; 937/549-2957. Mon-Thur 11:30-9; Fri-Sat 11:30-10. Closed
Sun except Mother's Day and Easter.*

THE OLDE WAYSIDE INN/WEST UNION—This 200-
year-old inn, a Blueplate Highway stop on the northeast corner of Main
and Cherry Streets, was once The Bradford Tavern and served Andrew
Jackson on his way to his inauguration in 1829, Mexican General Santa
Anna after his defeat by Sam Houston, and Statesman Henry Clay,
likely after a lengthy speech. The food is home-cooked and well-cooked,
served cafeteria-style. If you have a liking for whipped potatoes, skillet
gravy, old-fashioned dressings, homemade noodles, homemade apple
dumplings, homemade fruit and crème pies, and history, eat here.
*222 West Main Street; 937/544-7103. Tue-Fri 10-3, Sun 11-3; closed Sat and
Mon. Full meal $6-$8.*

ASIDE The Adams County engineer puts out a wonderful map—especially wonderful for visitors because on the back it has a Tourist Information map for the whole county. It shows foliage routes, Zane's Trace, the exact sites of the abandoned Mineral Springs Health Resort and the Counterfeit House, and all parks, preserves and trails. And more. You can pick one up at the county engineer's office, behind the courthouse at 116 Mulberry Street, or call 937/544-2943.

BLAKE PHARMACY/WEST UNION—A mild-mannered

drugstore outside, Blake Pharmacy on Courthouse square harbors one of Ohio's few remaining soda fountains and specializes in nickel Cokes. Things got really lively here when Bob Blake was mayor and officiated at 30 or 40 weddings in the sundry and Radio Shack aisle. Bob moved on to make Blake's a chain, adding stores in Peebles and Manchester, though they don't have soda fountains. His son Robert Allen Blake presides here and will be happy to make you an ice cream soda, malt, shake, or flavored Coke. Flavored Coke is five cents extra.
206 North Market Street; 937/544-2451. Mon-Sat 9 am-8 pm, Sun 1-5.

WILLIAM LAFFERTY MEMORIAL FUNERAL AND CARRIAGE COLLECTION/WEST UNION—The Lafferty

family have been in West Union since 1814, when two brothers arrived from Pennsylvania. As cabinet makers who produced coffins also, in 1848 they went into the funeral business, became transporters of coffins, producers of more elegant coffins, and, in the 1860s, embalmers as well. This funeral museum is a memorial to James William Lafferty (1912-1987), an undertaker for 59 years and a collector of professional paraphernalia. At present the big part of the exhibit is nineteenth-century horse-drawn hearses; the collection also includes old motorized vehicles, but there isn't room for them yet. Other exhibits include embalming texts and tools, and accessories, like lecterns, for home funerals. Front pages announcing the deaths of celebrated people, like Thomas Edison, President Reagan or Bob Hope, line the walls. The only really sad part is the little coffins.
205 South Cherry Street; 937/544-2121. After business hours (5 on weekdays, 1 on Sat) or after noon Sun, by appointment. Free.

ADAMS COUNTY HERITAGE CENTER/WEST

UNION—Originally a church, this crisp, well-landscaped brick heritage center also spent a good portion of its life as a funeral home, with entries widened for caskets and casket-bearing horse-drawn hearses. Now it houses the jewels of historic Adams County, from prehistoric Indian relics to Nathaniel Massie's surveying equipment (they fought for legal rights to it and removed it from the Warren County Historical Society); from an antique horn that belonged to the oldest band in Ohio (Liberty Band) to a display of murdered Sheriff Ben Perry's badges. The Adams County Genealogical Society and the Adams County Historical Society share the Heritage Center, and only genealogists keep regular hours here.
507 Heritage Way, two blocks north of Adams County Courthouse on State Route 247; 937/544-8522. Thur and Sat noon-4.

ASIDE It's appealing to fantasize about taking a very private guided tour of the eclectic Adams County with someone who can entertain, enlighten and organize 584 square miles of landscape, history and pie and leave you at day's end simultaneously lighter and heavier. In reality the person exists but his free time does not. Stephen Kelley has spent half his lifetime collecting, sorting and synthesizing Adams County. The tangible results are in a collection of ancient Indian relics he has found, bought or traded; newspaper columns beginning in 1981; four years of his published quarterly, *Ohio Southland*; the formation of the Adams County Heritage Center and many years as president of the Historical Society; self-published Adams County books and collections of photos, including *Landmarks of West Union, Ohio*; and the linguistic talent for informal, painless historical enlightenment. Kelley says that occasionally he'll do a bus trip, but because he has to take time off from work, he has to charge. *Write P.O. Box 208, Seaman, OH 45679-0208.*

COUNTERFEIT HOUSE/MANCHESTER—If you like
"drive-by chilling" wander past the house that Oliver Tompkins built in 1840; it's the only house in the U.S. designed and built to counterfeit money. It was here that Tompkins made his "funny" $500 bills.

Special door locks could only be operated by the "right" people; secret compartments over fireplaces gave Tompkins hiding places for himself, while slots inside doors hid money; five false chimneys gave off smoke and were used as spy towers to check on visitors; trap doors and a secret room with no obvious doors or windows concealed the money-making. If all this isn't spooky enough for you, take in the bloody fingerprints that appear through the painted walls, and the human bones discovered in a barbecue pit and on display by the front door. Jo Lynn Spires is the third generation of her family to own and manage the house; she also uses it as a showcase for the antiques she has to sell.

1580 Gift Ridge Road, five miles south of West Union just west of State Route 247; 937/549-2309. Open from first weekend in May until after first weekend in Oct. Call first; donations requested.

Counterfeit House

ASIDE Adams County Amish are in their fourth generation. In 1976 there were seven families living on Wheat Ridge Road and by 2006 there were about ninety families throughout the county. These Old Order Amish have divided into four congregations, Wheat Ridge East, Wheat Ridge West, Middle East and Middle West, with church services taking place, by turn, in family homes. The first generation, now in their 70s and 80s, brought a new life and productive order to an otherwise sagging countryside. They began growing wheat and corn, developed a cedar wood business, raised dairy cows and built homes. When their children took over and brought in tourists and thousands of dollars of added income, many of the older generation set off to do some sight-seeing of their own. Mom and Dad might head for Washington, D.C., on an Amish-filled tour bus, or even embark on a seven-week cruise to Europe, while we English show up to visit those still at home.

COUNTRYSIDE FURNITURE/WEST UNION—Like

us, the Amish are part of the global economy. An Amish bird-house manufacturer was so successful that the company was sold and sold again. The last owner moved all production to China. At this shop, owner Aaron Miller acknowledges that the steel-frame wicker furniture he sells is from China, and the "motion clocks" he has on display are from Japan. If you want to know what a motion clock is, stop in to see Mr. Miller and watch these clock faces turn around at the hour, and play music. After you've seen the wicker and the motion clocks, Mr. Miller, who in 1997 moved to Adams County from Holmes County in search of a less commercial place, also will show you the handsome locally made wooden furniture.
4153 Unity Road, West Union; 937/544-8019. Mon-Sat 9-5.

KEIM FAMILY MARKET/SEAMAN—After Roy Keim and

his family moved from Holmes County to Adams County, they began raising a little money by selling home-baked pies from a buggy alongside State Route 32. Soon enough, the buggy was too small. Now the Keims have a store just off the highway, and it's no longer Mrs. Keim and her daughters who are doing the baking, but half a dozen hired Amish girls who are producing breads, cakes, pies and the creme horns celebrated by a Cincinnati radio station. Candies are for sale, as well as deli sandwiches, which you're invited to eat in the picnic area outside. And lots of furniture is on display, including all kinds of gliders and rocking chairs and even a two-story children's play house. Tour buses are regulars here. Be sure to try the blackberry jam cake.
2621 Burnt Cabin Road and East State Route 32; 937/386-9995. Open year-round, Mon-Fri 8-6, Sat 8-5.

MILLER'S BAKERY, MILLER'S BULK FOODS AND MILLERS FURNITURE & BARNS/WEST UNION—

Daniel Miller's father was part of the first generation of Amish who in 1976 moved from Indiana to Adams County, where he raised beef and crops. The children were the ones who started baking; Daniel, for one, likes business better than dozing behind a plow. The Millers like running the store so much that they've propelled it into an enormous enterprise: three stores in separate buildings at one location, with a total of about 35,000 square feet. In a huge kitchen every week the bakery yields 40 dozen glazed doughnuts, 400 loaves of bread and 150 pies. Bulk Food has a wide array of goods, including Minnetonka moccasins, jams and jellies, spices, pretzel mix, a 17-pound bag of flour, and bargain groceries. But by far the biggest building is that for Furniture & Barns, where you can find everything from oak file cabinets, pie safes, bedroom furniture and complete diningroom sets, to sheds and barns. There are some frantic days now, Daniel admits, when behind a plow appears to be an attractive option.

960 Wheat Ridge Road; 937/544-8524. Open year-round Mon-Sat 9-5.

ZANE'S TRACE/STATE ROUTE 41—Cutting diagonally through Adams County is the road generally credited to Ebenezer Zane. Although he did survey and map the route that originated near Wheeling on the Ohio River and went across southeastern Ohio to Maysville, Kentucky, bison should really receive the credit for the original path. Indians followed, then early traders, settlers, important travelers, inns to accommodate them, and finally, asphalt. In July 1863 Morgan's Raiders followed Zane's Trace for part of their ride through the county. Watch for these historic sites, still standing but privately owned, along State Route 41: The Wickerham Inn (1801), just north of Peebles, was the first plastered house in the Virginia Military District. It's said to be haunted. The Treber Inn (1798), just south of Wheat Ridge Road, was built by the local gunsmith John Treber, because so many travelers pestered him for a place to stay. One of the oldest log buildings in Ohio, the Treber Inn served as an inn and stagecoach stop for forty years. Governor Kirker's Home (1805), southwest of West Union, is still owned by the family. Thomas Kirker was the first to leave Nathaniel Massie's fort in Manchester and build a home in the Adams County wilderness. Located on the original trace that veered off today's State Route 41 (the original ran parallel to today's road a little to the north; it was moved when West Union became county seat), the house is at the intersection of State Route 136 and Pixley Road. Kirker was later governor twice, though never elected. The house section in hand-hewn stone was his original home.

LEWIS MOUNTAIN HERBS & EVERLASTINGS/
MANCHESTER—The Amish aren't the only big tourist draw in the county. Judy Lewis has been growing herbs and everlastings (the "now" term for flowers that can be dried) since 1974, when she and her late husband, John, founded this business. In three spring months she sells over 150,000 live herbs in Ohio, Kentucky, Indiana and West Virginia. She carries over 600 varieties of herbs, everlastings and scented geraniums, which last are her specialty. She has 60 varieties of them, with fragrance options including rose, spice, pine and mint. The grounds, greenhouses, gift shop, and Melrose apple gazebo host garden club meetings, a couple tour buses a month, and weddings. You'll see quilt patterns on barns all over Adams County (and in other states too.) The very first quilt pattern on a barn, a memorial to a woman who quilted, was dedicated across the road from Lewis Mountain in 2001. (To see all 20 in the county, pick up the "Quilt Barn Trail" flyer from Adams County Travel & Visitors Bureau, 877/232-6764.) Energetic

Judy Lewis also has three rooms with private bathrooms that she rents on a B&B basis ($50 each) and a nice cottage with a kitchen as well as a bath ($65). *2345 State Route 247; 937/549-2484 or 800/714-3727; www.mtherbs.com Open year-round Mon-Sat 9-4. Closed Sun. Call about group tours and craft classes.*

OLDE THYME HERB FAIR—Over 30,000 people show up
at Lewis Mountain in the fall for two days of summer harvest. There are over 200 booths run by herb clubs; offerings include herb-related antiques, Amish crafts and food, herbal snacks, the Adams County Liberty Band, the West Union Steel Drummers Band, and enough herbs and everlastings to heal, spice, freshen and decorate unbounded floral cravings. Arrive with an empty car trunk.
Second weekend in Oct, Sat-Sun 10-5; 937/549-2484.

ASIDE Dr. Cornelia Dettmer would be amazing no matter where she lived; certainly Manchester hasn't been the same since she arrived. After retiring from her job as a radiation oncologist in Annapolis in 1993, she moved to Manchester. The lure was a fine 1856 red brick house always owned by a family named Ellison whose last member had died, leaving the house and its contents on the market. Dettmer bought it all, moved in, rescued the roof and other precarious elements, and studied up on the Ellisons, who were among the earliest families of Adams County. William, from the second Ellison generation and the builder of this house, became the county's richest resident following a profitable stay in the Ironton iron industry.

Among Dettmer's first moves in Manchester was to become unretired. The local doctor was leaving, so she bought the practice and became Manchester's primary care physician. And she took a good look at her new community. "I saw a terminal town," she says, "and all my cancer instincts came to the fore." After the flood of 1997 she volunteered to be floodplain administrator—two thirds of downtown Manchester is in the floodplain. Buildings began to be flood-proofed, and new construction was elevated above the 100-year flood level. Manchester's floodplain program won state and national awards.

As the town doctor, Dettmer got to know everyone, which helped when she ran for mayor in 2000; even though she was an outsider, she won by a good margin. Her slogan was "Restore Pride in Manchester"—the then ongoing fiscal emergency was nothing to be proud of. She was an activist mayor. Aside from becoming fiscally solvent again, Manchester launched events to attract tourists, cleaned up sidewalks and installed awnings. In 2004 Dettmer was reelected, but in 2005 she had to resign because of health problems. She kept on as physician until March, 2006, when she turned 75 and her insurance premiums skyrocketed.

That left Cornelia Dettmer, by now a serial retiree, with time on her hands. She repapered some rooms, went off on a trip, and began looking around for her next challenge. The next thing she knew, she was running for mayor again, and was elected again in November 2007 and took office in January, 2008. If she's available, Dettmer will show her house to visitors who make an appointment ahead. *503 East 8th Street; 937/549-2149. Charge is $5.*

EDGE OF APPALACHIA PRESERVE SYSTEM/LYNX—

Mostly on the east side of Ohio Brush Creek, there lies a land unique, beautiful and *protected*. It's an Ohio Galapagos, so to speak, where the unbridled enthusiasm of botanists collides with about 100 potentially threatened, threatened or endangered species and where the rare Allegheny wood rat, mollusks and green salamanders live on where farmers couldn't. Here, at the western flank of the Appalachian Plateau, are 14,000 acres protected by the Cincinnati Museum Center and The Nature Conservancy. This is the only place in Ohio where acidic Appalachian shale soils meet "sweet" limestone soils, so that at times plant communities change abruptly, in as little as ten feet, with plants like chestnut oak and red cedar preferring shale, and sugar maple, tulip trees and spring flowers preferring alkaline soil. The Edge of Appalachia System covers a 12-mile long, north-south stretch of land, making it the largest privately owned group of nature preserves in the state and a whopping piece of real estate for Chris Bedel, director, to keep an eye on. Bedel works for the Cincinnati Museum Center. He's the guy who chases off motorcycles, does PR, creates a budget, deals with illegal dumping, writes the grants, raises money, repels root diggers and runs eleven sessions of summer science camp. It helps to be enthusiastic and in good shape. But he's always looking for volunteers to help make trails, do repair work, check for unwanted debris, or share a spontaneous wonderment.
4274 Waggoner Riffle Road, (West Union post office); 937/544-2880; www. cincymuseum.org; www.nature.org; email: eoa@bright.net

Edge of Appalachia has three public access sites, Buzzardroost Rock Trail, Lynx Prairie, and Wilderness Trail, which may be visited without permission. They exist for research, education, passive recreation and preservation, so please stay on the paths and *don't pick or dig the flowers*. They have no facilities—no toilets, signs or picnic tables—except for parking areas. A 72-page spiral-bound booklet, *The Richard and Lucile Durrell Edge of Appalachia Preserve System, Adams County, Ohio*, by George Laycock, with some history of the region and detailed trail maps, is available for $10 at the Cincinnati Museum Center, Murphin Ridge Inn, or by email: eoa@bright.net For information on guided hikes for groups call 937/544-2880.

BUZZARDROOST ROCK TRAIL—This block of Peebles

limestone—75 feet high, 81-by-36-feet at the top—attracts more people for the view than for the 21 species of plants on it. Once almost trampled to death, the flora is now protected by a wooden walkway made and maintained by volunteers. Called Split Rock Hill by native Americans and settlers, Buzzardroost got its new name from the turkey and black vultures often seen roosting there or flying overhead. The rock rises 500 feet above the Ohio Brush Creek Valley. The trail to the rock and back is 3.4 miles with just one huffing-and-puffing hill.
Take State Route 125 east from West Union toward Lynx. Turn left on Weaver Road to parking area (north side of State Route 125). Trail then crosses State Route 125 heading southwest and zigzags, with a sharp right turn to the rock.

LYNX PRAIRIE—The best time to visit is during July, August and September when the prairie is in full bloom. If you want to experience the romance of your pioneer forbearers, try this. Put on jeans, hiking boots or sturdy shoes, insect repellent (chiggers and ticks can be aggressive) and sunglasses. Bring water and a camera. Look for signs of over 250 plant species on these ten prairie openings, some no bigger than a livingroom. Watch every step you take to avoid crushing something rare. When you get home, take a hot, soapy shower or bath to get rid of the chiggers and ticks. Envision your pioneer forbearers with a cold, soapy bucket of water and no calamine.

Take State Route 125 east from West Union through Lynx. Take Tulip Road, the first hard-paved road to your right. Go half a mile to East Liberty Church on the left. Turn into the drive and go past the church and park at the white picket fence. For trailhead, go to the right side (southeast corner) of the cemetery.

BUCKEYE TRAIL—The Buckeye Trail is over 1400 miles of Sherwin-Williams's #2408 "Sweeping Blue" paint blazes circling inside the Ohio borders. According to the very specific manual for Buckeye Trail Maintenance Volunteers, ideally a hiker should be able to see those blazes looking forward and backward from any point. And on each off-road stretch ideally the trail should be "a pathway with sound footing, reasonably free of vegetative hindrances and at least three feet wide." There are 26 detailed section maps and three—Sinking Spring, Shawnee, and West Union—are mostly in Adams County, though all three also spill into adjacent counties. The Sinking Spring-Shawnee sections are loaded with history and improbable wonders, like Mineral Springs Lake, the largest privately owned lake in Ohio; the entrance to GE Aviation's Peebles Test Operation; and the ruins of the former resort town of Mineral Springs.

Buckeye Trail Association, P.O. Box 254, Worthington, OH 43085; www. buckeyetrail.org/

WILDERNESS TRAIL—The renowned botanist E. Lucy Braun wasn't the first scientist to explore Adams County flora, but starting in the early 1910s she came as often as she could. Her students at the University of Cincinnati, where she was a Professor of Ecology, included Richard and Lucile Durrell, whom she introduced to Adams County. The Durrells, both ultimately University of Cincinnati faculty themselves, also helped buy land here to preserve it, and to encourage others to do so. They were leading progenitors of Edge of Appalachia. As for the land in the Wilderness Trail, they were the ones who gradually acquired it, starting in 1971. The detailed trial guide will point out exactly when you're at the junction of two bedrocks, two soils, and two different wildlife realms.

Take State Route 125 east from West Union to the left turn for Lynx Road. After .3 mile turn left onto Shivener Road (unpaved) and go to the parking lot at the end of the road.

ADAMS COUNTY NATURE YIN AND YANG—Eight different agencies own numerous natural areas (including Edge of Appalachia). What's legal at one will get you arrested at another. Some places do allow hunting, backpacking, or, at certain times of year, digging for ginseng; others allow none of these. For web sites contact www.ohiodnr.com which tells about preserves, wildlife, state forests and state parks. For more information on state nature preserves, call Martin McAllister, preserves manager, at 937/545-8313. State public recreation facilities in the county include the following:

Adams Lake State Park (937/544-3927) This day-use park offers fishing, picnicking, hiking and boating (no gasoline engines.)
Just north of West Union line on State Route 41.

Adams Lake Prairie State Nature Preserve (937/544-9750) Adjacent to Adams Lake State Park, at the end of the park road, these 25 acres have two quarter-mile trails. Post Oak Trail goes through the forest. Prairie Dock Trail goes through the xeric Prairie Remnant which includes 14 species of rare prairie plants.

Davis Memorial State Nature Preserve (937/544-9750). Scientists from all over the world have visited the 167-acre Davis Memorial. There are rugged cliffs, rich forests, prairie openings, even a sink hole. There is a portion of The Buckeye Trail plus two half-mile nature trails that are beautiful and informative. On the Agave Ridge Trail it's possible to see a geological fault line crossing a shallow stream bed, while on the far side two adjacent dolomites demonstrate that the Peebles variety is rounded and the Greenfield, jagged and layered.
From State Route 32 at State Route 41, go 1.2 miles east on 32; turn right/south on Steam Furnace Road and go .3 mile; turn left on Davis Memorial Road and continue 2.8 miles.

Tranquility Wildlife Area (937/372-9261). Tranquility has 4254 acres of public hunting, fishing, and hiking. There's also a shooting range.
Northeast of Tranquility (itself northeast of Seaman) between State Route 770 and County Road 100, which form a V that encloses two sides of the thousands of acres.

Brush Creek State Forest (740/858-6685; 877/247-8733). Hiking, picnicking, and horseback riding are the main activities in this 13,000-acre day-use forest, which has both hiking and bridle trails. The hardwood forest is usually thick with deer hunters in open season. Brush Creek, which has many disconnected areas, is administered at Shawnee State Forest.
State Route 73 south of State Route 32.

Chaparral Prairie State Nature Preserve (937/544-9750). This 66-acre nature preserve is spotted with prairie vegetation and mixed forests, with good displays of blazing star, rattlesnake master, and prairie false indigo. It has one three-quarter mile loop trail called Hawk Hill Loop.
From North Union go north on State Route 247 .1 mile from corporation line; turn left on Chaparral Road for 2.7 miles; turn right for .2 mile on Hawk Hill Road.

Whipple State Nature Preserve (937/544-9750). The 1.5-mile trail here offers nice early wildflower displays, dolomite cliffs, old second-growth forest and fine ridgetop views of the Ohio River valley.
From West Union corporation line go south on State Route 247 5.6 miles. Site is on left. Parking is a small gravel pull-off; no buses.

SERPENT MOUND STATE MEMORIAL/PEEBLES—One of Ohio's man-made wonders, the Serpent Mound undulates for 1,348 feet, and likely seems as amazing now as it must have when the Fort Ancient people built it around 1070 AD. That year was fixed in 1991 by radiocarbon dating, which made the mound about 1800 years younger than previously supposed. Since 1900 the Ohio Historical Society has owned Serpent Mound. About 18,000 visitors arrive every year to take the path around the mound and perhaps visit the museum.
3850 State Route 73 north of Peebles; 937/587-2796 or 800/752-2757; www. ohiohistory.com/places/serpent/ Grounds open year-round, Wed-Sun 10-5; closed Thanksgiving, Christmas, New Year's Day; museum, April-May and Sept-Oct, Sat-Sun 10-5; Memorial Day-Labor Day, Wed-Sun, 10-5. Groups year-round by appointment. Parking is $7 per car, more for RVs, buses; free for OHS members.

GOODSEED FARM/PEEBLES—In 1997 Steve and Marjorie Boehme pulled up stakes in suburban Trenton, New Jersey, and moved to Adams County, where they'd found just what they wanted: a 158-acre abandoned farm in a place where no lights are on all night, so they can see the stars. Besides, it cost about what they received for their three acres in New Jersey. In an old barn near the road, they set up a full-line garden store, the only one in the county. Trained in his family landscape business in New Jersey, Steve also runs a design-and-build landscape service; but he's in the shop on weekends. Keeping his eyes open in the rural setting, the Boehmes' teen-age son Stephen has identified sixty bird species on the farm. Stephen also has 48 hens, and sells the eggs at GoodSeed's shop.
200 Storer Road at County Road 100 (Old State Route 32); 937/587-7021; www.goodseedfarm.com/ From State Route 32 take State Route 41 north into Peebles. At the first light go left onto Vine Street; at the stop sign go right onto Marble Furnace Road/Old State Route 32 and continue west three miles; store is on the right. Mon-Sat 8-6; Sun noon-5. Open March 1-Christmas Eve.

ASIDE With a little down time in winter, Steve Boehme publishes "Crossroads", an Adams County booklet distributed by the Chamber and the Travel & Visitors Bureau. Among the best county visitors guides, "Crossroads" runs informative articles, lists of phone numbers and Amish craftsmen for hire, a big ad for GoodSeed, and lots more. You can pick up a copy at the Welcome Center, 110 N. Manchester St., West Union; 937/549-8515.

GE AVIATION PEEBLES TEST OPERATION—Like the Serpent Mound, this is one of the most unusual, most amazing places in Adams County. But unlike Serpent Mound, this is one that none of us without badges—which means, virtually none of us—can actually visit. It's a 7000-acre site used for testing and assembling GE jet engines, and though it has only about 250 employees, it has many of the earmarks of a small city, such as a ten-room motel, in this case reserved for visiting employees and contractors. There are forty miles of roads, 250 acres of mowed grass, and water, phone and electric systems. There are three fire trucks, an ambulance and a hazmat spill truck, all with trained personnel. And finally there are the eight active test sites, six of them outdoors—in 2007 two new ones were part of a $90 million expansion. At one test site a wind tunnel can produce headwinds, tailwinds and

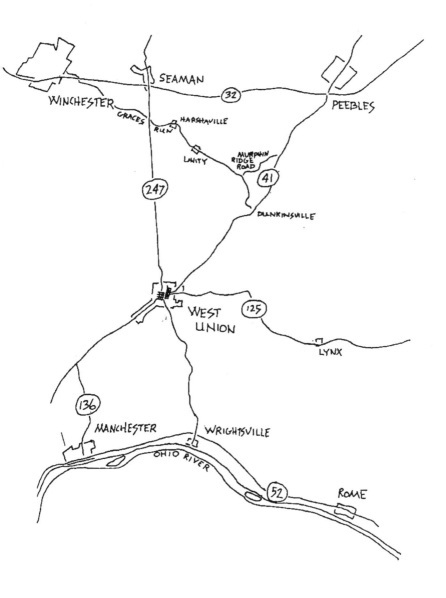

Trail Tavern

Yellow Springs

The most obvious and remarkable characteristic of Yellow Springs is its self-containment. Though the metropolitan sprawl of Dayton lies only a short highway hop away, the village remains isolated by broad expanses of farm fields and the Little Miami River, a hundred-mile-long waterway unspoiled and pretty enough to be designated both a State and National Scenic River. Two splendid National Natural Landmarks—Clifton Gorge and Glen Helen—border the Little Miami near Yellow Springs and along with John Bryan State Park, form a continuous three-mile belt of woodland that almost entirely cordons off the village's eastern flank. The residents consider themselves the virtual stewards of the Glen and the Gorge. In recent years the Tecumseh Land Trust, which helps landowners set up conservation easements, has only enhanced the greening of Yellow Springs' environs.

Although finding Yellow Springs on the map is relatively easy—east of Dayton, south of Springfield, north of Xenia—locating its true coordinates is something else entirely. Beyond geography, Yellow Springs is a state of mind. Long-time villagers think of themselves as artists, artisans, scholars, social and political activists living the rational lifestyle. Many outsiders aren't too sure about that, but there is no question the village is luring new residents--including some commuters, particularly to the south side, where some distinctive modern housing is springing up.

There was a time in the mid-nineteenth century when outsiders thought of Yellow Springs as Sodom and Gomorrah on the Little Miami, for a group of free-lovers had taken up residence in nearby hills. Then the renowned educator, Horace Mann, chose this part of the Ohio hinterland for his experiment in egalitarian education. Mann launched a crusade to run the free-lovers away—he didn't want them sullying his fledgling Antioch College.

While other Ohio towns developed on seed corn and elbow grease, Yellow Springs began with a health spa that boasted a resort hotel. The iron-laden waters gave the village its name and attracted both the afflicted and those afflicted with wealth, who came by the trainload to avoid the heat, escape the cholera and partake of the "medicinal" mineral springs.

Eventually the hotel disappeared, but the college has endured for more than a century and a half. The twenty-first century, however, has not dealt kindly with the unstructured curriculum and nontraditional approach to learning that ultimately evolved. Enrollment plummeted, an attempt to revamp college programs failed, and finally the college announced a plan to suspend operations in 2008, in hopes of reopening in 2012. Then, as alumni pledged millions of dollars, the trustees agreed not to close after all. With or without the college, the village of some 4,000 retains a strong tradition of self-expression and intellectual interests. It may be one of the tiniest places anywhere with its own public radio station. There is also a locally organized chamber music concert series, which brings notable ensembles to the village for Sunday evening concerts, and there is the coolly elegant Shirley Jones Gallery on Corry Street, which exhibits the work of contemporary artists who often have a connection to the region.

ARTHUR MORGAN HOUSE—This bed and breakfast with six guest rooms, each with private bath, was the home of Arthur Morgan, president of Antioch College from 1921 to 1936, and his wife, Lucy. The large stucco house is located on a quiet, tree-shaded street a short distance from everything visitors would want to see in Yellow Springs. Innkeeper Susanne Oldham specializes in made-to-order breakfasts—eggs, scones, locally roasted coffee and more, with the emphasis on organically grown ingredients. The rooms have no telephones or televisions. However, all communication is not lost: free wireless internet is available throughout the house. One of the real treasures of the place is Oldham herself. She grew up in Yellow Springs and arguably knows more about the village and the surrounding area than anyone else you are likely to meet. Those lucky guests who are adept at the grand piano in the living room, may even be able to convince her to accompany them on the flute.
120 W. Limestone Street; 937/767-1761; www.arthurmorganhouse.com No smoking; pets only for special circumstances. Rooms from $95 to $115.

EDEN HALL/XENIA—This Greek Revival mansion was built in 1840 by Abraham Hivling, a prominent Xenia businessman. The story goes that Hivling's father, while building homes for each of his eight daughters, told his soon-to-be-married son that he was obliged to build his own house. And so Abraham set about building "a bigger house than any of the girls have," and the result was a 9,400-square-foot mansion. Its ownership stayed in the Hivling family until it was sold to Paul and Evelyn Cozatt in 1972. Mrs. Cozatt filled the 32 rooms with the international antiques and artifacts that she collected and opened up for tours by appointment. In 2003 Rick and Tracy Gerhardt purchased Eden Hall and began restoring the home and grounds. Three rooms are now a B&B.
235 East Second Street; 937/372-8750 or 800/930-3881; www.edenhallmansionbedandbreakfast.com Rooms are $100.

YE OLDE TRAIL TAVERN—Aptly named, Ye Olde Trail Tavern has stood vigil since 1927 on what once was the trail linking Springfield and Xenia. And while the route has now been paved and given a state highway number, once inside at the bar or at one of the dark wooden tables in the rear room, customers can be forgiven for imagining they left their horses tethered outside. The back room, incidentally, was originally a log cabin. In recent years, both a glass-enclosed eating area and a deck have been added to the tavern, much to the chagrin of preservationists. However, the clientele still comes for some simple food—maybe a beer and a burger—and also for such rare libations as black and tan on tap.
228 Xenia Avenue; 937/767-7448. Mon-Thurs 11:30-10; Fri-Sat 11:30-11; Sun 12:30-5:30. Inexpensive.

THE WINDS—What started out as a collectively owned and operated café that made its own yogurt and baked its own bread has evolved into a restaurant with a reputation throughout the region for fine food and wine. Owners Kim Korkan and Mary Kay Smith have cultivated a loyal cadre of customers with an eclectic menu that weans the taste buds away from meat 'n potatoes and toward imaginatively prepared dishes featuring in-season produce. There are small plates— such as stuffed calamari or Thai beef salad; and large plates --- grilled tuna or a springtime special of chive crepes stuffed with local asparagus and house-made ricotta or porcini dusted game hen. The dinner menu changes monthly, introducing diners to different entrées matched with different wines. Wednesday evenings are designated as "bistro nights" with a prix fixe menu that includes four courses, salad through dessert, and a half bottle of wine. Featured wines—actually, an entire inventory of fine wines—are for sale at the wine cellar next to the restaurant. Reservations are recommended, especially for bistro nights and weekends. Small plates range from $5 to $10; large plates average $25. *215 Xenia Avenue, 937/767-1144; www.windscafe.com Tue-Sat 11:30-2 and 5-10; Sun brunch 10-2. Wine Cellar Tue-Sat 11-9.*

QUICK EATS—Unlike most towns of its size, Yellow Springs has no tradition of the "greasy spoon" diner. And while a couple of fast food restaurants have located there, villagers hit with hunger or too busy to cook head to Current Cuisine, a gourmet deli with fine cheeses, prepared foods, salads, sandwiches and soups. There are a couple of tables inside and, in warmer weather, a few out on the sidewalk. Incidentally, the deli's name refers to the name of the owners, the Currents, rather than the faddishness of the menu. Also on Xenia Avenue is the Sunrise Café, whose menu lists a number of vegetarian dishes and carries the warning "We Do Not Have A Microwave." Items are made from scratch so don't be in a rush.

CHAMBER MUSIC YELLOW SPRINGS—Yellow Springs is home to one of the nation's premier chamber music concert series, primarily because so many talented music-lovers live there. The village virtually constituted an audience waiting for an ensemble, and in 1982 they came together with the creation of Chamber Music Yellow Springs, a presenting organization that invites musicians from the United States and abroad to give one of the five performances in a season. The season runs from October through March or April and always ends with a competition with two groups competing for a cash award. The concerts, which usually take place Sunday evenings in the First Presbyterian Church, are very popular and often sold out. *314 Xenia Avenue (U.S. 68). For tickets and times call 937/374-8800; www.cmys.org*

LITTLE ART THEATRE—When the online magazine Salon asked for nominations for the "greatest art-house theater in an unlikely spot," it didn't surprise Yellow Springs folks when their Little Art Theatre came up a winner. Tucked inconspicuously between storefronts on Xenia Avenue, the theater is one of the rare places where the medium of film is regarded with respect. There's a good variety of films—foreign, art and independent as well as Hollywood productions. Like most art theaters outside major metropolitan areas, this one struggles along, but each week it succeeds in bringing remarkable cinema to the village. Schedules are available by calling the theater or checking its website. *247 Xenia Avenue, 937/7671; www.littleart.com*

ASIDE—The renowned—to cyclists at least—Little Miami Scenic Trail runs from Springfield to Cincinnati, some 77 miles. The hub is the Xenia Station, at the junction of U.S. 68 and U.S. 42, three blocks south of the Greene County courthouse, which provides plenty of parking and restrooms. From the hub, it's just a short ride—less than ten miles—north to Yellow Springs and then on to Springfield. The southern route more or less follows the Little Miami River, toward Spring Valley some seven miles away and then on through Warren and Hamilton counties to the Queen City. Portions of the trail are well shaded, others run along farmland and meadows; and there are numerous staging areas, and restrooms, along the trail. The surface is paved and even attracts hearty hikers for various segments. www.miamivalleytrails.org

---

GLEN HELEN—This thousand-acre nature preserve serves unofficially as an enormous community backyard for the villagers of Yellow Springs, who take to these verdant hills with great frequency, enthusiasm and affection. There are more than twenty miles of trails, all open year-round during daylight hours. In 1975, the 1886 Cemetery Road covered bridge was moved to the Glen and can be viewed from Grinnell Road; to walk through it, follow the path from the highway. You'll find that graffiti scribblers have gotten there first. Having been developed originally in the nineteenth century as a health resort where the mineral-laden Yellow Spring promised a "cure", the Glen predates the village. Today, as its donor intended, it's a wild preserve. Benefactor Hugh Taylor Birch, who gave the Glen to Antioch College in memory of his daughter, wanted a living wildlife laboratory. It offers forests, meadows and prairies amid three-hundred-year-old oak trees, massive sycamores and the lovely sweep of the Little Miami River across the floor of the Glen. Children especially like to hike these rocky hills and many of the field trips and educational programs are geared to them. Since 1961, some 60 acres of the Glen has been set aside for a Riding Centre, for horsemanship at any level.
405 Corry Street; 937/769-7375; www.glenhelen.org Open daily dawn to dusk. Free

REVIEWER'S FAVORITES/GLEN HELEN

1. The Inman Trail, the heavily forested loop that begins near Corry Street and drops—via steeply terraced steps—into the Glen for eye-popping views of natural and historic landmarks, including the Yellow Spring, which gave the village both its name and early medicinal fame. An 80-ton memorial boulder marks the burial site of Arthur Morgan, Antioch's long-time president, and his wife.

2. The Raptor Center at 1075 State Route 343 opened in 1970 for the rehabilitation of injured birds of prey, including owls, hawks and falcons. Those which couldn't survive in the wild are kept for educational uses and are on display in outdoor enclosures. 937/767-7648.

3. Trailside Museum, 505 Corry Street, is a perfect introduction to the Glen. Constructed of materials found in the Glen, it offers interpretive displays and a small menagerie of indigenous turtles, snakes and mice.

4. The Horace Mann Statue on Bryan Park Road was erected in 1935 to commemorate the centennial of public education. It's a replica of the famous Mann statue in Boston—Hugh Taylor Birch tracked down the original German molds.

Antioch Hall

Antioch College Campus—

Approaching Yellow Springs from the south of U.S. 68, the twin spires of Antioch Hall are visible in the distance, rising above the treetops like brick beacons to Horace Mann's ideal of democratic education. Because of those romantic spires, Antioch Hall—one of the first Victorian Gothic buildings in the United States—is an architectural cousin of the Smithsonian Institution. Along with the adjacent North and South Halls, it was one of the original buildings erected when Mann took charge of the fledgling school in 1853, one year after its founding. Mann's campus was a barren field, which, unfortunately, also described Antioch's coffers. He struggled valiantly but by 1859, the woes of Antioch College had killed the Father of American Education. An obelisk on a small mound behind Antioch Hall now marks his original burial site—the body was later removed to Rhode Island—and bears the moral exhortation that was the last sentence of his last address to his students: "Be ashamed to die until you have won some victory for humanity." Achieving victory for Antioch was thus left to Mann's successors at the college's helm. Then in the 1920s, President Arthur Morgan developed the first collegiate work-study program. It was Morgan's belief that the combination would keep the curriculum alive and allow students to apply what they learned in the classroom. The program remained at the heart of an Antioch education for more than 80 years. The remarkable Antiochiana Collection in the Olive Kettering Library attracts serious researchers with its volumes of original Morgan and Mann documents. Among the documents are the letters of Massachusetts's famous Peabody sisters (one married Horace Mann; the other, Nathaniel Hawthorne); a bust of Morgan made by students working in the foundry; and a clock and diningroom table belonging to Horace Mann. The Antiochiana Collection is open Mon-Fri 10-4:30. 937/769-1237; www.antioch-college.edu

SHOPPING IN YELLOW SPRINGS—Individually owned shops along Xenia Avenue (U.S. 68) and Corry Street are the focus of commercial life in Yellow Springs. Although the highway brings in a constant parade of traffic, pedestrians crossing from the shops on one side of Xenia Avenue to the other bring cars to a halt and lend a civilized note to the rhythm of commerce. It's easy to walk almost anywhere in the village center, and on-street parking, though not always easy to find, is usually free. The most uncommon aspect of Yellow Springs shopping is that the stores are locally owned, either by the villagers themselves or by residents of nearby Springfield. As befits a town that is home to many craftspeople, there is no shortage of shops featuring handicrafts made here and elsewhere. A popular stop is Unfinished Creations, which sells art and jewelry-making supplies. It also serves as a center for locals to trade information—after all the *Yellow Springs News* is only a weekly. (At noon some brown-baggers often gather to exchange news and hold impromptu discussions.) You'll find places to buy books and Birkenstocks, herbs, wines, distinctive toys. And, in the Kings Yard, an enclave of shops made user friendly with brick walks and strategically placed benches, you'll find handmade jewelry, a glass studio and a pottery collective run by local ceramists. Another store that deserves a visit is Julia Etta's Trunk on Corry Street, a women's shop that offers distinctive clothing in natural fibers.

ASIDE There are no shopping centers in Yellow Springs, which doesn't stop the perennial anxiety that someone is planning a strip center somewhere at sometime. Anyone with such an idea would be wise to read the history of the Whitehall Farm, close to 1,000 acres on the northern edge of the village, whose imminent sale at auction galvanized Yellow Springs in 1998-99. Fearing untoward development, the villagers pooled resources and persuaded the owners of the old Whitehall mansion to make a bid that would preserve the land. Just imagine the scene outside the auction hall that February evening as residents of Yellow Springs—hearkening back to the heyday of the sixties—sang "This Land Is Our Land" and "We Shall Overcome".

YOUNG'S JERSEY DAIRY—The Young family has been using the big red barn near the road since the end of the Civil War; by now, after generations in the dairy building, they know ice cream and how to make it. On any given day servers are dishing out some three dozen varieties and flavors of the cold, creamy dessert, including gelato and sugar free ice cream. Monday through Friday the visitor can peek through the glass of the white building south of the barn to watch ice cream in the making. But just as it's a far cry from the Civil War, so is Young's now a far cry from a simple dairy. They do sell ice cream and milkshakes, as well as baked goods and sandwiches. But there is also a restaurant, the Golden Jersey Inn, which offers country-style cooking— try the house specialty of baked potato soup with cheese for lunch ($4) or, perhaps, fall-off-the-bone barbecued pork ribs for dinner ($15 a half-slab). And then there is miniature golf and a driving range—called, of course, Udders and Putters—and batting cage. As a special treat for city or suburban kids, there are farm animals waiting to be fed and petted. Incidentally, Young's has such a loyal following in the region that on any day—especially a warm one—you're likely to find it crowded. Fortunately, there is a large parking lot.

6880 Springfield-Xenia Road/U.S. 68 North; Dairy Store 937/325-0629;
www.youngsdairy.com Sun-Thur 6 am-11 pm; Inn 937/324-2050, Mon-Fri 11-9,
Sat-Sun 8 am-9 pm.

ASIDE Founded in 1941 by a small group of Antioch College faculty,
the *Antioch Review* is one of the oldest and most prestigious literary
magazines in the United States. While it began as a forum for political
and social commentary, the *Review* quickly expanded its mission
to include short fiction and poetry. Its catalog of contributors is a
pantheon of contemporary thought and literature, stretching from John
Dewey through Ralph Ellison, from David Reisman and Daniel Bell to
Sylvia Plath to Rod Serling to Joyce Carol Oates, T.C. Boyle, Raymond
Carver and on and on. The *Review* also continues to serve what may
be its most important role, directing a spotlight on talented writers in
the early stages of their careers. Supported by Antioch College during
its initial decades, the quarterly now is funded through an endowment
and contributions to the Friends of the Antioch Review, as well as
annual subscriptions. www.review.antioch.edu

Clifton Mills

CLIFTON MILL/CLIFTON—Given the power of the Little
Miami River as it churns through the Clifton Gorge, it is no wonder
that Clifton was once the locus of a strong milling industry. There
was a linen mill, a saw mill, a paper mill and more. Today, the Clifton
Mill, built in 1802, is still in existence as the largest water-powered grist
mill in the United States. Not only are visitors invited to tour the mill,
but they can buy the freshly ground flour in the gift shop. Of course
there is the Millrace Restaurant in the building that once served as the
flour warehouse. The pancakes made from the corn and wheat are a
specialty—so much so that some years ago *Bon Appetit*, the gourmet
magazine, put the Millrace on its list of best breakfasts in the United

States. Since the mill perches on the rim of the Clifton Gorge, diners are also treated to an incomparable view through the back windows. Although the Clifton Mill is often busy, the crowds peak between the Thanksgiving and New Year's holidays when owner Anthony Satariano exhibits an awe-inspiring light display. Millions of lights are installed to illuminate the mill, the gorge and the grounds, and create a miniature replica of the old village. Mr. Satariano also displays his collection of over 3000 Santa Clauses, ranging from the very old to the very odd. And, for the delight of the children, there is a live Santa Claus, as well, who makes a trip down the chimney every 15 minutes.

75 Water Street, off State Route 72, seven miles south of Interstate 70; 937/767-5501; www.cliftonmill.com The restaurant is open Mon-Fri 9-4; Sat-Sun 8-5; it closes at 2 pm during the Christmas lighting season and through January. Inexpensive. The mill and gift shop remain open for an hour after the restaurant. Closed Christmas Day, New Year's, Easter and Thanksgiving Day.

ASIDE Perhaps no image in Yellow Springs better expresses Arthur Morgan's educational work-study concept than the mural in the lobby of the Yellow Springs Post Office on Corry Street. Axel Horn's painting, like hundreds of others done in public buildings across the country, was a byproduct of the Depression, when the Works Progress Administration doled out work to otherwise starving artists. Their commissions, being regional, focused on local themes: the Yellow Springs scene portrays a young man in a cornfield, who, having finished his work of felling a tree, lays aside his ax to study from a book.

JOHN BRYAN STATE PARK AND CLIFTON GORGE STATE NATURE PRESERVE/CLIFTON—Since Glen Helen

must be left wild and wonderful, campers, picnickers and fishers head, instead, to the abutting John Bryan State Park, which is named for the farmer who willed the land to Ohio in 1918. Initially, however, the state turned down the gift because Bryan, an atheist, had attached a proviso banning religious services. His generosity eventually overshadowed his philosophy and the state accepted his land for a park where the only worship today is to the glories of Mother Nature. But that doesn't keep the area at the eastern end of the park from an other-worldly atmosphere. Therein lies Clifton Gorge State Nature Preserve, a 269-acre realm that safeguards a spectacular canyon carved by erosion from a melting glacier. The dolomite and limestone gorge, with its rapids and waterfalls, is one of the most stunning geological sites in Ohio. Rare plant species have emerged from its shaded recesses, including the red baneberry and wall rue, a unique fern. The Little Miami River runs through the gorge, slowly, very slowly, widening it, but not making it deeper. The history of the area, of course, is not limited to geology. During the nineteenth century, the water power of the gorge enticed mills to the area. Before that, however, the gorge was the province of the Shawnee, who late in the 1780s captured frontiersman Cornelius Darnell, a crony of Daniel Boone. Darnell escaped by jumping across the gorge, a feat that made him a local legend. Today, the state's Division of Natural Areas and Preserves reminds visitors that the trails are steep and always slippery and that proper footwear and clothing are recommended.

Off State Route 343 west of Clifton and east of Yellow Springs; 937/767-1274. Open daily dawn to dusk.

FAVORITES/CLIFTON GORGE AND JOHN BRYAN STATE PARK

1. The Falls of the Little Miami at Clifton show water making one of the biggest splashes in Ohio.
2. The Narrows along Rich Trail is the neck in the river where Cornelius Darnell allegedly made his 22-foot leap to escape from the Indians.
3. The Blue Hole is a pool in the Little Miami near the gorge's Rich Trail. Another name is Spirit Pool, for the Indian maiden who drowned there, a victim of unrequited love. Legend has it that once a year her spirit rises at midnight and wails with grief.
4. The wildflowers offer the uncommon diversity of more than 300 species.
5. The Tecumseh Tree is a grand specimen several hundred years old. It witnessed the growth of another grand native of the area, the Shawnee Chief who is its namesake.

ASIDE Famous comedian Dave Chappelle makes his home in Yellow Springs when he is not traveling as one of the top stand-up comedians of the times. He comes upon the location quite naturally, having spent much of his youth in the village—his father taught voice and music at Antioch College. Those who have seen the documentary "Dave Chappelle's Block Party," may recall the opening scene featuring the marching band from nearby Central State University.

NATIONAL MUSEUM OF THE UNITED STATES AIR FORCE—More than a million people a year visit what is generally called the Air Force Museum—the name was changed officially in 2004—making it the most popular non-commercial (free) attraction in the state; the three hangar-sized buildings comprise the world's largest museum dedicated to military aviation. History buffs will find it difficult to tear themselves away from the buildings dedicated to the early years of flight—check out the cloth covered biplanes—and the craft of World Wars I and II. Among them are the plane that dropped the atom bomb on Nagasaki; the German Messerschmitt, the first operational turbojet; the Japanese Zero, and the V-1 and V-2 rocket-powered long-range missiles, which scared the living daylights out of Londoners. For a sense of the progress of aviation over the last half century, see the galleries dedicated to modern flight and the Cold War years. You'll see big-bellied military air transport planes; the heavy airlift C-124 cargo plane, affectionately called "old shaky"; the stealth bomber, which looks like a massive bat from an alien territory; and the SR-71A, an aircraft able to fly more than three times the speed of sound. It had to be built of titanium because air friction generated enough heat to melt aluminum. For real "wow!" power, nothing beats the giant silo at the end of the museum. It houses multi-story missiles and launch vehicles, including the 65-foot Thor intermediate range ballistic missile, the Titan I Intercontinental Ballistic Missile at 98 feet, and the Titan II at 108 feet. Visitors who arrive early enough can sign up for a shuttle to tour four Air Force One presidential airplanes, those used by Presidents Roosevelt, Truman, Eisenhower and Kennedy. There is also an IMAX theater, a café, and a book and souvenir shop. Wheelchairs and strollers are available.

Enter Wright-Patterson Air Force Base at Area B off Springfield Pike, east of Woodman Drive; 937/255-3268; www.wpafb.af.mil/museum Daily 9-5. Closed Thanksgiving, Christmas and New Year's Day.

REVIEWER'S FAVORITES AT THE NATIONAL MUSEUM OF THE UNITED STATES AIR FORCE

1. The P-40 "Flying Tiger" was the plane with painted shark's teeth. It was flown by the American Volunteer Group assembled by Claire Chennault to face the Japanese Air Force during World War II.
2. The Memphis Belle, B-17, was the first heavy bomber to complete 25 missions over Europe during World War II.
3. The Stealth fighter was computer designed with hidden exhausts to deflect radar.
4. The first operational hydrogen bomb measured 24 feet, 10 inches long, which explains why the bombers of the Strategic Air Command were so big.
5. A slab of the Pentagon from the rubble of the 9/11 terrorist attack of 2001.

NATIONAL AFRO-AMERICAN MUSEUM AND CULTURAL CENTER/WILBERFORCE—The selection of

Wilberforce as the site for this significant museum could not have been more appropriate. The village was the site of seven Underground Railroad stations that brought people from Southern slavery to freedom. It also is the home of Wilberforce University, founded before the Civil War as the nation's first private college for black students. The museum's permanent exhibition focuses on the changes and struggles in African-American life from the end of World War II through 1965, following the passage of the Voting Rights Act. Examples of 1950s lifestyles in predominantly black communities are enhanced with recorded recollections and gospel music. Shown in the small theater is the award-winning 27-minute video, "Music As A Metaphor", which traces the roots of African-American music through to the music of the 1950s. There also are changing special displays, often featuring the great artists in literature and music, as well as the work of visual artists represented in the museum's collection and presented in the Rotating Gallery.

1350 Brush Road, off U.S.42 north of Xenia; 937/376-4944, 800/752-2603; www.ohiohistory.org Tue-Sat 9-5. Nominal admission charge. Tours by appointment.

GREENE COUNTY HISTORICAL SOCIETY/XENIA—

Greene County was one of the original seventeen counties when Ohio became a state in 1803, which helps the county historical society celebrate a longer-than-average past. The museum has several parts, including the Victorian Town House, 1876, with its unique round turret, and the Galloway Log House, a two-story white oak home built by James Galloway about 1799. It was in this house that Galloway's daughter, Rebecca, was wooed by the great Shawnee leader, Tecumseh. While she considered him "the most brilliant man" she had ever met, it is said she refused to marry him unless he forsook his Indian heritage. Unwilling to comply, Tecumseh forged ahead with his plan to unite the Indians to stem the white tide westward. During the war of 1812, Tecumseh sided with the British, the fair-weather friends of the Indians, who made him a brigadier general. He was killed at the Battle of the Thames, where the British finally lost all claim to the Northwest Territory and the Indians lost all hope for a nation of their own. *74 West Church Street; 937/372-4606. June-Sept Tue-Fri 9-12 and 1-3:30; tour hours 1:30-3:30 and Sat 1:30-4; or by appointment.*

BLUE JACKET/XENIA—In the late 1700s, a young white man with the unlikely name of Marmaduke Van Swearingen left his home and his people to fulfill a dream of becoming part of the Shawnee Nation. His story, and his rise to the role of principal war chief, has become one of the most popular outdoor dramas in the nation, presented each summer in the amphitheater of Caesar Ford Park. Van Swearingen, called Chief Blue Jacket, led the Shawnee in the battles between the tribe and encroaching frontiersmen, and the play, written by W. L. Mundell, seeks to dramatize the history of the Shawnee Nation through the life of this one man. Staged here each summer since 1981, *Blue Jacket* offers the audience plenty of frontier excitement and the legendary figures of Daniel Boone and Simon Kenton. And because the Shawnee once thrived in the Xenia area, the play offers a wonderful dose of romanticized local history. *520 Stringtown Road, off U.S. 35, east of Xenia; 937/376-4358 or 877/465-2583; www.bluejacketdrama.com Performances 8 pm Tue-Sun from mid-June to mid-Aug. Backstage tours available for a small fee at 5 pm before each performance. Pre-performance dinners served outdoors in a screened pavilion beginning at 5:30 pm.*

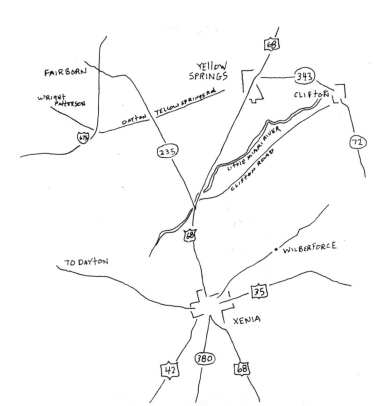

Golden Lamb

Lebanon

The town of Lebanon is a charming and unfatigued place—this even though its population almost doubled between 1990 and 2005, rising from 10,000 to 19,978. In Lebanon this has been to the good. While the outskirts have expanded to accommodate newcomers commuting to Cincinnati or Dayton, the historic downtown stays pristine and even becomes better, because more customers flock the streets.

Lebanon was settled early in the nineteenth century, and from 1805 a Shaker colony grew four miles away in Union Village. The Shakers provided Ohio with a model of order, thrift and industriousness. But the Shaker colony was doomed from the outset, for they practiced the ultimate frugality—celibacy—and their beliefs, which included property held in common, were too unsettling for the Great Unwashed nearby. The colony ultimately grew to 600 people, and in the early years whole families moved in. This was the first Shaker settlement in the west, and founders of Shaker colonies in Kentucky, Cleveland and Dayton all came from Lebanon. So says John Zimkus,

Warren County Historical Society historian, who adds that Lebanon was never very hospitable to the Shakers—mobs from town would go out to terrorize Union Village. Finally, around 1819, by command of what they said was a vision from God, two of the Shakers rode through Lebanon and placed a curse on the town. Conversely, they blessed Dayton, which was proving more hospitable. For quite some time the curse worked, or appeared to.

Lebanon has an appearance of order, thrift and industriousness; the historically-minded like to think that some of it is continuity. The locals esteem the memory and artifacts of those early sojourners. Antique dealers seek out those honest, plain pieces of furniture; museums prize and exhibit them; local artisans reproduce them for the tourist trade. Even the sober Shakers might find some humor in their latter-day vindication.

Old Lebanon today is ardently handsome, with leafy streets, orderly neighborhoods, distinguished older houses, and a downtown of brick sidewalks and well-tended storefronts overhung by awnings and more trees. Lebanon is famous across this part of the state for, of course, the Golden Lamb, its museums, its antique shops, its railroad excursions, its horse-drawn-carriage Christmas parade and its proximity to both the picturesque Little Miami River valley and the Kings Island amusement complex. It has all the loveliness of an older town, alongside an array of attractions with modern appeal.

HARDY'S BED & BREAKFAST SUITES—Al and Phyllis Hardy live in a neighborhood of attractive nineteenth- and early twentieth-century houses, and now they've bought up four in their immediate vicinity, fixed them up, and turned them into a popular bed and breakfast. Al is also in the furniture business, so all the furnishings are for sale, in case a guest sleeps on something, or unpacks into, or sits on something, he can't live without. Al just wonders why he hasn't been doing this since before 1992. The rooms are all attractive and appear comfortable. The Hardys can accommodate up to 20 people in three- to five (including kitchen)-room suites; cable television is available for all. There's a public golf course across the street, tennis courts behind, and downtown Lebanon a short down-hill walk away. Breakfasts are all in the dining room of March Manor, the biggest house, which is centrally located. March Manor has just one B&B suite and is where the Hardings live. The chef has 17 breakfast menus, so you have to stay 17 days to have a repeat.

212 Wright Avenue; 513/932-3266 or 877/932-3266; www.hardysproperties. com No smoking, no children, no pets. Each suite is $145 a night or $170 for the entire 1860 Wright Place house—the whole house, including two bedrooms, two baths (one down), and even a laundry.

SILVER HIGH MANOR—This is an attractive 1847 brick house

with some original features, including an ornate crown molding. There are two parlors downstairs, which guests may use, and two bedrooms and a bath on the second floor, with a half bath off the stair landing. Hostess Celeste Stark makes breakfasts featuring gourmet omelets and pancakes. Celeste has two hobbies whose benefits guests may enjoy in season. One is her garden, which she started in 2004, when she and her husband, Nick, moved in here and rescued an overgrown yard. The other is Christmas decorations.

22 North High Street at Silver Street; 513/228-2200; www.silverhighmanor. com Rates are $125 a couple on weekends, $100 during the week; $70 for a single during the week.

THE VILLAGE ICE CREAM PARLOR AND
RESTAURANT—Remember those phosphates you used to get as a kid, and the malts, and the tin roof sundaes? The kind that make modern soda jerks screw up their faces and say, "Whaa?" They didn't go out with ration stamps and rayon stockings after all. They're right here, in a 1940s-style ice cream parlor, surrounded by venerable Lebanon. Malts are a meal in themselves, tin roof sundaes are smothered in chocolate syrup and Spanish peanuts, and sodas come with a good squirt of whipped cream and enough ice cream to last all the way to the bottom. The lunch and dinner menu includes soup and sandwiches; $8 dinner offerings include fish, hamburger, chicken. The menu may be old-fashioned, but this shop is monitored by a web cam. If you want to know how busy they are at this very moment, go to the web site and click "See us online."

22 South Broadway; 513/932-6918; www.villageicecreamparlor.com Open seven days 11-8; closed major holidays. A malt is $4.15; a cone with one dip is $1.95.

BROTZEIT DELI—Susie Murdoch seems so happy running this

shop, making sauerkraut, pretzels, German potato salad and strudel, that it's hard to believe she was trained as a mechanical engineer and spent twenty years working on motors. But when her employer left the area, and the tenant in this building, which Murdoch already owned, moved, it seemed like the moment had arrived to realize her dream to open a deli. She says the name "brotzeit" means "bread time," but it's really like wishing someone a good appetite. Murdoch and her husband Ted own Brotzeit Deli, but she does most of the work because he has a job in Wilmington. She flies in frozen pastries and rolls from Germany. She has a large stock of German sausages (made in Sarasota) and imported foods, like mustards, chocolate and so on. But the mainstay of daily life here is sandwiches and platters like ones you might find in Germany. For example there are German ham or liverwurst sandwiches ($7), weisswurst or bratwurst on a bun ($3) or German hot dog ($2.50), black forest cake ($3.50 for a slice), or apple butter crumb cake ($3.) No beer, alas, but you can try German coffees or a full array of soft drinks. *30 East Mulberry Street; 513/282-6500; www.brotzeit-deli.com Tue-Sat 9-6; closed Sun and Mon.*

GOURMET ON BROADWAY—Gourmet on Broadway is just two blocks north of The Golden Lamb but light years away in food and temperament. Each, in its own way, is a local institution—The Golden Lamb being Aunt Gladys' favorite place while Gourmet steals away her nontraditional niece and nephew who have vegetarian leanings, a Mediterranean palate, a love of homemade soups, and a nose for homemade pastries. The owner, Mahnaz, is a young woman who took the entrepreneur part of her Xavier University MBA seriously enough to hang her degree in a kitchen—her own. She's great with stews— lamb or chicken, vegetables, rice or couscous seasoned with fresh herbs, which make everything aromatic. Salads of all kinds, made-up soups (such as her roasted tomato pesto), everything homemade, no preservatives, and a low-fat accent (until you get to her pastries). Even after a decade and a half, she still cooks as if she were back at Xavier, in the dorm kitchen, cooking for her friends.
32 North Broadway Street; 513/933-8377. Open Tu-Sat 11-5; closed Sun & Mon. Dinners Th-Sat from April through year-end holidays. Call ahead.

BRANDYWINE INN/MONROE—This restaurant, in one of Monroe's oldest buildings (originally a tavern and a coach stop between Dayton and Cincinnati), is an experience for the discerning diner. German-born chef George Bernas loves French food, and three nights a week he demonstrates what he loves. He prepares everything from scratch and does everything himself—even down to filleting the fish. It's possible to order a la carte or to opt for a *prix fixe* dinner with four courses and a choice of entrees. Poached salmon, stuffed chicken, lamb, duck and filet mignon are all menu features. The restaurant is small, with just 20 tables. Doris Bernas is dining room host. There's a wine list and full bar. And though the restaurant is normally open just three nights, it will open any time for groups of 12 or more. Remember that this restaurant doesn't take credit cards. Personal checks are all right.
204 South Main Street (six miles west of Lebanon on State Route 63. Cross the interstate, then look for Monroe's Main Street, to the left.) 513/539-8911; www. brandywineofmonroe.com Thur-Sat, with reservations from 6 on. Reservations preferred. Entrees from $17 to $25.

THE GOLDEN LAMB—The Lamb is an inn suffused with its own history. Merely walking its hallways causes the traveler to lose a century or so, becoming lightheaded in the rarer air of the inn's upper floors. The rooms have private baths now and air conditioning, but otherwise the guest could be his own great-grandfather, just off the stagecoach.

For over 185 years, The Golden Lamb has been perhaps the best known inn in Ohio, as well as the oldest. Opened two days before Christmas in 1803 by Jonas and Martha Seaman, who kept vegetable gardens and a pigpen out back, the inn "set a good table and had comfortable beds," according to those who knew. One reason for its early popularity was that it found itself at an important intersection; travelers could be going north, south, east or west.

The rooms are all named after previous guests, a weighty list that includes Mark Twain, James Whitcomb Riley, Harriet Beecher Stowe and ten of the twelve U.S. presidents who have visited the inn. In 1842, Charles Dickens was also a guest. According to the reports, Dickens, wearing a brown frock coat and a beaver hat, alighted from the stage in front of the inn and wanted a drink. It was a reasonable request from a man climbing off the unreasonableness that stagecoach-riding must have been at the time, but the inn was a temperance inn in those days.

Afterward, when he recorded his Ohio sojourn in *American Notes*, he said that he had nothing to drink here at this inn in Lebanon but tea and coffee. "This preposterous forcing of unpleasant drinks down the reluctant throats of travelers is not uncommon in America," he wrote. He intimated that the inn cheated on food prices to make up for the lost liquor revenue. He didn't seem to care much for the whole of Ohio, actually, complaining that not only was there nothing civilized to drink but the natives spit a lot and didn't keep their hedgerows neat.

A former landlord furnished the inn from country auctions, buying what he liked, which happened to be Shaker antiques. Now the inn is one of a handful of acknowledged Shaker museums in America. Several of the rooms are solely for the viewing of collections, but most of the inn is a "live" museum, that is, guests eat and sleep in rooms that also contain artifacts, a somewhat radical but imminently appealing approach to museum management. The old Federal-style brick in downtown Lebanon is one of southwest Ohio's perennial favorites, especially during the Christmas season.

27 S. Broadway; 513/932-5065; www.goldenlamb.com The inn has 18 rooms. A room for two is $67-$133.

Favorite rooms include the DeWitt Clinton room and, because it is one of the largest, the Martin Van Buren room. The Rutherford B. Hayes is a suite, with sitting room, bedroom and bath. The Golden Lamb has two restaurants. At the rear the Blackhorse Tavern has live entertainment and its own menu. *The main dining room is open Mon-Sat 11-3 and 5-9; Sun noon-8. Lunch $8-17; dinner $17-30.*

VALLEY VINEYARDS/MORROW—An invitation on a

stupendous barrel lid ushers you into the tasting barn of the Schuchter family, which in the late 1980s was the first Ohio winery to take home a gold medal in international competition. Second largest of the state's 100 plus wineries, Valley Vineyards wines recently earned thirteen gold medals in national and international competition. They're best known for their ice wine, which they launched in 1992. The grapes are left on the vine until after the third frost, when they're picked and then pressed while frozen, yielding a sweet dessert wine. All year the winery runs Friday night Grill Outs featuring steak, salmon and sides (reservations required; $55 for two).

2276 U.S. 22-State Route 3 (Montgomery Road); 513/899-2485; www. valleyvineyards.com Mon-Thur 11-8, Fri-Sat 11-11, Sun 1-6.

THE HORSE-DRAWN CARRIAGE PARADE—Lebanon celebrates Christmas with a parade of horse-drawn vehicles: a procession of old-fashioned carriages, wagons and carts set amid the old-fashioned facades of downtown Lebanon. Unique in the nation, this parade draws 70,000 people, who in 2006 saw some 350-400 animals pulling 126 vehicles. It's a demonstration of horse power, with some donkeys too, but no oxen or llamas or riders on horseback. The horses range from miniatures pulling small carts and a driver, to a team of eight Clydesdales hitched to a show wagon. Perennial volunteer Arla Tannehill says that when the Clydesdales pass, "striding in cadence, they shake the pavement." It's as if the world trembles in awe.

The parade vehicles show how people and goods and services used to get around. They include farm carts filled with dressed-up people; an old-time fire engine restored by a retired fireman in Gahanna who has to hire horses to pull it; stage coaches (not every year); a hotel limousine from Mackinac Island; passenger carriages; a restored Kroger delivery cart (the Lebanon store manager always rides in it); milk trucks. In the beginning the parade had to hire horse-and-vehicle teams from out of town, but now more and more local horse-owners are getting into the act, and 85 percent of all participants come from Southwest Ohio.

It all sounds and mostly is, wonderful. But, says Tannehill, "It's a parade with horses, so anything can happen." Besides, all the antique vehicles mean a rig can break or a shaft can splinter. That's one reason a person called a "head walker" walks alongside every animal. And some 50 people in green vests—all experienced horsemen—are around, ready to help if needed. No helium balloons, which might pop, are allowed; no candy throwing. Not spooking the horses is rule number one.

Every year there are two parades, each lasting about an hour, both with largely the same lineups but completely different atmospheres. The first, at 1 p.m., is in full daylight, with animals, vehicles and hitches fully visible. The second, at 7 p.m., is after dark, romantic and awesome. Between parades teachers serve a big lunch for all participants and the hundreds of volunteers. Arla Tannehill has been volunteering since 1988, the second year, and if she'd known ahead of time about the first parade she'd have been on board for that too. An erstwhile horsewoman, she has a green vest. She's done everything for the parade, but for years she was backstage, charged with getting rigs in line. She was the one at the assembly point hollering "ONE", pause, "TWO", pause, "THREE", pause, and finally going home exhausted.

At night carriages are rigged with lights and spectators participate also, for high-school students hand out candles and ultimately thousands of faces along the route take on the glow of candlelight. Tennehill sees all downtown Lebanon emerge as a living, breathing Norman Rockwell panorama. She says, "If this parade won't put joy in your soul, there's not a thing that will." Annual event first Saturday in December; parades at 1 and 7; 513/932-1100. Free. From Fairgrounds parade goes down Broadway to Main, and then returns on Cherry and Broadway again. Gift and food vendors on Mulberry Street; stores open late. A shuttle serves a remote parking site.

SHOPPING—Broadway, the main drag, is full of shops, as is the East Mulberry cross street. Antiques are the main theme, but you'll also find choices in clothing and linens, for example. Twice a year, in late January and early October, there's the **Lebanon Antique Show**, with some 70 dealers. Recognized as one of the better and more diversified shows in this part of the state, the Lebanon Antique Show is at Bowman Primary School, at *State Route 123 and Hart Road. Sponsor is the Warren County Historical Society (513/932-1817; www.wchsmuseum.com).* Among Lebanon's better shops are **Oh Suzanna** *(16 South Broadway; 513/932-8246),* which has antiques, quilts and linens, jewelry, and a Vera Bradley line; and **Charles Gerhardt** *(33 North Broadway; 513/932-9946),* noted for furniture, oriental carpets and tribal art. If you like old-style furniture but not someone else's scratches, check out **Knickerbocker Gallery**'s large showroom, where all the furniture is new; some pieces are exact reproductions of antiques. You'll also find lighting and accessories *(41 East Mulberry; 513/933-9222; www.knickergallery.com).* **Ambassador's Antiques** carries new linens, silver flatware, antiques from Europe and North America *(40 East Mulberry Street; 513/934-5677).* **Miller's Antique Market** is a mall, open every day and located in a handsome yellow-brick building. Miller's has 72 dealers, with period antiques, fine art, and porcelain *(201 South Broadway; 513/932-8710).*

WARREN COUNTY HISTORICAL SOCIETY MUSEUM

—In the early part of the twentieth century, when schools didn't have gyms, this building was the equivalent of the downtown Y. But when the local historical society took it over, it became a model hometown museum. Out came the gymnasium bleachers and in went a village green surrounded by tiny shops and craft houses. Elsewhere in the building are prehistoric Indian items, farm tools, pioneer clothing, antique toys, reproduction Victorian rooms, and a seven-room Shaker collection, said to be the largest anywhere and known worldwide. The Historical Society has spent much of this decade renovating the former post office next door for additional space, a project that in 2007 awaited one last burst of funding for completion.
105 South Broadway, just off the corner of West Main; 513/932-1817; www.wchsmuseum.com Tue-Sat 9-4, Sun noon-4. Adults $4, seniors $3.50, ages 5-18 $2. Closed Mon and holidays.

LEBANON MASON & MONROE RAILROAD

—The Lebanon Mason & Monroe Railroad—the LM&M for short—runs four-car excursions of all kinds between Easter and the day before Christmas. As it happens they could go to Monroe but don't normally, and they only go to Mason when chartered for trips to the Brazenhead Irish Pub there. Since new management arrived in 2005, they've mostly dropped rides to other towns and made every trip an excursion, including, on the quieter side, a lot of half-hour rides to a picnic grove. The biggest event is Day Out with Thomas, for young children and their families, which over two three-day weekends in September brings 25,000 people to Lebanon. In October, the LM&M runs Murder Mystery dinners for grown-ups, who during a 45-minute trip witness a pretend murder followed by clues and dinner at the Golden Lamb, where the mystery is solved. Though some excursions do sell out, the railroad tries always to have some tickets for people who just walk up, but it's best if you can plan ahead.

127 South Mechanic Avenue; 513/933-8022; www.lebanonrr.com All season, Easter to Christmas, rides are Sat at 10; Sat and Sun 12:30 and 3; adults $17, 2-12 $12. Intermittent (call or see web site) Tue and Fri one-hour rides leave at 10:30 and noon; adults $12.50, 2-12 $7.50. Tickets at 127 South Mechanic or call 866/468-3401.

THE GOLDEN TURTLE CHOCOLATE FACTORY—Joy and Ted Kossouji know a lot about candy-making. They ought to. Joy's family was in the business in Norway and Ted's made candy at home. There's wonderful almond toffee and chocolate-covered Oreo cookies. The moldings represent seals, alligators, dinosaurs, dolphins and turtles, all in chocolate. It's a great-smelling showroom, decorated with antiques, and the wares are scrumptious.

120 South Broadway; 800/345-1994 or 513/932-1990; www.goldenturtlechocolatefactory.com Mon-Sat 10-5.

GLENDOWER—Glendower is one of several fine old houses along this wooded hilltop overlooking the remnants of the last canal built in Ohio, but it is the only one that's a state memorial. Built in 1836 by a young lawyer of Welsh ancestry, it was named for the Welsh hero Owen Glendower, who revolted against Henry IV starting in 1400. When the house's last private owner died in the 1940s, her heirs sold the house to the Warren County Historical Society, which donated it to the State of Ohio. Then at the end of 2007, the State gave it back to the Warren County Society, along with 5700 items of local interest. It's a grand house, with central porticoes front and back and one-story wings on both sides. The elaborate furnishings include a crystal chandelier and furniture made by early cabinetmakers and local craftsmen.

105 Cincinnati Avenue/U.S. 42 just south of downtown; 513/932-1817; www.wcsmuseum.com Adults $3; 5-18 $1. June-Labor Day Wed-Fri noon-4, Sat-Sun 1-4; Sept-Oct weekends only. There's a ten-day candlelight tour at Christmastime.

ASIDE Much to the relief of the tourist bureau, Warren County is no longer called "Hog Heaven", as it was in the mid-nineteenth century, but it's the home of one of America's most notable breeds—the Poland China. The breed began early in the 1800s when the Lebanon Shakers, starting with a Philadelphia variety called Big China, began the tedious process of selective breeding. By mid-century the Shakers had their hog—a docile creature that was a miracle of protein conversion and sturdy enough to walk to Cincinnati markets. The first pedigree was written in 1876 by a farm owner, W.C. Hankinson, and a recorder, Carl Freigau, for a sow named Lady Pugh. There's still a monument to it all, a bronze plaque on a shaft just north of State Route 122, on the Dixie Highway (and today behind a Meijer's), on what was once Lady Pugh's farm.

THE LEBANON CEMETERIES—Pioneer Cemetery is the smaller, older cemetery and home of the Harner sisters—Sarah, Elizabeth, Mary and Ann who, according to Ripley's Believe It or Not, were simultaneously killed by a ball of lightning that came down the chimney of their farmhouse and struck all four even though each was in a different room. Lebanon Cemetery, the town's ongoing

burial grounds, is nearby. This spacious and lovely park-like grove is the permanent address of Lebanon's most noted native son, Thomas Corwin. Corwin was an extraordinary public servant: legislator, Ohio Governor, five-term U.S. congressman, U.S. Senator and Secretary of the Treasury. He was witty, elegant and courageous, delivering in 1847 an impassioned speech in the Senate denouncing the Mexican War as an act of conquest. He died in 1865, after jokily suggesting his own epitaph: "Dearly beloved by his family; universally despised by Democrats; useful in life only to knaves and pretended friends."
Pioneer Cemetery is at the west end of Mulberry Street. Lebanon Cemetery is two blocks north, off Silver Street.

PINES PET CEMETERY—More than 15,000 pets—goldfish, birds, skunks, dogs, cats, horses, a duck and a ferret—are buried on the grounds of this 35-acre park, which also has the cremated remains of sixty people who chose to repose into eternity beside their pets. There is a small chapel in the park; a bench in front of it reads, "If Christ had a little dog, he would have followed Him to the cross." It is indeed, a lovely, tranquil place, giving testimony either to the tenacity of our relationships with pets or the tenuousness of our human ones.
764 Riley Wills Road, off U.S. 48 north two miles north of State Route 122 and just before Hidden Valley Farm; 513/932-2270. Grounds open daily, daylight to dusk.

LEBANON RACEWAY—Just outside the business district, on grounds leased from the Warren County Fair Board, standardbred trotters and pacers push out of the starting gates from January to May and from September to December. It's a half-mile track, with times that will respectably beat 1:57, and fans cheer their favorites and place their bets in the glass-enclosed grandstand. This harness-racing track opened in 1948, and its biggest crowd ever was 5,295 in 1967.
665 North Broadway Street; 513/932-4936; www.lebanon-raceway.com Parking and admission are free.

FORT ANCIENT STATE MEMORIAL/OREGONIA—
Long recognized as one of the outstanding prehistoric sites in America, the Fort Ancient Earthworks rise in a 760-acre park overlooking the Little Miami gorge. The site has three-and-a-half miles of earthen walls enclosing over a hundred acres. The earthworks were built by the Hopewell culture, which prevailed here from 100 BC to 400 AD and constructed these walls between 100 BC and 290 AD. The Fort Ancient culture, the first here to support itself on agriculture—corn, beans and squash made up 80 percent of their diet—dated from 800 AD and lasted until Europeans came. Their diet, heavy in corn which contained sugar and particles of grit from grinding, caused tooth disease, a mark of advancing civilization. In the last few years archaeologists have found a previously unidentified 200-foot circle on the northwest corner of the site. Exploratory digs, yielding the likes of a bear tooth, arrowheads and other artifacts, began in 2006 and were expected to continue for five to seven years. This site has a museum that dates from 1998 and has some virtues, but tries to cover too much world and along the way doesn't tell enough about Fort Ancient. But there's a very good and helpful flyer available, and the trails around the grounds are wonderful.

6123 State Route 350; 800/283-8904 or 513/932-4421; www.ohiohistory. org/places/ftancien/ Memorial Day-Labor Day Wed-Sat 10-5, Sun and holidays noon-5; April-May and Sep-Oct Sat 10-5 and Sun noon-5. Closed November-March. Adults $7, 6-12 $3; Ohio Historical Society members, free.

FORT ANCIENT TRADING POST/OREGONIA

FORT ANCIENT TRADING POST/OREGONIA—A sign on the door of this former church reads, "Come on in. We'll be right over." Sure enough, in about three minutes, you've got company from across the road, either the second or third generation of Elsbernds, or perhaps even the fourth generation in the person of Joseph, who was born in 1995. Six rather startling rooms are piled to the ceiling with enough castoffs to sink the Delta Queen. All sorts of chandeliers dangle in cockeyed fashion; tinware and military remnants are quietly aging everywhere; odd boxes store about a thousand arrowheads. There are enough old tools to supply a dozen primitive workshops, along with items labeled "S coil fosele," and "qurtz." A person could spend several hours rummaging and never get to the back door.

5254 State Route 350; 513/932-3109. Daily 9 to dark. Credit card all right "about half the time," for father William is reluctant to deal with them, but son John has no problem.

MORGAN'S FORT ANCIENT CANOE LIVERY/OREGONIA

MORGAN'S FORT ANCIENT CANOE LIVERY/OREGONIA—In 1957 the Morgans chose this part of the Little Miami River—six miles from any town—for their canoe business. Fifty years later they are still here. Now they're running tours, renting kayaks as well as canoes and giving lessons, even though most people think they already know how to canoe. They run eco tours on the river using rafts, and a naturalist goes along. They need at least 20 people for that, at $25 a person. Company president Gary Morgan, for one, is qualified to give tours; he's trained as a river biologist. (He also keeps busy. Morgan's runs a winter business in Costa Rica.) Typical canoe outings are an hour and a half, going three miles downriver, or an all-day trip of 18 miles, also downriver, catering available. (Upriver trips are all by road vehicles.)

5701 State Route 350; 513/932-7658 or 800/WE CANOE (932-2663); www.morganscanoe.com/ftancient/ Weekends April and Oct; daily May-Sept from 8 am. Canoes are $20-$40 depending on length of trip. All special or raft trips require a reservation; canoeists will save $6 by making one.

KINGS ISLAND—Last year about three million people visited this amusement park where the main attraction is The Beast, the world's longest wooden roller coaster. It undulates its way across 35 acres, through three tunnels and a 540-degree helix, goes nearly 65 mph, and is 7,400 feet long. Another famous ride here is the Racer. When it was built in the early 1970s, it was the first twin-track wooden coaster in many years; that alone was enough to stimulate a renewed interest in coasters nationwide. One of the Racer's tracks is turned around, which made it the first coaster to travel backward. Altogether Kings Island has 14 roller coasters, including also the Vortex, a six-loop coaster guaranteed to rearrange your basic molecules, and the Firehawk, meant to give you the sensation of flying by flipping you over. They are among 80 rides altogether, as well as 30 water slides in the park's Boomerang

Bay. The park has six themed areas, including a rivertown, the Coney Mall section (which depicts Cincinnati's old end-of-the-trolley stop amusement park,) and International Street, a European-style village crowned by a 33-story, one-third replica of the Eiffel Tower. There are also stage shows (five different ones a day) and 80 places to buy food. Other attractions have grown up around Kings Island as well: a golf course, a tennis stadium for international competitions, a Kings Island inn and conference center and two water parks, the Beach and Great Wolf Lodge. The great wooden coaster, The Beast, is still the draw; people come from all over to ride it, including one man who left his loving mother in Boston in order to buy a house near Kings Island from which on summer evenings "he can hear the sweet tunnel-roaring of The Beast."

6300 Kings Island Drive, at I-71; 800/288-0808; www.pki.com Daily Memorial Day through Labor Day, 10-10; weekends in Oct and Apr-May. 2007 admission $44.95 for adults and kids over 48 inches tall; over 3 and seniors $29.95; two-day pass $54.95.

Kings Island

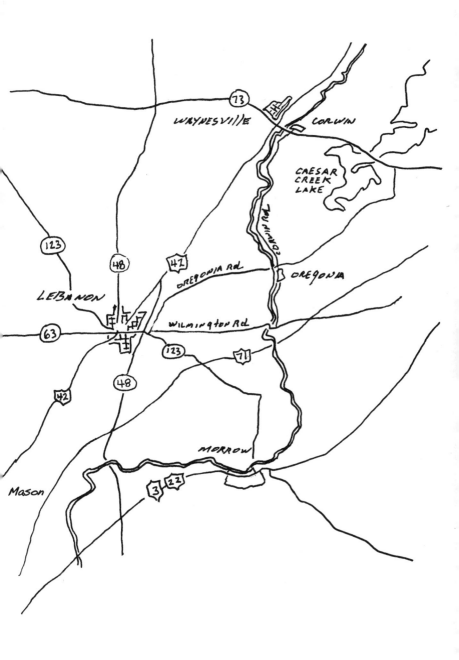

The Buxton Inn

Granville

Granville is a splendidly flawless Ohio village: leafy, tranquil, and guarded by magnificent architecture and an air of decorum. It is wonderfully intact—much of the village is on the National Register—and its good geography has held the menace of shopping malls and franchise strips at bay. Newark, its larger neighbor only six miles away, has taken on the various vagaries of heavier commerce which leaves Granville unspoiled and decorous. It is, in short, the kind of small town that people dream into existence, which frightens Granvillians somewhat as they are aware of their good fortune. Looking to the west, they see Columbus eyeing them with a lazy, predatory gaze as the first four-lane highway from Columbus, State Route 161, is scheduled to arrive in Granville in 2009.

For now, two-lane highways, State Routes 37 and 161, enter the village quietly. Route 37 comes in from rolling hills to the south, pausing momentarily while the traveler gazes at the picturesque scene: a panoply of trees stretching longitudinally, punctuated by church steeples and nestled against the hill that the college envelops, looking parochially down upon the village.

The town itself, with just under 5,000 residents, was unusual from its moment of inception. Instead of being established by the usual hodge-podge of settlers, Granville was brought into being by a group of New Englanders who all were from the same place—the over-populated and thin-soiled Granville, Massachusetts—and largely of one mind. Their first ceremony involved felling the first tree, the stump of which was the pulpit for the first Sunday church service. A certain ceremonious sense has thus always pervaded the village.

Some Welsh came too; a few of their descendants are still around. Not too many years ago, you might even have found a villager or two who could speak a little pickup Welsh, even though Bill Utter, the late town historian, called it the most villainous language on Earth. Occasionally someone or another might celebrate St. David's Day—the patron saint of Wales—on the first of March. The old Welsh, of course, did most of the splendid stone and slate work around the village. The Granville Inn, for instance, was built by a family of Welsh stonecutters. The other village historian, the late Horace King, once contended that he knew who the real village aristocracy was—his mailman, a seventh-generation Welshman.

Time has changed Granville's main street into one dominated by aromas from several local eateries. There are also working stores here—a book store, a printer, banks, clothiers and others. But with its downtown post office and library, Granville has a town center that functions like a real town center—an anomaly itself and probably reason enough to see a dome placed over the whole of it. The village's farmer's market brings throngs of shoppers to the village center each Saturday morning from late spring through mid-October.

Granville plies its nineteenth-century feel, and it has good food—even the little places are good. It is impossible to get out of Granville weighing the same as when you entered. Traveler, gird thyself. Thus tradition, of one kind or another, does continue in Granville, Ohio. And its major observable tradition endures: it remains one of Ohio's loveliest, most pristine and intact villages, a place for all seasons, whether you are living there, or merely passing through.

ACCESS—While some Granvillians view Columbus as a megalomaniac whose expansion is devouring it, others rejoice that improved routes permit shorter commutes and better traffic flow. From Columbus to Granville, it is easiest to take I-270 to the east side to pick up the newly reconstructed State Route 161 (Dublin-Granville Road). On the Granville end exit onto State Route 16 West, which turns into Columbus Road and leads into the heart of Granville. From the south take State Route 37 north from I-70; on the final hilly approach you'll come upon one of the best overviews of the village itself.

Granville Inn

THE GRANVILLE INN—The place was a gift to Granville, no matter what John Sutphin Jones' intentions were. One story is that if the village paved the street, he'd build an inn to be proud of. Another is that he was tired of entertaining out-of-town friends at his farm, Bryn Du, even though he had 52 rooms. Jones, according to local history, was an ex-railroad conductor who received astute tips on the location of Ohio coal lands from traveling businessmen. He became president of the Sunday Creek Coal Company, and his farm on the east edge of Granville covered a thousand acres. In 1924, when he decided to build his inn within the grove of trees once occupied by the Granville Female College, he had the sandstone dug out of the hill behind the farmhouse. These hills behind the village were known then as the Welsh hills because of the Welsh families who lived there, many of them stonemasons, it being a common and encouraged craft in Wales. The inn took two years to build and cost half a million dollars. It has carved oak paneling, tapestries and rugs, carved and upholstered furniture of walnut and mahogany, and "the atmosphere of a palatial home." For opening night, Mr. Jones sent an engraved invitation to everyone in the Granville telephone book; a newspaper account said 2,000 people attended. In the inn's early years, there were white-gloved attendants and guests dined on pheasant under glass. If the enterprise lost money, Mr. Jones made up the difference. But before the 1920s were out, he died and the Depression struck. Eventually, a Denison graduate from nearby Newark purchased the inn at a sheriff's sale and began a five-year restoration program on the building. The inn is long since fully revived. Rooms are comfortable and the dining room is both elegant and casual, depending on the season and your table. The menu is contemporary with a focus on French cuisine and, in most cases, quite healthful. Specialties range from steak to pasta to seafood. The kitchen is known for serving fresh meats, breads, seasonal produce and delightful desserts.

314 East Broadway; 740/587-3333; www.granvilleinn.com Thirty rooms, including three suites; all have high-speed internet access. Rates range from $120-$200. Lunch, Mon-Sat 11:30-2:00; dinner, Mon-Thur 5-9 and Fri-Sat 5-10. Restaurant closed on Sunday. Dinner entrées are $16-$30.

VILLAGE BED AND BREAKFASTS—The B&Bs of Granville are something like the old Underground Railroad—you may need luck and references to get in. They aren't widely advertised, if at all, and there are houses that open rooms only to Denison alumni on special occasions. **The George T. Jones House Bed and Breakfast Home** is one of the more architecturally splendid houses in the village, a richly detailed Victorian Tuscan built by a wealthy village merchant for his bride. Today, it has been immaculately restored by Steven Katz and his wife, Constance Barsky, even down to the period wall coverings. It's the most elegant B&B in the village, sitting on a quiet, tree-shaded street just off of Broadway. There are three rooms, all with double beds and private baths. Breakfast is "elaborately" continental. Rate as of 2008, $110. *221 East Elm Street; 740/587-1122; www.geocities.com/gtjhouse* No children. No pets. No smoking. **The Porch House** is located in a quaint turn-of-the-century home in the historic village. Proprietors Bruce and Lisa Westall provide charming guest rooms with private baths, as well as a delicious full breakfast. Located near downtown and adjacent to the bike path. *241 East Maple Street; 740/587-1995; www. porchhouse.com* By reservation only. Credit card to reserve. $85-95 per night. The **Follett-Wright House** is the large yellow Victorian on the hill just two blocks east of the center of town. Kirsten Pape is Danish, which informs the traveler's breakfast, and when she found her house to be too large, she turned the servant's quarters into guest accommodations, and they have their own part of the house. There are two guest rooms with air conditioning and private baths. Breakfasts include Danish rolls and coffee cake, and her dining room table looks down on the other village inns. *403 East Broadway; 740/587-0941; www. bbonline.com/oh/follett-wright No smoking. Does not accept credit cards. $80 per night. By reservation only.*

THE BUXTON INN —A good inn should be as unpredictable as a country road. A good inn, actually, should be on a country road. The inn-seeker is propelled by a picture. This picture may vary but, broadly, it consists of a kind of historical elegance. The inn-seeker desires a historical context but without community sleeping rooms, a bath down the hall, or drafts that topple the gravy bowl. After all, we are in the twenty-first century.

The habitual inn-seeker's hard definition combines architecture, food, lodging, and that most nebulous of features—tmosphere —into the splendid eccentricity of the inn-keeper's craft. The innkeeper himself—or herself —does not likely choose such a profession rationally. He or she is ordained into it. Anyone who knows anything about the obsessive personalities of innkeepers, chefs, and other tormented craftsmen knows this. It is no surprise, therefore, to learn that Orville Orr, keeper of the Buxton Inn, is an ordained minister. It was good training for all higher callings.

All in all, The Buxton is bsolutely nonpareil. In winter, it's articularly cozy eating in the stone cellar where the bar is, by the fireplace. The upstairs front rooms are most formal, and the brightest is the conservatory out back, which looks onto Mr. Orr's little pond and splendid gazebo. The lodging begins upstairs, then goes down the street where Mr. Orr has expanded his domain by purchasing other homes in the neighborhood. The gardens provide a perfect venue for small weddings.

The Buxton was built as a tavern in 1812 and was also Granville's first post office and a stagecoach stop on the line between Columbus and Newark. President William McKinley was a guest here, as were, at one time or another, Harriet Beecher Stowe, John Phillip Sousa, and Henry Ford. There's a legend that President William Henry Harrison, in a bit of unrehearsed gaiety, once rode a horse up the stairs and into the ballroom.

The Orr family kitchen sets a table that is richly varied, from luncheon quiches and crepes to dinner items such as roast duck and fresh fish. The kitchen leans towards healthier selections and uses salt sparingly; it serves white bread but prefers whole grain ones. The desserts are fresh and original, including a peach Melba widely recognized for its decadence.

A visitor may still find Mr. Orr on the premises, the soft-spoken man with the hint of humor about him, moving here and there, observing everything. He is the sort of man who will—and has —apologized to a guest because somehow an errant fly found its way into the inn. Mr. Orr is a consecrated man, and so is his admirable hostelry.
313 East Broadway; 740/587-0001; www.buxtoninn.com Breakfast, Mon-Fri 7-9, Sat-Sun 8-10, Sun brunch 11-3. Lunch, Mon-Sat 11-2. Dinner, Mon-Thur 5:30-9, Fri & Sat 5:30-10, Sun 4-8. Dinner entrées $15.95-$25.95. Room reservations a must and require a credit card. Room rates $95-$105.

OTHER DOWNTOWN SUSTENANCE—Victoria's Ole Tyme Deli & Ice Cream *(134 East Broadway; 740/587-0322. Mon-Fri 11:30-9; Sat-Sun 10-9, moderately priced)* looks as though is has grown a posy—leafed-out sprouts form a nosegay between croissants, and the potato salad, tomatoes, lettuce and pickles merely add more appeal. Ice cream parlor tables and chairs—and the umbrella tables outdoors—add "a touch of Paris in Granville." The food is so good that *Gourmet Magazine* asked for the broccoli soup recipe. *Columbus Monthly* once ordained its San Diego Club as one of the best sandwiches in the area. Up the street a few doors is **The Aladdin** *(122 East Broadway; 740/587-0253. Mon-Sat 6 am-9 pm; Sun 7-9, $4.50-$7.50)*, is an unpretentious little café that ladles out a substantial vegetable soup along with apple pie. In appearance, the place is like a diner with its booths, stools, and a great row of smart-mouth restaurant retorts hanging over the short order grill: "Prices subject to change according to customer's attitudes," and "People who believe the dead never come back to life should be here at quitting time." Just a few steps away, **Brews** *(128 E. Broadway; 740/587-0249. Mon-Thur 11 am-10 pm; Fri-Sat 11 am-11 pm; Sun noon-10)* has become a village hotspot. The moderately priced food and drinks and comfortable atmosphere have made Brews a popular watering hole for college students and families alike. Dinner specials: $13.95-$18.95. Visitors should also swing by **Whit's Frozen Custard** *(138 East Broadway; 740/587-3620)*, where the sinfully sweet custard desserts will remind you of the good old days. Although seating is extremely limited and most diners just stand out on the street to eat, the custard is worth the crowd.

ANTIQUES—Granville is an interesting place to shop for antiques. Try these: **Green Velvet** *(130 E. Broadway; 740/587-0515)* features vintage jewelry and home décor items that add a classic touch to any room. Among items carried here are the fabrics of nationally known designer Amy Butler, a local resident, as well as the hats of local milliner Amy Hamilton, who has also garnered national attention. **B Hammond Interiors** *(123 E. Broadway; 740/587-3700)* provides a wondrous mix of furniture, novelties, flowers and more. **Wee Antique Gallery** *(1630 Columbus Rd; 740/587-2270)* has an assortment of classic furniture pieces as well as a nice collection of china and silver items. **The Wooden Box** *(4584 Columbus Rd; 740/321-1170)* showcases primitive Victorian antiques. For the sports fanatic, **Cream Station Antiques** *(1444 Newark Granville Rd; 740/587-4814)* has an impressive collection of sports memorabilia as well as early advertisements. Lastly, **Greystone Country House** *(128 S. Main St.; 740/587-2243)* specializes in primitive furniture and European antiques, especially those from Germany. Brochures may be found all over town that will provide detailed descriptions of these and other shops.

GRANVILLE LIFE-STYLE MUSEUM—The late Hubert Robinson wanted a front porch, so he tore out the bay window and built one. A sign out front reads, "Hubert's porch, adults welcome" and so they come and sit, reflecting on the memory of Hubert and Oese Robinson, people who saved everything. The house is as they left it, an unorthodox monument to, as one visitor put it, "this woman who saved all her stuff." It is also a gentle, genuine, and somehow touching museum of the lives of two ostensibly ordinary people. When the family fortune—and its goods—fell to the Robinsons, Oese did what any self-respecting woman would have done in those post-war times: she modernized the kitchen, even to providing herself a view, which she painted on one wall and put a window frame around. The museum wisely kept the kitchen exactly as Oese left it, as well as their early-1950s television, which is still sitting anachronistically in the Victorian parlor. *121 South Main; 740/587-0373 or 587-3350. Open second Sat mid-April through mid-Sept, 1-4. Granville Chamber of Commerce sponsors a Christmas open house, first Sat (6-9 pm) in Dec. Victorian undergarment program and the house/garden tour available to groups by appointment mid-April to mid-Nov.*

THE ROBBINS HUNTER MUSEUM—This 27-room mansion

has been in architectural books since the turn of the twentieth century. In fact, it is so impressive that the Smithsonian says it has one of the two best Greek Revival interiors in America. It's an exacting copy of two ancient Greek temples, and visitors can still browse through the period-decorated rooms filled with Robby Hunter's collections of early furniture, paintings, carpets, silver and china, and items of Ohio craft. Hunter was a master forager—among his other accomplishments he collected for Henry Ford's Dearborn Village—and he filled the old mansion with his expert finds. It also has what curators have called an outstanding example of Greek Revival outhouse architecture. It is a small building to the rear that, indeed, contains the museum facilities, and was once a bank building.
221 East Broadway; 740/587-0430; www.lchsohio.org/robbins-hunter_house.htm Open April through Dec, Tue-Sun, 1-4 and by appointment.

THE GRANVILLE HISTORICAL SOCIETY MUSEUM—

This is the village museum, which has an extensive collection of woodworking tools that were donated by a notable village craftsman. Some were so arcane that they couldn't, for a time, be identified, especially the "devil" used to break up sugar or salt that had hardened in a barrel. There are wooden lathes, a wooden plow, and a sausage-stuffer made of wood; all filling most of the basement and strong testimony to a time when the mind, hand, and eye were still connected. In the museum is also a splendid photograph of the local Welsh Hills Band, which was said to be able to outplay any three bands in the county and "needed no music since they knew only one piece but could play it ten different ways."
115 East Broadway; 740/587-3951; www.granvillehistory.com Mid-April to mid-Oct, Sat and Sun 1-4.

Robbins Hunter Museum

DENISON UNIVERSITY—Denison's campus, a great unsullied retreat of educational privilege, will never be used as a movie location; it would be rejected immediately as looking too much like the quintessential ivy-covered college. And the Big Red football team? The Deeds Field-Piper Stadium underwent huge renovations that were revealed for the 2006 football season. Seventy-five-foot candle lighting will allow Big Red to host evening games as well as practice after dark. An Olympic-size track surrounds the newly installed turf and there are new bleachers for the visiting fans. For game schedules as well as ticket prices, visit www.denison.edu/athletics/

BRYN DU—This mansion, one of Ohio's notable landmarks, was built as an Italian villa in 1865 then made famous by coal baron John Jones, who reconstructed it and added an adjoining 18-hole golf course. The house, after Jones, had 52 rooms and 12 fireplaces; it also had a great Federal-style, three-story portico. The architecture was second only to the family itself, who built the Granville Inn, for Mr. Jones' daughter, Sallie, also was a notable local landmark. Having learned to ride on her father's coal ponies, she loved horses, loved to swear in his stables, and sometimes ran her hunting dogs down the halls of the inn. Heifetz played at Bryn Du, and Paderewski played Mrs. Jones' Steinways. Today the Village of Granville owns the house, and manages it through a commission as an events locale. The sprawling historical grounds provide the perfect location for a fairy tale wedding. The Welsh descendants, by the way, know the correct pronunciation of the name is Bryn Dee.

537 Jones Road (State Route 539), just east of town on the north side of the road. Bryn Du is not regularly opened to the public, but reservations for special occasions can be made by calling 740/587-7053.

ASIDE It is said that the village contains 29 different styles of architecture. The best way to take it all in, should one be so dedicated, is to walk the village with Horace King's book, *Granville, Massachusetts to Ohio,* which lovingly draws and details the village architecture. It's for sale at the Robbins Hunter Museum and Granville Historical Society Museum. Mr. King provided the documentation that placed a substantial part of Granville on the National Register.
For those looking for more detailed history of Granville, in 2005 the Granville Historical Society published a three-volume history, in honor of the village Bicentennial. The title is, *Granville, Ohio: A Study in Continuity and Change*. Both books can be ordered from the historical society at www.granvillehistory.org

---

BIKING—Licking County has one of the best biking trails in all of Ohio with 14 miles of paved railroad right-of-way that runs along Raccoon Creek, much of it through woodland. The trail has benches along the way, scenic overlooks, portable potties, and lots of wildlife—everything, thus, in the way of creature comforts. There is so much wildlife, in fact, that early-morning bikers are advised to watch out for deer, which aren't spooked by bikes and tend to stand and watch. The trail is used by bikers and hikers alike and, even on most weekdays, you'll be within sight of someone most of the way. The trail runs from Newark, through Granville and Alexandria, and on to Johnstown. The two best accesses in Granville are from the bottom of the hill on South Main Street near the old train depot and on the west end of the village near Bicentennial Park.

ASIDE A dozen miles north of Granville on State Route 661, is the humble crossroads of Homer, Ohio, a tiny footnote to national history because of the accidents of birth. A marker at the library and across the street from the Homer Cemetery gives the barest facts: Victoria Claftin Woodull, the first woman candidate for president of the United States, 1872. Victoria was a spiritualist, stockbroker, and an advocate of women's rights, Free Love, and legalized prostitution. She was also a newspaper publisher who printed the first English translation of the Communist Manifesto. Wrote a Homer woman in 1979, "Her greatest success was as a hornswoggler, which is why some people think she would have made a good president." She didn't become president, of course, Grant did, another Ohioan. Victoria moved to England, married a wealthy banker, and became, finally, something many presidents do not—a legend.

LICKING COUNTY COURTHOUSE/NEWARK—

Newark's town square is one of the larger in Ohio; plunked in the middle is a splendid old courthouse surrounded by a well-treed lawn filled with picnic tables. Broad benches edge the sidewalk and older men congregate here to exchange world views. The religious paintings in the west courtroom leave little doubt that the Italian architect who designed the place didn't really have the United States' constitution in mind. People here point out that their courthouse, unlike scores of others, is only a tribunal, free from city and county offices. They did pitch the brass spittoons, but the heavy, carved chairs, hardwood walls, frescoed ceilings, elaborate light fixtures and ancient fire hoses on reels are still here. *75 East Main Street, Newark; 740/670-5778.*

ASIDE The legend of Johnny Clem asserts that he ran away from Newark at the age of ten, attached himself to a Union regiment where he became a drummer boy, and rallied the troops at the 1862 Battle of Shiloh. The next year—during the Battle of Chickamauga—the four-foot, 40-pound lad managed to shoot a Confederate colonel off his horse. He became the youngest Army sergeant and, after the war, was commissioned a second lieutenant by his friend, General Ulysses Grant. Said one writer, "Though he lived to age 85, he was in the end remembered for what he had done at 12." In fall 1989 the young Johnny Shiloh found himself facing a court martial, 127 years after the fact. A historian charged the boy wonder was a fake, and a local attorney arranged for a mock trial, the key players fitted in period costumes, including the young Clem. After charge and counter-charge, he was found not guilty. The legend became true.

LOUIS SULLIVAN IN NEWARK—The traveler has to be

only so much of an architectural maven to appreciate a Louis Sullivan building, so one of the nicest surprises in central Ohio is to stumble upon a little noted Sullivan not found in the usual publicity handouts. It's just across the street from the Licking County Courthouse, a much more imposing structure, which might be why Sullivan is often overlooked. But it leaps out of the block to startle you with its wonderful symmetry in which Sullivan was consummately modern,

though with one foot still planted in the classical traditions. The building was one of a series of small Midwestern banks designed late in his career, after both business and personal reverses. The one most aficionados in Ohio know is the bank building in Sidney; this building is not quite as grand but every bit as interesting.
One North Third Street. In late 2007 building was unused.

THE MIDLAND THEATRE/NEWARK—First opened on
December 20, 1928, as Newark's version of an opulent theater palace, this auditorium soon after presented the town's first movie with sound. The landmark house went dark after the blizzard of 1978, which capped an ongoing decay. Local arts patrons helped bring about a recent renovation and the Midland has reopened to host national performing artists, as well as performances of the Granville-Newark Symphony Orchestra.
36 North Park Place, 740/345-5483, 9-4 for ticket information; www. midlandtheatre.org

NATOMA RESTAURANT/NEWARK—The oldest restaurant
downtown has been in the same family over 70 years, attracting judges and lawyers to the Courtroom Lounge, "where justice is served." Founded in the 1920s by George Athan, who immigrated from Greece in 1910, the restaurant today is run by his three grandchildren. The name Natoma was that of an Indian princess featured in a Victor Herbert operetta. Food and service here are good; the spinach salad is a noonday favorite.
10 North Park Place, 740/345-7260; www.thenatoma.com Mon-Thur 11-9:30, Fri 11-10, Sat 5-10. Dinner entrées range $12.95-$25.95.

SHERWOOD-DAVIDSON HOUSE MUSEUM/
NEWARK—The fact that eager old ladies in period costumes sometimes squabble over whose turn it is to guide you through this 1815 Victorian home can't help but make visitors feel special. This museum is filled with Licking County artifacts, including a wonderfully sensuously-shaped Coke bottle that was the company's fledgling design. It was created by a Newark fellow, Alexander Samuelson. The house had a porch closet where folks could leave borrowed books if the Davidsons weren't at home. According to the guides, no books ever went on the missing list. In 2004, the museum underwent a $500,000 restoration project that included constructing a new foundation for the historic home as well as improved access and lighting.
6 North Sixth Street; 740/345-6525; www.lchsohio.org/sherwood-davidson_ house.htm March-Dec, Tue-Sun 1-4.

NATIONAL HEISEY GLASS MUSEUM/NEWARK—Glass
is one of those ubiquitous items that is everywhere in our lives without our giving it much thought. In the hopeful dawning of new consciousness, glass—as a container—may even be making a comeback. Therefore, a notable haven for the cognoscenti of handmade glass is surprisingly close to most of us, in Newark, Ohio, the home of the Heisey Museum, the national museum, if you will, for this is the significant public American collection of what is arguably the finest

handmade tableware ever produced in America. It's here because this area was the center of America's glassmaking industry, for it is here that both quality silica and cheap natural gas were found. The museum itself is an 1831 Greek Revival house filled with eight rooms of glass made by the Heisey Company during its productive years, 1896-1957; and even to novice eyes this is an impressive collection. With the company's closing, the handmade industry was virtually ended in this country. It was doomed by cheaper imports as well as a society that had quite unwisely decided to be "throwaway." In its time, Ohio's Heisey was sold only by jewelry shops and the best department stores. It was such glass-with-class that it is likely the only folks of modest means who drank from its famous stemware were the people who made the glass and took the seconds home (not all of it legally). In Newark, for a time, people of ordinary means supped egalitarianly from fine crystal. Today, many aficionados, who have both Heisey and Waterford in their cabinets, will choose Heisey as the better-made glass. Some Newark dealers contend the antique Heisey cutters and engravers were, of course, noted for their perfection, particularly the master engraver of the 1930s, Emil Krall, an Austrian who was considered one of the finest engravers in the world. Heisey's extra process of fire-polishing—done in what glassmakers call "the glory hole"—was a notable process that lent the glass its brilliance. The Cambridge Glass Company was nearby and also made fine glass, but the Newark contingent contends Heisey is a bit superior. A gentle rivalry exists between the sister groups, but every June, Newark is mecca to the nation's Heisey collectors and the entire place is viewed through a glass, lightly. It's the annual convention at which time there are auctions, flea markets—a notable one is held on the courthouse lawn—and swap meets. The museum has most of the original Heisey molds—some 4,400 of them—and a few are used to make small pieces for the museum shop. The old company is still standing, off East Main at Oakwood, although the great smokestacks are gone and there is not much to see. Where many people have seen Heisey glass, even through they may not have known, is in both the stage and film versions of *The Glass Menagerie*; Laura's famous menagerie was a Heisey menagerie. *169 W. Church Street, Newark; 740/345-2932; www.heiseymuseum.org Open Tue-Sat 10-4, Sun 1-4; closed on major holidays. Museum can provide more information about the Heisey Convention along with a dealer directory.*

GOLF WORKS/NEWARK—Come and learn how to build your own golf clubs in a 40-acre setting so pastoral that one worker keeps her horse here. It began as a mail-order business, but now, owner Ralph Maltby, author of five books and a consultant to other writers of the sport, teaches pros and beginners from as far as Indonesia, Canada, Japan and South Africa, how to fit, repair and assemble clubs. The largest supplier of quality golf supplies in the world provides greens only for testing, and the only birdies here are in a nearby pond. *4820 Jacksontown Road (State Route 13 south); 740/328-4193; www.golfworks. com Call 800/848-8358 to register for Maltby Clubmaking Academy. Clubs with Maltby components range from $23.95-$149.95 plus labor costs.*

Longaberger Headquarters

LONGABERGER CORPORATE HEADQUARTERS/

NEWARK—The gigantic basket situated along State Route 16 in
Newark has astounded more than one person who looked up from the
road and saw it looming ahead. This basket is an architectural wonder,
the dream of the late Dave Longaberger, founder of The Longaberger
Company which he opened as J.W.'s Handwoven Baskets in 1976
in nearby Dresden, Ohio. The basket stands seven stories high and
features two 75-ton handles on the top. Corporate executives run the
large company from within, and the newest Longaberger products are
featured in the basket's 30,000-square-foot atrium. Company officials
say the building is an exact replica of the company's Market Basket,
except exaggerated 160 times. In 1999, when Dave Longaberger died,
daughter Tami was running the largest manufacturer of handmade
baskets in the country. Still privately-owned by Longaberger family
members, the company has struggled in recent years, frequently
laying-off some of its many basket makers. Yet, Longaberger sales
representatives across the country continue to bring in orders for
hordes of baskets each year. The company has also spawned the
Longaberger Golf Club and Longaberger Village—both located farther
east on State Route 16.
*1500 East Main Street, 740/322-5588; www.longaberger.com Tours Mon-Sat,
8-5 and Sun, noon-5.*

THE GREAT CIRCLE EARTHWORKS (PREVIOUSLY
MOUNDBUILDERS STATE MEMORIAL)/NEWARK—

This 66-acre park contains the remnants of what has been called "the
most elaborate and complicated earthworks in prehistoric times in
America," which, while anachronistic, serves to suggest its importance
in the inventory of Ohio earthworks. The white man's encroachments
destroyed much of it but, fortunately, left segments, including the
great ceremonial circle, 1,200 feet in diameter with walls 8 to 14 feet
high, enclosing over 26 acres. Ohio's first state fair was held in the
circle, which, ironically, helped save it. It's a wonderful natural area
now, wooded with maples, dogwoods and old beeches, and the best
time to visit it is in early spring or late fall—before or after the 75,000

annual picnickers—when the visitor can walk the circle and ponder our connection to this ancient people. The works were built by the Hopewell, Ohio's first great architectural firm, probably about 2,000 years ago. Archaeologists think the works were "civic centers" for the Indians of the area, used in a seasonal context for ceremony, religion, and trade. There is also a museum—America's first devoted exclusively to prehistoric American Indian art—where the history of Ohio's prehistoric cultures is carved in rock, pottery, pipes and ornamentation. The circle is one part of the Newark Earthworks State Memorial. A second part is the Wright Earthworks, a 50-foot-long mound that was one side of a square. (It's just north of the Great Circle; take Grant Street west from State Route 79 and turn right on James Street, from which Earthworks are visible.) The Octagon Earthworks, roughly a mile and a third in a straight line northwest, are a preserved circle and an octagon, six to eight feet high, tied together, covering 70 acres. But they are also in a private golf course with part of the greens inside the enclosures, demonstrating conclusively the correlation between religion and recreation. As far as can be determined, this is the only Ohio memorial to irony.

99 Cooper Avenue, off State Route 79 on the south side of Newark; 740/344-1919 or 800/600-7178; http://ohsweb.ohiohistory.org/places/c08/greatcircle. shtml Museum is expected to re-open in Spring 2008, following renovation. Great Circle and Wright are accessible all year. No admission charge. The junction between the Octagon Earthworks octagon and circle is visible at all times from a viewing platform in the Moundbuilders Country Club parking lot, 125 North 33rd Street, accessible from West Main Street. Also, there are four open houses a year, and earthworks may be seen at other times by prearrangement; call 740/344-1919.

DAWES ARBORETUM/NEWARK—Ohioan Beman Dawes struck it rich when he hit oil in West Virginia and started the Pure Oil Company. In time, however, his enduring legacy might prove to be his 1,000-plus-acre arboretum on his great swell of Licking County earth, sloping wonderfully down into well-tended farms. Dawes had five homes at one time, but Daweswood was his favorite. He found it one day when he had driven out from Newark and saw some lumbermen cutting trees, and bought the land to stop them. His commitment to trees never waned and today, a large part of the arboretum is stately with old hardwoods. After seeing a tree dedication in England, Dawes initiated the ritual here, calling upon his notable friends, and first plantings were gifts of Admiral Byrd, Orville Wright, General Pershing, Red Grange, and over 60 others. It's a custom that is carried on still; John Glenn, Jack Hanna and Governor Bob Taft have given plantings in more recent years. Second in size in Ohio only to Cleveland's Holden Arboretum, the arboretum is deeded to increase the general love and knowledge of trees and shrubs, so it is not as "showy" as arboretums given to flowering displays. It has a lovely driving or walking tour, one of the northernmost Cypress swamps, the world's largest lettered hedge (complete with a tower to climb and take a good look), and what has been called one of the best Japanese gardens in America. Among its peers, though, Dawes is known for being a pioneer in the use of computerized plant records—for example, its plant list is computer accessible. It is a great area resource, offering more and cheaper horticultural education than any arboretum in the country. It has a splendid array of programs, aids both amateurs and professionals in propagating unusual species, and maintains a 3,000-volume library. Dawes and his wife are buried in the arboretum.

7770 Jacksontown Road SE; 740/323-2355; www.dawesarb.org Daylight-dusk except Thanksgiving, Christmas and New Year's. No admission charge. Visitors Center and gift shop hours are Mon-Sat 8-5 and Sun and holidays, 1-5. House tours are Sat and Sun at 3:15, $2 adult, $1 child.

YE OLDE MILL/UTICA—What turns your head is the 2,000-pound overshot water wheel that once ground grain in an 1817 mill. What turns a profit is the Dager family ice cream business, where you can see how everything but the cow works. The Dager family restored the mill to use as their headquarters, but in 1986 a fire destroyed everything except the mill's foundation. The family pitched in and rebuilt what is one of the largest mills on the new Ohio frontier. And once again they grind out ice cream in a scenic 20-acre park that serves as a campus for a mill museum, an ice cream parlor and gift shop, and a place to picnic, fish, and meditate. The Ohio-sanctioned Ice Cream Festival draws up to 20 tour buses on Memorial Day weekend. The Buckeye Tree Festival, in September, is a family reunion sort of affair with an 1840s theme and music, honoring Ohio's statehood.

11324 Mt. Vernon Road, State Route 13, 10 miles north of Newark; 740/892-3921; www.velveticecream.com

CRANBERRY BOG/BUCKEYE LAKE—This bog is one of Ohio's treasures, a living remnant of the ice age that is believed to be the only "floating" cranberry bog in the world. When the canal was built in 1825, the bog was 50 acres surrounded by 4,000 acres of marsh. Today—miraculous that it remains at all—it is about 14 acres surrounded by 2,000 acres of the lake. Described as "a big green sponge," it is a monument to both the tenacity and fragility of nature. Because the bog is largely an acidic environment surrounded by an alkaline one—the lake itself—it is slowly disappearing. The bog is teeming with rare plants, including some carnivorous ones, but because of its fragility, visitors must obtain special permission to visit, or they may stop in on the last Saturday each June when the Division of Natural Areas and Preserves holds an "open bog," which usually attracts upwards of a thousand people.

Near the village of Buckeye Lake, off State Route 79 just south of I-70. For a guided tour or more information about boat transportation, contact the Buckeye Lake Historical Society at 740/929-1998. Individual visitors must provide own boat transportation and receive permit. For permits, complete an online application at www.dnr.state.oh.us/dnap/location/cranberry.html

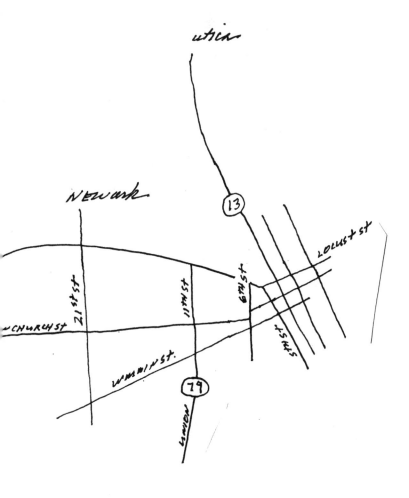

Mount Vernon

There is something suspenseful in the geography—
the way the road twists and turns, giving way to
surprising vistas as the land rises and falls on the hilly
approach from the north on the old 3C Highway.
Then it passes Academia, the Seventh-Day
Adventists' settlement, now the headquarters of the
church's Ohio conference. The most noteworthy
building is the all-brick Mount Vernon Academy, a
boarding school for grades 9-12 and descendant of
the school that gave Academia its name.

Then the road makes the long, slow descent to town,
past the overhang of maples and dogwoods, to the
surprise of antebellum houses on narrow brick
streets. From this perspective, the town appears more
Southern than Midwestern—an unexpected pleasure
in heartland Ohio.

This is a town of uncommon beauty—as genteel as a
well-bred Southern lady of a certain age: her wealth
displayed, but discreetly, and her troubles hidden by a
veil of propriety. The old homes are well maintained,
their cupolas and verandas intact, betraying a steely
resolve beneath the Southern charm.

Mount Vernon was founded by Virginians who named it, and influenced by Marylanders who followed. But Pennsylvanians and Connecticut Yankees pushed in from the North and here, democratic theory was tested, as Northerner and Southerner met headlong to fashion a workable society—a new frontier, so to speak, in the wilds of central Ohio.

Mount Vernon had a keen aesthetic sense and an eye for the finer things; even as it prospered through the decades its gentler aspect endured. When librarian Mary McGavick came to town to interview for her job, she first spent some time driving around, admiring the fine houses, the Public Square, the ornate storefronts. After she'd looked the place over, she told the library director, "I'd pay you for a chance to live here."

Mount Vernon has that effect on people. But its attraction goes beyond the physical attributes, as McGavick discovered once she'd moved in: "It's the only town in central Ohio where you will encounter left-wing intellectuals, right-wing intellectuals, good old boys in pickup trucks and sweet old ladies who smell of sachet."

Russell Cooper House

RUSSELL-COOPER HOUSE—The Russell-Cooper House is a wonderful composite of Victorian excesses—adding onto it was the hobby of Colonel William Cooper, who returned home to Mount Vernon in 1888 and spent the next 14 years ordering changes to his house. Inside, this bed and breakfast has six guest rooms, including one called the Colonel's Room, which aside from spaciousness and a comfortable bed (two beds, in fact; one is a single) has a few Civil War mementos. The proprietor is Tom Dvorak, whose late wife Mary was a descendant of the Colonel's. Be sure to ask to see the big dining room's painted ceiling, which the Dvoraks discovered by accident a few years ago and then had restored. In the corners it has the female faces of the four seasons, and of them all only winter has a smile. Go figure. *115 East Gambier Street; 740/397-8638; www.russell-cooper.com Rates are $85 Fri-Sat and $75 Sun-Thur.*

KENYON INN & RESTAURANT/GAMBIER—It took more than good planning and a pile of bricks to make this port in a storm look like it's always been a part of this old college. Actually, it's relatively small, looking more like an old country guest house outside, full of the latest modern amenities inside—except for an elevator. Thirty-two walk-in and walk-up rooms are all done in contemporary décor, with light wood furniture and painted ceilings. The one ground-floor room is reserved for the handicapped. As for the Kenyon Inn Restaurant, it's an area favorite, reliably good; the only catch is that the dining room really is small—just ten tables with 32 seats, and often all of them are filled. On warm days the restaurant expands with more tables just outside on the porch, which becomes a very pretty place to eat, across the road from the beautiful Kenyon campus. Dinners offer fresh fish and one of the better prime rib dinners in central Ohio. The restaurant is on one side of the inn lobby; the other side has a well-stocked barroom. *100 West Wiggin Street; 740/427-2202; www.kenyoninn.com Room rates range from $80-$150. Restaurant offers breakfast Mon-Fri 7-9:30, Sat 8-10, Sun brunch 10-2; lunch Mon-Sat 11-2; dinner Mon-Thur 5-8:30, Fri-Sat 5-9, Sun 5-8. Reservations strongly recommended. Dinner entrees $6.95-$22.95.*

The Gambier House

THE GAMBIER HOUSE/GAMBIER—The Gambier House is in a small, very attractive house: two levels under a slate gambrel roof, white frame with black shutters, a row of dormers upstairs, and all tucked in behind a cast iron fence. The interior is comfortable, attractive and never overwrought. There are four bedrooms upstairs and one down; all have double or queen beds and private baths. Toward the back a carriage house holds a suite that sleeps four to five, has a small kitchen and the inn's only television-VCR. Proprietor E.J. Heer makes fine breakfasts, with the likes of pear crisp, buttermilk waffles, bacon. She uses local organic eggs and, if possible, local produce. When the season is right, she promises, "The innkeeper will pick the blueberries." This is Gambier's only bed and breakfast.

107 East Wiggin Street; 740/427-2668; www.gambierhouse.com Rooms are $99-125.

The White Oak Inn

THE WHITE OAK INN/DANVILLE—This true "destination" inn—there's nothing near it but the Walhonding-Kokosing Valley flood control district—is an elegant 1915 farmhouse built with six bedrooms by a wealthy farmer who wanted his sons to marry and then bring their brides home. (They didn't.) Present-day owners, Yvonne and Ian Martin, have ten bedrooms, six with fireplaces, including three in the guest house, plus two log-cabin cottages. The 14-acre setting is wooded, and the front porch overlooks the Kokosing River. Yvonne promises gourmet breakfasts with Amish style peppered bacon, dishes like stuffed French toast, and the fragrance of fresh-baked muffins every morning. Dinners are also available for guests, though only by reservation.

29683 Walhonding Road/State Route 715 12 miles east of Gambier; 740/599-6107 or 877/908-5923; www.whiteoakinn.com No young children. Main-house room rates range from $95-185.

THE ALCOVE—Cloth napkins are the first hint that a restaurant might be a cut above average. Clean carpeting is the second. Throw in a mural with scenes of historic Mount Vernon painted on the wall, some greenery for an English garden profile, good food and vigilant waitresses, and you've got a place nice enough to score points with your mother-in-law. The dinner favorite is prime rib, and the lunch special is always popular. Another favorite is fudge pecan balls for dessert.

116 South Main Street; 740/392-3076; www.alcoverestaurant.com Mon-Thur 11-9; Fri-Sat 11-9:30. Dinner entrees $12-18.

INTERNATIONAL DINING IN MOUNT VERNON—"I'm thrilled that there's ethnic food in Mount Vernon now," says a long-time resident who arrived in the meat-and-potatoes era. Here are some of the places that delight her—and others—looking for virtual travel at nearby tables. **Fiesta Mexicana**, *308 West High Street; 740/397-6325 and 740/397-6329.* This very popular Mexican restaurant serves both lunch and dinner, with, for example, a beef burrito $5 at lunch, a flan custard for dessert at $3, and the favorite entrée, two chimichangas for $8.50. The building is pumpkin-colored stucco, Mexican style, and the colorful accents carry on into the interior. Mon-Thur 11-2:30 and 5-10; Fri 11-10; Sat noon-10; Sun noon-9. **Henry's on the Square**, *6 Public Square; 740/397-5603.* Located in the Curtis Inn, a hotel, Henry's welcomes all comers with two menus, one American and one Indian. Thus you can find, for example, an American Rack of Lamb, $20, or Tandoori style chicken, beef, shrimp or fish, all under $20. Mon-Fri 11-9, Fri 11-10, Sat 4-10. **Mazza's**, *214 West High Street, 740/397-2076; www.mazzassince1939.com* Opened in 1939, Mazza's is a Mount Vernon tradition dating back into the meat-and-potatoes era. Menu offerings include an Italian sausage sandwich for lunch for under $5; a dinnertime chicken marsala is $12. The buzz in spring 2007 was that Senator John Glenn, his wife and family came to Mazza's for Easter dinner. Mon-Thur 11-9, Fri 11-9:30, Sat 3-10; Sun closed (except major holidays).

VILLAGE INN/GAMBIER—On the outside the Village Inn is brick and white trim, a sort of ersatz colonial, so the inside comes as a pleasant surprise: a cozy bar with dark wood paneled booths along the wall, and a second room filled with tables. The Village Inn closed early in the 2000s, and then in early spring 2007 reappeared with a set of enthusiastic new owners, one of whom, Jerry Kelly, was tending bar when we arrived. Lunch is sandwiches and salads; dinner offerings include mac and cheese, Greek salad, and hoisin-chili glazed shrimp skewers.
102 Gaskin Avenue; 740/427-2112; www.villageinngambier.com Hours are 11 am-midnight Tue, Thur, Sun; Wed, Fri, Sat 11 am-1 am. Lunch noon-2; dinner 5-9; bar menu other times; closed Mon. Lunches $4-7; dinners $5-9.

PUBLIC SQUARE—The symbol of Mount Vernon's singularity is the square right under its nose—Public Square. It's circumnavigated by anyone driving into town as all roads lead here. Entering and exiting this rotary could be a nightmare, as it is some places. But in Mount Vernon it occurs with the ease of a well-oiled turnstile, and out-of-towners have been known to enjoy the process so much, they've been seen circling the square a half dozen times or so. (They could just be lost.) If you stand in the square and look out you'll see the roads going off in four directions, uphill and downhill and with little slope. But you'll scarcely be able to see the figure on top of The Monument, for it's very high and from here, you'll have no perspective on it. It depicts a Union soldier facing the Southern battlefields. If you get into town and are lost, he makes a great compass, at least when seen from a distance. He was put in place, with some difficulty, in 1877, and remains steadfast even now, when they drape him and the rest of the circle in white lights at Christmas. The Cooper Fountain was donated by Charles Cooper, the founder (with his brother Elias) of Cooper Iron Works. It preceded the monument and was so magnificent that initially it became a tourist attraction. Bronze and marble, it's 12 feet high and has three storks each spurting two jets of water.

KNOX COUNTY HISTORICAL SOCIETY MUSEUM—In a town with so many fine old houses as Mount Vernon, it comes as a surprise that the Knox County Historical Society Museum is in a more ordinary building on a highway outside of town. But as it turns out, this museum exhibits some very heavy machinery originally made here, and, as Museum Director Jim Gibson explains, no one wanted to see a seven-ton machine crashing through a lovely old floor into the basement. So since 1987 the Museum has been housed in what was once the local Yamaha Motorcycle dealership. Cooper Industries, the local company that made the heavy machines, helped buy the building because it was suitable for exhibiting the company's early steam engines—and you can't look a gift iron horse in the mouth. (Cooper has been bought by Rolls-Royce and is now Rolls-Royce Energy Services.) The museum has four six-to-seven-thousand-pound Cooper steam engines, which look something like locomotives. As three additions have helped the building grow from its original 6000 square feet to 15,000, the museum also had room after the turn of this century for a couple Cooper compressors, built to pump natural gas through pipelines. These are really big—the biggest, in service from 1944 to 1999, is 70,000 pounds and about 12 feet tall. "These machines," says Gibson, "are pretty unusual for a county history museum." We agree. He goes on to point out that the museum also has some of the more usual stuff, for the large showroom is divided to resemble late nineteenth-century roomfuls of items made or used locally. Collections include a wonderful old switchboard; an overhead cashier system; newspapers back to 1852; memorabilia from entertainer Paul Lynde, including his 1964 Thunderbird; Indian artifacts.
875 Harcourt Road/U.S. 36 just west of town; 740/393-5247; www. knoxhistory.org Open Mar-Nov; Thur-Sun 2-4 and Wed 6-8. Adults $2.

MOUNT VERNON SHOPS—**Aunt Bee's Quilts & More**, *(229 South Main Street, 740/393-3900; 800/393-1893)* has quilts and wall hangings, fabrics, sewing machines and notions. Mon-Fri 10-5; Sat 10-3. **Bead Therapy Bead Shop**, *(227 South Main; 740/393-2323 or 877/362-2323.)* Owner Patty Harrell opened the bead shop in late 1999. She offers an extraordinary collection of beads—glass, metal, crystal, stone, pearl, and so on, all in many sizes; customers select the ones they want and put them in muffin tins adapted for the purpose with price levels. Strings available too, as well as suggestions on how to use beads. Mon-Sat 10-6.

DOWN HOME LEATHER—This handsome shop is just on the other side of the square. It's redolent of leather; you'll see purses, briefcases, belts, wallets and every imaginable leather product on display. What's really amazing is the fact that everything is made on the premises. It seems there's a workshop downstairs where Laurel and Duke Wagoner, their son and her sister make leather products. "We make everything," Duke says. "Even the snaps, we make the snaps that go on purses." What about zippers? No, he admits. "The zippers are from Chicago. But I know the man who makes them." Most clientele learn about the shop when they're in the area attending college. That's how it happened that Duke had just shipped four brief cases to four

Kenyon alumni working in Tokyo. It can even happen that a reporter who steps in to find out about Down Home Leather (founded 1969) leaves with a new purse. (Prices are reasonable too.)
9 North Main Street; 800/393-1186; www.downhomeleather.com Mon-Sat 10-6.

G.W. Armstrong House

THE HOUSES OF MOUNT VERNON—Mount Vernon is a wonderful place for old houses. You'll find street after street of them, for walking or slow driving; some of the best are East High, East Gambier and North Main. As of 2007 the Knox County Historical Society and the Visitors Bureau were out of their old supply of walking tour guides, but they were preparing three new ones. The first, on Gambier Street, was due by spring, 2008 and should be available at the Visitors Bureau, 103 South Main Street at Vine, 800/837-5282; or the Historical Society Museum, above, 875 Harcourt Road/U.S. 36. Here are a few suggestions for starters.

On East Gambier Street, at number 115, you'll see the **Russell-Cooper House**, also a B&B listed above. It was originally built in 1829, but that's not something you'd ever guess by looking at it. Colonel William Cooper married into the house and then, in the late nineteenth century, recreated it.

On East High Street just above Public Square you'll find **Knox County Courthouse**. Perched proudly up on the hill, it dates from the mid-1850s. The **G.W. Armstrong House**, *601 East High,* was built in 1889. Designed by mail-order architect George Franklin Barber of Knoxville, it's been called Mount Vernon's best Queen Anne style house.

From Public Square drive up North Main to East Lamartine Street, and turn right. After one block, at the corner of Gay Street, you'll find two almost-twin Italianate houses from the early 1880s. The one at 506 North Gay has a mansard roof, which its companion at *600 North Gay* lacks. Continue on Lamartine to the end of the street, where you'll find **Round Hill**, one of the famous old houses of Mount Vernon, built in the early 1850s in an Italian Villa style.

MEMORIAL PARK—Since the 1970s, Mount Vernon has had a very active girls' softball program—for girls 5 to 18 years old—and all the games are played at Memorial Park. There you'll find four lighted softball fields, scoreboards and a loudspeaker system. From May through June, 500 girls play in a local recreational program. Then on July 1, eight all-star teams start playing other towns. They have never won a national championship, but they often finish very respectably— second for girls ten and under in 2005, for example. Local businesses, like T-shirt Express, Charlie's Body Shop or Presley Construction, sponsor team trips. *In May and June games start at 6 on weekdays and at 10 on Saturdays. There's also a web site: www.leaguelineup.com/mvgs/*

MOUNT VERNON THEATERS—Go up the East High Street hill from Public Square and you'll come to the Memorial Building, which houses the **Memorial Theater**. The 993-seat Memorial opened in 1925 and has been refurbished several times, most recently in 2006; it's now the home of the Central Ohio Drama Club and dance recitals. 112 East High Street; 740/393-6704. Then there's the **Woodward Opera House**, which originally opened in 1851 and is thought to be the country's oldest mostly intact theater. Since the late 1990s, the long-closed theater has been a project, the stuff of dreams coming true. It started with a goal of $4 million, and over the years, as the building next door was acquired too, the price tag ballooned into $14 million—a lot for a town the size of Mount Vernon. But at least by now much of that money has been spent and what remains is $6.7 million for interior restoration; of that $1.2 million is in hand from a state capital budget appropriation. Opening is now set for 2009. Tenants, including the Convention and Visitors Bureau, occupy retail space in the adjacent building, so the Woodward already has an income. In summer and fall the theater is open for public tours on Saturday mornings 10-noon; free. (It's a third-floor walk-up.) *103 South Main Street at Vine; 800/837-5282 (CVB) or 740/392-6142; www.thewoodward.org*

ASIDE Actors had been appearing in blackface since the Revolution but it was Mount Vernon-born Daniel Decatur Emmett who organized the first minstrel show, in New York in 1842. When he wedded skits and songs to a black persona, he started an entertainment craze that lasted for over half a century. He is more famous for writing Dixie, the unofficial anthem of the Confederacy. Daniel was neutral about the Civil War but he was not happy that the Southerners had appropriated his song. "If I had known to what use they were going to put my song," he said, "I will be damned if I'd written it." Copyright being a nebulous concept in the 1800s, the largely unacknowledged Father of the Minstrel Show (as well as its stereotype of black Americans) last toured at 80 in 1892 and then retired to Mount Vernon, where he died in 1904. Now every year during the second weekend in August, Mount Vernon closes its downtown streets for the Dan Emmett Music & Arts Festival, with lots of music and juried artisan exhibits. *740/392-3378; www.danemmettfestival.org*

KOKOSING GAP TRAIL—The Kokosing Gap Trail, a rail trial from Mount Vernon to Danville, is one of the jewels of Knox County. Altogether it is 14 miles long, with three paved four-and-a-half-mile segments. The first is from Mount Vernon to Gambier; the second, from Gambier to Howard; the third, from Howard to Danville. It follows alongside the Kokosing River most closely in the first part, which makes a nice walk from Mount Vernon to Gambier, where you can leave the trail at Laymon Road and head up the steep hill (the only taxing part of this walk) to Gambier, take your pick of two inns, the deli or the organic-food café, mosey around the old campus south of Wiggin and then walk back. Half a mile past Laymon the trail has restrooms in season and an exhibit of a 1940 locomotive and a 1924 caboose. Really good walkers can go on to Howard or Danville, but most people who do the whole trail are cyclists. The Kokosing Gap Trail says that it is the country's largest rail-to-trail park maintained solely by donations and volunteers.

Access in Mount Vernon is in Phillips Park; from East Gambier Street, go south two blocks on Liberty Street. Trail never closes. www.kokosinggaptrail.org

LIONS RACCOON DINNER/DANVILLE—"It started out as a prank," says Pat Crow, who's executive director of the Knox County Visitors Bureau and is the perennial master of ceremonies for the Danville Lions Raccoon Dinner. In 1944 a few friends concocted a surprise meal featuring raccoon. It happened again the next year, and as time passed people in the community expressed interest. Now it's an annual event the first Monday in February, with a hundred volunteers preparing a meal for 600-800 people, always including some from out of state. It's a full meal too—not just raccoon, but also potatoes and raccoon gravy, vegetables, dessert and beverage. The animals are felled by a couple of men who hunt them for fur. They freeze about 230 raccoons, which amounts to 625 pounds. The cooks stew the meat like pot roast for four to five hours in 18-quart roasters. Pat Crow says it tastes something like pot roast too, but there's ham available for culinary wimps. For most people the dinner provides a chance to brag that they actually ate raccoon. "The stories go on and on," says Crow. "I've been MC 20 years and it's the funnest thing I do every year."

The dinner is at St. Luke's Community Center, 100 South Main, 5-7:30; afterward the Danville Jazz Band performs across the street in the High School Auditorium, and an Ohio sports figure gives a speech. *Contact Knox County CVB to get on the mailing list; 800/837-5282; www.visitknoxohio. org/calendar/ Price was $11 in 2007; reservations not necessary.*

BROWN FAMILY ENVIRONMENTAL CENTER/ GAMBIER—This environmental center is part of Kenyon College, which uses it for classes, but it's also open to the public. The main attraction is a network of trails; a flyer has been issued for one, the BFEC Attractions Trail, which is about a mile long. It has prairie areas, a pine plantation, a hilltop view that takes in the Old Kenyon Steeple. Other trails, each about a mile, are in wooded areas and a wetland on the north side of State Route 229.

9781 Laymon Road (south of State Route 229); 740/427-5050; www.kenyon.edu

KENYON COLLEGE BOOKSTORE/GAMBIER—It's not every bookstore that offers 23,000 trade books, 10,000 texts, a snack bar, over-stuffed chairs, and a book castle that kids can enter and climb in. Alongside the expected display of Kenyon merchandise, there's a corner in front for faculty authors and student artwork on the walls. Since Gambier is so small, the Bookstore also functions as a community

center, a place where people can read, meet or study. It's open every day of the year, except June 30, when it closes for inventory; on Christmas and January 1, it closes at noon. You'll find a quirky delight in back, a cottage named Denham Sutcliffe Bookseller in honor of a professor. It accepts donations of used books, which are sold at bargain prices: 25 cents for paperbacks, 50 cents for hard cover, all on the honor system. Because it has a student manager, it's open only when classes are in session, noon-4.
106 Gaskin Avenue; 740/427-5710; www.kenyon.edu/bookstore.xml Hours are 7:30 am-11:30 pm.

KENYON COLLEGE—In the words of one perspicacious writer, Kenyon is "an assertively high-toned, militantly liberal-arts, quintessentially eggheaded place, draped in social history and overgrown with ivy." (The ivy is not in evidence today, but the remark has such a sonorous quality that we'll let stand.) Kenyon is the oldest private institution of higher learning in the state of Ohio. Its first six graduates were in the Class of 1829 and graduation exercises were led by the founder, Philander Chase, a Dartmouth graduate and educational entrepreneur who raised money for Kenyon in England. Hence, the British influence in architecture. One professor has described it as "a sort of medieval Hamlet with modern plumbing, a kind of St. Disney-in-the-Fields." Kenyon has 1654 students, became co-ed in 1969, and as of 2007-08 52 percent of the students were women. The campus has seen come and go poets, philosophers, prime ministers, a president and very good swimmers. Actually its swimming program is the most successful collegiate swim program in national sports: in 2007 the men's team won its 28th consecutive national Division III championship, and the women's team won its 21st; and since 1976 Kenyon swimmers have earned 1500 All-American designations. Kenyon is the home of the famous literary journal, *The Kenyon Review*. Well-known graduates include poets Robert Lowell and James Wright, novelists Peter Taylor and E.L. Doctorow, actor (and now benefactor) Paul Newman, President Rutherford B. Hayes, birth-control pill developer Carl Djerassi, the late Swedish Prime Minister Olof Palme, and cartoonists Bill Watterson and Jim Borgman.
740/427-5158; www.kenyon.edu

MIDDLE PATH—With its lawn and old buildings, the old campus south of Wiggin Street is one of the most beautiful man-made places in Ohio. Visitors should take time to walk Middle Path, the gravelly institution built by students a century-and-a-half ago. It runs north-south for one mile from Old Kenyon to Bexley Hall, the full length of the campus, and has carried the weight of many Kenyon traditions, especially having to do with paving. There are always rumors that Middle Path, surfaced with a fine gravel, is to be paved. They are always unfounded. Its tributaries, though, have been "poured," making alumni and students nervous that logic will outweigh tradition and the closest distance between two points will no longer be their lovely, gravelly, straight Middle Path. Be sure to stop in Ascension Hall along the way, and climb up to see the restored literary rooms at the front in the central tower. Nineteenth-century literary societies had ornate meeting rooms in many Ohio colleges, but these are the only ones that

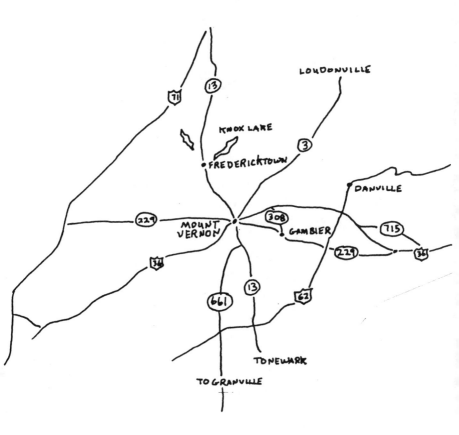

Roscoe Village

Coshocton

U.S. Route 36 and State Route 16 in Coshocton are to travelers today what the Tuscarawas, the Walhonding and the Muskingum Rivers were to the Indians in 1750. Easy access and exit still make it a fine spot for the amenities of a settlement. Perhaps the best entry is via State Route 16, a road carved into a hole, offering no long views until you get to Chestnut Street. There, the sky opens and you turn east—into Goshogunk—the Delaware Indian word for "black bear" and what is now downtown Coshocton. Here, in a setting that's hilly and beautiful, we find the old town, both prehistoric and historic, where the Tuscarawas and Walhonding Rivers flow together to form the Muskingum, and where modern commerce first arrived in the 1830s, with the opening of the canal.

It was here that Christopher Gist, while checking out the landscape for the Ohio Company, led Ohio's first Protestant Christmas service for a wary group of ragtag French traders, Englishmen, and curious Indians. Gist was there for another historical event as well. He visited with Mary Harris, a white woman who, having been captured by the Indians at an early age, was now married to Chief Eagle Feather. She was well-respected and well-remembered, and many places in Coshocton and Roscoe now named "Whitewoman" carry her legacy. Yet one day the chief brought home another woman, and the story is that Mary was not happy about it, nor was the other woman. What happened was that *someone* put a tomahawk in Chief Eagle Feather's head. The Indians blamed the new wife and carried her back to Coshocton where she was given one chance to escape, was tracked down, tortured and beheaded, a somewhat sobering event for the visiting Gist.

The natives are much friendlier these days. In the heart of downtown is the courthouse, where on a warm Friday night 60 years ago, Marshall Jacobs may have been seen scaling the building. He'd climb *down* too, which of course is much harder. None of the other wall-walkers of his day ever climbed *down*. Now, Marshall has passed on, and everyone stays on the ground on summertime Friday nights for band concerts on the courthouse lawn. The courthouse forms a handsome backdrop. It's a fancy red brick with a mansard roof and an ornate clock tower whose bell was transported here by canal boat well before the Civil War.

Coshocton, then, melds two towns, Coshocton proper, begun by the Indians, and the now-annexed Roscoe, born of canals and Ohio's first canal-town restoration. Roscoe Village will satisfy the tourist, but there is a charm to Coshocton that lies in the geniality of those who live there.

ROSCOE HILLSIDE CABINS—These comfortable cabins are on a wooded hillside; they're new, dating from 2004 on; and they have all the comforts of home except maybe better. Each cabin has central air and heat, a livingroom, bedroom or two, kitchen and bath with Jacuzzi, and non-woodsy features like TV, VCR and DVD. They also have ladders leading up to lofts where there's an extra bed. Linens are provided and kitchens are fully equipped. If you're used to a dishwasher, the only roughing it comes in when you wash up after meals. *46971 County Road 495, near Roscoe Village; 866/582-8146; www.hillsidecabins.net One bedroom unit $150; two-bedroom $275; second night lower.*

APPLE BUTTER INN—Apple Butter Inn occupies an 1840 house, white with red shutters and a front porch, and located on Hill Street overlooking Roscoe Village. Four guest bedrooms, all with private baths, are in the house, and two more are a little downhill in the carriage house, where visitors have more space, kitchenettes and Jacuzzis, but less sunlight. Kim Simmons, her husband Brian, and her father Tim Veatch, have all been helping to run the inn since 2003. Full breakfasts. *455 Hill Street; 740/622-1329; 888/279-0247; www.applebutterinn.net Rates from $85 weeknights up to $140 for the carriage house on a weekend.*

INN AT RAINBOW HILLS BED & BREAKFAST/
NEWCOMERSTOWN—In spite of some genuine old-time log-cabin siding, this B&B is all brand new, built of woods from the property, and open only since January 2007. It has four bedrooms with queen beds, fresh *hand-ironed* sheets, private baths and private balconies. All have use of the large lounge on the first floor, and breakfasts—big breakfasts that start with champagne and orange juice. *26349 Township Road 251, 1.5 miles west of State Route 751, 2.5 miles north of U.S. 36; 740/545-9305. No children, smoking or pets. Three rooms are $165 each; one is $175.*

Rainbow Hills

RAINBOW HILLS VINEYARDS/
NEWCOMERSTOWN—The vineyard spawned the B&B. The only vineyard between Ironton and Wheeling when it opened in 1988, Rainbow Hills has an idyllic country setting. Lee Wyse chose the site from seven possibilities east of the Mississippi; he was looking for "marginal" farmland with south-facing hills, high-acid well-drained soil, four seasons, streams, and substantial towns within 30 miles. Previously an agricultural research biologist who had worked in Australia and East Africa, Wyse confirmed his choice by inspecting every inch of this property on foot. Ultimately he and his wife Joy built this jewel in the woods, with rows of vines curling over hills, a pond and comfortable spaces for tasting, drinking and dining. Wyse says that 99 percent of the grapes they use are grown on his property or in the area; his specialties are cabernet franc and seyval blanc. In summer he and Joy host outdoor wine and steak-fry dinners on Fridays and Saturdays, by reservation only. *Same address and phone as the B&B. Mon-Sat 11-6 except winter holidays. Steak fry and wine, $28.*

THE OLD WAREHOUSE RESTAURANT & LOCK 27—

This handsome old Roscoe Village building houses a restaurant with an unusually attractive adjacent courtyard. Menu features include homemade soups, handcut steaks, and fresh fish. King Charles Tavern is upstairs, Lock 27 dining room and bar are downstairs. Menu is the same all day. *400 North Whitewoman Street; 740/622-4001. Lunch and dinner $5-19.*

RAVEN'S GLENN WINERY AND RESTAURANT/WEST

LAFAYETTE—In 2004 Renee and Robert Guilliams traded their long-term health care business for a winery and restaurant that accommodate individuals and bus tours. As Coshocton County natives, the Guilliamses surely had a good eye for a setting: both the dining room and a large deck overlook the Tuscarawas River, which is very beautiful in this area; a golf course on the far bank keeps the view perennially green. This is a family business, with the restaurant's Italian menu reflecting grandparents who came from central Italy and son Beau at work as winemaker. *56183 County Road 143, off US 36 9 miles east of Coshocton, West Lafayette; 740/545-1000; www.ravensglenn.com Tasting room Mon 11-6, Tue-Sat 11-8; restaurant Tue-Sat 11-8. Tasting alone, $2. Lunch $7-12; dinner entrees $15-24.*

COURTSQUARE CAFÉ—One thing Larry Garabrandt has is

energy; he starts his days at 5:30, milking at his family's dairy in West Lafayette. He opened this Main Street family restaurant in September 2003 with nine people in the kitchen. Before long he had winnowed that down to one, himself, and his mother, who makes rolls and buns. (His sister comes in when they're very busy and does the dishes.) Garabrandt learned to cook from his late grandmother, who shared her recipes with him. Now he's serving up the likes of lasagna ($13) and chicken cacciatore ($13.99) and, in season, pumpkin stew from scratch. *241 Main Street; 740/295-3663; www.courtsquarecafe.com Tue-Thur 11:30-9, Fri 11:30 am-2:30 am, Sat 5-2:30 am. Closed Sun-Mon.*

SERENITY TEA HOUSE—Former teacher Jeanne C. Keenan used

to entertain her students at the Montessori school with tea parties. Then she included parents; then she was doing teas at home. "I could see how people calmed down and connected," she says. Serenity Tea House is her way of providing that kind of serenity for everyone, though it was hard the first day she opened because her chef didn't show up; then the second chef didn't work out either. Today's chef is serving up dishes including crepes ($7.29 with salad) and panini for lunch and orange-flavor pancakes ($4.29) or oatmeal ($3.79) for breakfast. Keenan herself makes lemon bread, muffins and scones every morning, and boasts about offering thirty different types of loose-leaf tea. A pot of hot tea is $2.25. *611 Main Street; 740/623-0094; www.serenityteahouse.com Mon-Sat 7-3.*

ROSCOE VILLAGE—The 308-mile Ohio-Erie canal from Cleveland

to Portsmouth, with 146 locks, cost $4.7 million and took seven years to build. Ohioans used to boast that together, this canal and the parallel one and its branches in western Ohio, gave the state over 1000 miles of canal by the late 1840s—more than anywhere else in the world. Thank Alfred Kelley and his crews of Irish laborers for this. The Irish immigrants got 30 cents a day and a jigger of whiskey every five hours.

With picks, shovels and wheelbarrows they completed mile after mile of canals, aqueducts and locks. And because of them there evolved the little town of Roscoe, one of the pivotal points on the Ohio-Erie Canal. Its success lasted twenty years, until the railroad, whose pieces were shipped in by canal, put an end to the need for a canal system. As water breathed life into the canals, water also finally washed them away. The 1913 flood ended the declining system for good. Fifty-five years later Roscoe Hill residents Edward and Frances Montgomery mourned these remnants as they drove through the village. Edward Montgomery had made a fortune by inventing a process to put rubber on gloves, so he and his wife had the wherewithal to restore the canal's tollhouse and then the Old Warehouse; they also set up a foundation to restore the whole village. Today Roscoe Village draws 250,000 visitors annually; by now, it's prospered almost twice as long as the original. Over twenty homes and buildings have been upgraded and filled with sweets, clothes and gifts. Most buildings are brick, with stepped gables typical of the canal era, gardens flourish, and festivals are frequent May through December. In summer visitors on the easy walking tour are greeted by shopkeepers in canal-era costumes. At the north end of Whitewoman Street the traveler can see the Parthenon of the canal era—Triple Locks—gateless and grassy, but with "well built sides, straight and true." From here, follow the path from the end of the parking lot to the footbridge on the site of the Walhonding Aqueduct—it once carried boats, mules and passengers *over* the Walhonding River—to the restored mile-and-a-half stretch of canal that now carries the Monticello III. *600 North Whitewoman Street, off State Routes 16 and 83 near U.S. 36 junction; 800/877-1830, 740/622-9310; www.roscoevillage.com Living History Tour: adults $9.95, students $4.95, seniors $8.95, under 5 free. Group rates when prearranged. Tour takes 1 1/2 to 2 hours. Open all year. Shops and exhibits closed Thanksgiving, Christmas, New Year's Day, Easter.*

THE MURALS—As the birthplace of specialty advertising—the seed was planted in 1887 when Jack Musil put advertising slogans on burlap school bags—Coshocton has had a subtle, long-term exposure to the graphic arts. The result seems to have created a desire to perpetuate Coshocton history in that larger-than-life style—the mural. Coshoctonites may take this for granted, but with six murals on local history in one small town, they should not.

1. *Chase Bank Canal Days Mural*—Originally in 1960 this 8' x 24' mural was in the lobby of the Coshocton National Bank; some nine years later it moved across the street to where it is now, in Chase Bank; customers can deposit and withdraw under the most aesthetic circumstances. Artist Dean Cornwell used bright colors for a canal town scene that\ in real life was rather drab. The mural caught the eye of Edward and Frances Montgomery and inspired them to launch the Roscoe Village restoration. A smaller version is in the Roscoe Village Visitor Center. 120 South 4th Street; 740/623 4950. Mon-Fri 9-6; Sat 9-2.

2. *Bouquet's Treaty with the Indians*—In 1764 Col. Henry Bouquet and 1,500 British regulars and American militia crashed through the wilderness to a place on the Walhonding River just north of today's Coshocton. Though prepared for war, Bouquet tried a new tactic—talk. With it, he subdued the Delawares, Wyandots and Shawnee without firing a shot, obtained freedom for every captive (whether they wanted it or not) and got a promise of peace. This triple coup was unequalled for its time and was put to canvas

144 years later, in 1908, and glued to the wall in the Common Pleas Courtroom of the Coshocton County Courthouse. The artist was Arthur William Wolfle, says Irene Miller, Clerk of Courts, who will give tours if she's not too busy. She knows what it's like to visit courthouses; she's been to and photographed every one in Ohio. Coshocton County Courthouse, Main Street; 740/622-1456. Open during the week.

3. *Colonel Bouquet's Receiving of Prisoners from Indians at Coshocton, Ohio, October 1764*—Commissioned as a gift by the class of 1964, this mural was to have been done by the famous illustrator Benton Clark, but he died after doing the original sketch. The mural was finished during the summer of 1964 by the late Benjamin Blackson, whose brother Lewis "Pooch" Blackson survives to remember watching the painting process during his lunch hours, and even adding some paint to the horse's tail. The mural is 7' x 28' and, Blackson says, weighs 500 pounds. It was dedicated exactly on the 200th anniversary of the prisoner transfer. "Bouquet's treaty," Blackson adds, "is probably the most historic thing that ever happened in our county." Central Elementary School, 724 Walnut Street. The mural is inside the 8th Street entrance; go to the office first for permission.

4. *Painting of Roscoe Village* One of the best homemade items at Spitler's Family Restaurant is the 5'x16' mural on the back wall of the dining room. Robert Spitler commissioned George Young to paint it from a

photograph—a view from Spitler's house. Presumably, Mr. Spitler liked the view so well that he wanted the pleasure of it at work as well as at home. He didn't anticipate it would take five years: "Patrons came in and *talked* to him while he painted. I thought he'd *never* get done." It's a 20th century view of Roscoe that muralist Young finished in 1978. 585 South Whitewoman Street; 740/622-3688. Sun Thur 6-9, Fri-Sat 6 am-9 pm.

5. ***Benton Clark Mural***—In the 1930s Benton Clark was a nationally known illustrator. When alcohol and marita problems brought him home to Coshocton, he became close friends with the town firemen, procured a piece of 1.5'x14' plywood from a friend at the lumber company, and went to work in the fire department kitchen on a three-part mural depicting firefighting in Coshocton in 1803, 1905 and 1962. In May of 1990 it was given a place of honor, under lights, in the lounge of the new fire department on South 7th Street. Coshocton Fire Department, 325 South 7th Street.

6. ***First Presbyterian Sermon Preached West of the Alleghenies, September 21, 1766***—Not to be outdone by general historians, the Presbyterian church commissioned a mural by Mr. and Mrs. William Lucas, which shows two Presbyterian ministers, Charles Beatty and George Duffield and an Indian interpreter, Joseph Peepy, meeting with a group of Delaware Indians along the Tuscarawas River. 142 North Fourth at Chestnut Street; 740/622-0486. In the church parlor; enter through door at parking lot.

MONTICELLO III—While "Mad" Marshall Jacobs, Coshocton's flagpole climber, steeplejack, inventor, problem solver and free spirit, could keep his feet firmly planted periodically, his mind and hands could not lie idle. It was he who hand-built the Monticello II, a perfect replica of the first canal boat to dock in Roscoe Village in 1830. It took Marshall two-and-a-half years and 1,648 hours to build his boat. He began with a borrowed blueprint and a dollar's worth of lumber. When it was finished someone else became captain but Marshall would ride along and tease the passengers; a more authentic nineteenth-century man could not have been conjured up. He claimed the Monticello would last seven years. It lasted nineteen, plus almost fifteen after that on land as a popular picnic shelter. The county's Lake Park hopes that Monticello III, launched in 1990, will last even longer. Monticello III is a stainless-steel-hulled, 100-passenger boat that came from Indiana via Kentucky and West Virginia, up I-77 and west onto U.S. 36 through Newcomerstown, at times along the original canal bed. It's a handsome boat, plying along the restored canal to Mudport Basin and back, with draft horses doing the pulling.

Lake Park, 740/622-7528. Take U.S. 36 east of Coshocton 1.5 miles to State Route 83 North. Turn left. Go 1/4 mile to parking lot and sign. Memorial Day-Labor Day. Boat leaves every hour on the hour, with three trips Tue-Thur 1-3 and five Fri-Sun 1-5. Adults $7, 5-12 $4, under 5 free.

ASIDE Marshall Jacobs climbed his first pole—telephone—while being chased by his sister. He had just broken her watch. It was a minor foreshadowing of what was to come. A grammar-school drop-out, he lived life by The Marshall Plan—do whatever you feel like doing, but don't hurt anyone. Within the confines of that limitation, Marshall handbuilt the Monticello II canal boat that carried tourists for 19 years; he got married atop a 176-foot flagpole (*Life* Magazine carried the story); he scaled local courthouses to raise money for the handicapped; he lived and slept wherever he pleased, becoming particularly fond of two old railroad cars; and he spent 260 hours on a 12-inch square piece of plywood perched 140 feet above Zanesville during a blizzard in 1955. When his electric blanket failed at minus 15 degrees, he came down. A publicity fanatic with a big heart, he was known locally as the world's champion flagpole sitter. Two weeks before he died, a friend pulled up below his fifth-story apartment where he was convalescing and beeped. Marshall just climbed out the window, hung from one balcony to the next until he reached the ground. The optimism and fingers were strong to the end.

THE JOHNSON-HUMRICKHOUSE MUSEUM—Wealthy bachelor brothers David and John Johnson spent their time collecting. On their excursions to the Orient they gathered trunks filled with jade, cinnabar and oxblood porcelain. They lugged back Samurai swords and suits of armor. Between travels, they concentrated on tools of the Ohio moundbuilders. They were partial to Indian baskets and collected hundreds of examples. But none of their acquisitions aroused such interest as the mysterious "holy stones"—stones with Hebrew inscriptions discovered in Newark in the nineteenth century. Some people said they were relics of a lost Israeli tribe; among those who claimed they were fakes, one of the latest is the Ohio Historical Society's Brad Lepper. Perhaps the holy stones could be called the holy scams.

300 Whitewoman Street; 740/622-8710; www.jhmuseum.org May-Oct, noon-5, seven days. Nov-Apr, Tue-Sun, 1-4:30. Adults $3, 5-16 $2.

Galley in the Alley

GALLEY IN THE ALLEY—Lewis "Pooch" Blackson is one of the unifying forces of Coshocton. He knew the commercial artists whose names were linked with the town—one was his brother Ben. He helped curate a 2006 show at Johnson-Humrickhouse on art by brothers Benton and Matt Clark. And he used to know the legendary Marshall Jacobs—for over a decade Pooch had breakfast every day with Marshall and he can describe in robust detail exactly how Marshall ate his meal. Since he has a good collection of the work of Coshocton artists, and others, including many lithographs, Pooch has opened a gallery in a garage behind his nineteenth-century house. He also has a phonograph there, and some old records, and samples of his own recent drawings, and he can provide all the talk you'd like.
617 Chestnut Street; 740/622-6578. By appointment. Free.

BEST VIEW—Halfway down Whitewoman Street, the main street of Roscoe Village, is a street that turns *up* and is properly called Hill Street. It's a hard climb by foot and a low-gear drive by car, but the reward comes .2 miles up when you turn around to face the most picturesque view of Coshocton across the rivers. The most outstanding landmark will be the lovely cap of the Victorian Coshocton County courthouse.

LIBERTY POTTERY—"We," says Becky Lowe, potter and owner of Liberty Pottery, "are one of the last handthrown potteries in Ohio." With that, she throws what is really clay but looks like a two-pound chunk of chocolate on a potter's wheel and within 80 seconds she has shaped it into a bowl and put it up on a shelf with other bowls that are similar but not exactly alike, which is the point of handthrown pottery. After firing, the brown turns black, just one of the many colors produced here. Lowe has been squeezing, pushing and coaxing clay in Coshocton for 30 years. She works in the back of what was originally Roscoe Village's hotel, where the likes of bowls, mugs and plates are shaped, painted and fired. The shop is across the street.
403 Whitewoman Street; 740/622-6767; www.libertypottery.com/ Mon-Sat 7-5:30, Sun, 10-5. Retail shop: 416 North Whitewoman Street, 740/622-4601. Mon-Sat 10-6, Sun 10-5.

WILDWOOD MUSIC—"We're like a shop that sells Rembrandts and Picassos," explains Marty Rodabaugh of Wildwood Music. But what her store carries is not paintings but top-of-the-line high-end guitars, mandolins, banjos and dulcimers—she claims that Wildwood is one of the few stores in the country with a selection of dulcimers. But the real reason this shop, located in an 1840 house near the Roscoe Village Visitor Center, is doing well is that, Rodabaugh says, "We're the lowest prices in the world." Customers come from all over, making on average an eight-hour drive to get here; most are amateurs who love to play. Most but not all. Johnny Cash was here, and Jimmy Buffett. Visitors can lay eyes, at least, on hundreds of instruments, including some worth thousands of dollars.

672 North Whitewoman Street; 740/622-4224; www.wildwoodmusic.com Wed-Fri 12-6; Sat 12-5.

POMERENE CENTER FOR THE ARTS—In a Greek Revival house lovely enough to qualify as the jewel of Coshocton, the Pomerene Center for the Arts offers eight to nine exhibits a year featuring local and regional visual arts. Called the Johnson-Humrickhouse House, the home really was owned by the Johnson Brothers, who developed the Roscoe Village museum across the river, though they lived on the west coast. When they died in the 1930s, leaving the house empty and neglected, their executor, Warner Pomerene, renovated the building, and he and his wife Lara lived in it for almost 50 years. In the early 1980s they left the house to the community, and in 1985 it opened as the Pomerene Center. It has four galleries, and director Anne Cornell says the house's rooms are so handsome that they inspire artists.

317 Mulberry Street; 740/622-0326; www.pomerenearts.org Tue-Fri 1-5; weekends by appointment; free.

MILLER PHARMACY SODA FOUNTAIN—Miller Pharmacy is a drugstore with a genuine soda fountain, dating from the last remodeling in 1956. It's one of only a handful left in the state. So says Elise Miller, the pharmacist, who followed in her father's professional footsteps and promised to come back to Coshocton if he wouldn't take out the soda fountain. She's since founded another business, located next door and providing home IV services all over Ohio. One person working in the original drugstore is Lynn Addy, who makes the floats, malts and shakes; extra thick costs an extra quarter. Addy admits that she represents a new generation: she'd never heard of sodas before she started working here.

234 Main Street; 740/622-1806. A malt is $3.

COSHOCTON ANTIQUE MALL—Twenty-five dealers show off their stuff in what was once the Montgomery Ward store on Main Street. There's some furniture, lots of dolls, framed mirrors, vintage ladies hats, lamps, and so on, spread out across the main floor and downstairs in the lower level. Three dealers handle Coshocton memorabilia; Erma Miller's specialty is advertising in historic Coshocton County yearbooks; the ads tell about long-gone local manufacturers.

315 Main Street; 740/622-7792. Mon-Sat 10:30-5.

ASIDE Colonel Pren Metham became a Coshocton hero—almost. On April 14, 1865, he attended the same play as President Lincoln, the First Lady and John Wilkes Booth. After the President was shot, it was Metham who reacted the quickest, avoided the crowds and ran for a side door to catch the assassin outside. Unfortunately the door he chose led to the ladies' dressing room, leaving Metham only a brief mention in local history while Dr. Samuel Mudd, who treated Mr. Booth's broken leg without knowing who he was, went on to become an idiom—"His name is mud."

HELMICK COVERED BRIDGE—Helmick Covered Bridge

is a little out of the way but the drive is worth it for the scenery: State Route 60 winds its way north in a canyon of tall leafy trees. In 1863 bridge builder John Shrake of Newark erected this 168-foot-long multiple kingpost bridge, which proved sound enough to carry traffic over Kilbuck Creek for 118 years. It had to be closed in 1981 and then slipped into a decade of neglect. But covered bridges work their way into people's affections, and, loath to lose this one entirely, local residents raised $250,000 for its restoration, which reused some of the original, handhewn timbers on the north end and was finished in 1996. *County Road 343, 1.4 miles east of State Route 60 at Blissfield.*

TEMPERANCE TAVERN MUSEUM/
NEWCOMERSTOWN—Fifteen miles east of Coshocton off U.S.

36 is the consummate small-town museum, the Temperance Tavern Museum, a hands-on personal repository of the townspeople's past, perpetuated with their time, money and artifacts. For this, thank the founder, the late Dorothea Marshall, and her worthy successor, today's Barbara Scott, who claims that when this building was a tavern in 1841, *temperance* did not mean abstinence from alcohol. At least not for this saloon. The Ohio-Erie Canal ran by the front door, and travelers were taken down the stone steps to the kitchen. Collections include a dress worn to Warren G. Harding's inaugural and an original trombone used in the Newcomerstown Hyperion Band. It doesn't hurt that legendary Boston Red Sox pitcher Cy Young and Ohio State coach Woody Hayes were both from Newcomerstown. Cy Young, who toted up his 511 victories in the 1890-1911 era, retired to his farm nearby, where he died in 1955 at 88. The museum has the largest collection of his memorabilia, including the pair of shoes he had on when he died and the wood he chopped the last week he was alive. The Woody Hayes exhibit includes his bronzed baby shoes and pictures of Hayes as a high school athlete. After watching her work on this museum, Scott's husband Vane founded one himself: the USS Radford National Naval Museum, right across the street, in honor of the ship he served on during World War II. Officials from Washington have come and told him that his was the finest naval museum they'd ever been in. *221 West Canal Street; 740/498-7735 or 740/498-8803 or 740/498-8792. Memorial Day-Labor Day Tue-Sat 10-3, Sun 1-4. Free; contributions appreciated.*

OLD STONE FORT/ORANGE—When Isaac Evans arrived in

what is now Oxford Township in 1800, the old stone fort was already an antique. History says at least one French fort was located northeast of the Ohio River, and the National Society of Colonial Dames believes it was here. If so, this small stone shanty, sitting off the curve of a country road and restored in 1952 by the local historical society, is the oldest building still standing in Ohio. Supposedly, the French explorer d'Iberville built it between 1679 and 1689 while following the nearby Tuscarawas River. He placed it far enough from the river to avoid flooding. He was more foresighted than Evans, whose house was soon washed over by flood waters. When he rebuilt his home, he put it near the fort.

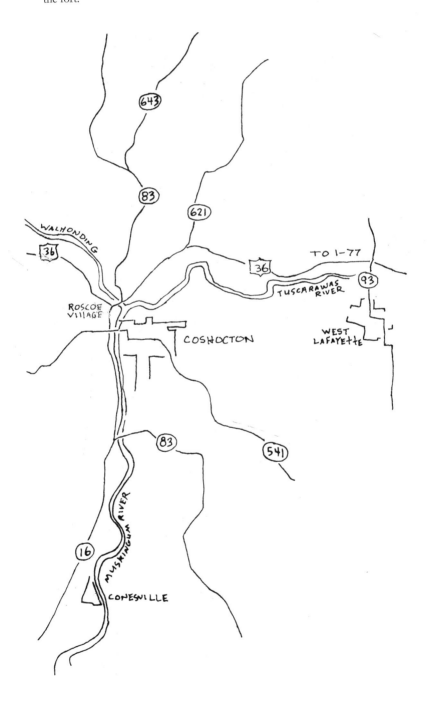

Victorian House

Amish Country

Holmes County and its bordering territories are so attractive that chances are, had the Amish not chosen the area to replace their European homeland, others would have. Actually, others did. The Amish were not the initial settlers—families by the name of Grant and Butler arrived first. But by 1809 an Amish man named Jonas Stutzman had settled in Holmes County. He was the first of thousands. Today, Holmes County, with adjoining areas of Wayne, Tuscarawas, Knox and Coshocton counties, has an Amish-Mennonite population of 35,000, enough to qualify as the world's largest concentration. A corollary is, that there are more horses per capita here than anywhere else in the world.

The further we get from the past, the more important the Amish become. The Amish life is our Ohio past in continuum. Old Order Amish, living largely without electricity or telephones, with schools only through eighth grade, thrive on hard work and strong faith, much as our Ohio ancestors did. And they chose a most beautiful part of Ohio in which to do it. Holmes is the only county whose state highways are *all* state scenic byways (a fact perhaps too remarkable, but not really misleading.) But it's mostly the Amish, their crafts and their cooking that have made the county a major tourist destination. That gives residents two options, either get out of the way or find some profit in it. So, some Old Order Amish keep to the back roads and come to town either early or late to avoid being run down in their buggies, which on occasion has occurred. And of course some find profit in it.

Holmes County countrysides undulate in all directions. Hills and valleys are covered with lush meadows, pastures and woods unbroken, with enough clothesline in sight that, if joined together it could reach from one Ohio border to another. Buggy and draft horses dot the landscape, wagons of hay are topped with men and boys in straw hats, and bonneted women shuck corn in the yards. It's a visual medley allowing passersby to glimpse their imagined pasts with twenty-first-century impunity.

Even so, this isn't historic Williamsburg. It takes visitors a while to shed a certain voyeuristic discomfort. But with great care, a trip through the Amish settlements and countryside can be mutually beneficial, a cultural exchange in our own backyard. So go to Amish Country. For if Ohio today is the tomorrow we talked of yesterday, then Holmes County is the yesterday we talk of today.

The Inn at Honey Run

THE INN AT HONEY RUN/MILLERSBURG—This

is one of Ohio's premier inns—a luxurious retreat on 70 wooded acres in the heart of Amish Country, just 3.3 miles from Millersburg. Founded in 1982, the inn started with the main lodge, a country inn of contemporary wood and glass. A honeycomb of rooms built into the side of a hill came later, and later still several cottages and Monarch House for especially posh suites. A staff of 60 keeps things running like a cruise ship. The restaurant seats 75 and requires reservations for white-tablecloth fine dining amid wall fountains. The menu features regional cuisine, with local produce and meats. Dinners offer, for example, orange-glazed duck, walleye, pasta, filet and ribeye (entrees are $17-32), while lunches, with menu items including trout, sandwiches, and ham loaf, average $15. Marge Stock, the inn's doting founder, attentively minded its day-to-day operations for 20 years, and then sought out and persuaded the best innkeeper she knew, Phil Jenkins, to take over when it was time for her to retire. Formerly the owner of two award-winning B&Bs in Georgia, Jenkins arrived in 2003 and has put his own stamp on the Inn—for one thing, it has a liquor license now—which operates as smoothly as ever. Amenities range from gardens of trilliums and daffodils, to hiking trails, to an on-premises spa. And, from the hill where the view from the honeycombs is a sheep-covered valley, the sounds of buggy wheels and hoof beats gently muffle the final cost of the bill.

6920 County Road 203; 330/674-0011; www.innathoneyrun.com Rooms range from $114 on weekdays off-season to $335 for a cottage for four at peak season. Continental breakfast included.

FIELDS OF HOME/MOUNT HOPE—In the mid 1990s Ruth

and Mervin Yoder noticed that lots of visitors came to their area, but there was a dearth of places to stay. So they built and opened Fields of Home in 1995, behind their own house. It has five rooms, some with kitchenettes, all spacious and attractive with wood-paneled walls, private bathrooms (some with Jacuzzis), air conditioning and bucolic views of green hills, grazing horses, growing crops. In 2001 the 20 acres that were providing that view came on the market, and the Yoders foresaw that all of it might be turned into houses if they didn't buy it. The moral, says Ruth, is that if you want to call your B&B Fields of Home, you'd better own the fields. The two new and adjacent cottages help to finance the view. Breakfast is an elaborate continental left out from 7:30-9.

7278 County Road 201 (Millersburg post office); 330/674-7152; www. fieldsofhome.com Rooms are $75 weeknights, $85 weekends, $10 less in winter; cabins are $120-$130 weeknights, $135-$145 weekends.

FARMSTEAD LODGING/MOUNT HOPE—This is the only

genuine Amish farm lodging in this area as these pages are prepared—it must be a national rarity, because after we were there a family from California was scheduled to arrive. Farmstead Lodging has only one room, with a queen bed and an extra bed for children—this is one of the few B&Bs anywhere that welcomes children. Hosts are Kathy and Willis Miller—Willis, the farmer, also lets guests who are interested accompany him to bring in the cows for milking. Kathy is a hospitable woman. If they wish, guests may join the family for dinner ($14 a plate). One day, a family was stranded here when their car broke down. While the father was off seeing about the car, Kathy asked the mother if she and the children would like to escape the scorching heat by swimming. She popped them in the buggy and they all trotted off to a neighbor's pond. (A *lined* pond, Kathy stressed.) The room, which is not fancy, is in back of the house at grade level, has its own entrance, a kitchenette, a bathroom and gas lighting. A breakfast of pastries, coffee and juices is left in the kitchen the night before.

8457 County Road 77 (Fredericksburg post office); 330/674-0603; www. amishbusiness.com/FarmsteadInnBnB (Amish web sites are subcontracted with non-Amish.) Room is $95 a night, $85 second night; lower in winter. No smoking; cash and checks only.

COUNTRYSIDE CAMPER'S PARADISE/CHARM—

Finding Township Road 356 off State Route 557 is worth the hunt. In summer, 2007, it cost $16 per adult to stay in one of Millers' spotlessly clean, fully furnished log cabins. They sit high on a hill overlooking the Doughty Valley where the only sound is the clip-clop of horses and the honking of geese. Each of the four cabins sleeps six—kids under 6 stay free, under 12 have reduced rates. The cabins come with a wood stove, kerosene lamps, linens, a nearby pump, and an outhouse without spiders, wasps or odor. Mornings, guests walk the few steps up to Miller's Bakery for juice or coffee and just-made rolls and doughnuts— all included in the price. Camper's Paradise has a Millersburg address but is closer to Charm.

4280 Township Road 356, watch for sign along State Route 557; 330/893-3002. No pets or alcohol. Cash or checks only.

HOTEL MILLERSBURG/MILLERSBURG—Here's an agreeable place to stay if you're bed-and-breakfast shy but hate the idea of a chain motel. Built in 1847, it's Millersburg's oldest large building, remodeled in the 1980s and again in 2006 when an elevator was added. The lobby area still emits a mysterious hotel aura where strangers seem to wear the cloaks of secret spies, regardless of the fact that they're probably insurance salesmen from Parma. There are 27 rooms, all with baths, on the second and third floors. The restaurant, called the Tavern, is known for its mushroom chicken, $10.

35 West Jackson Street; 330/674-1457; www.hotelmillersburg.com Tavern hours Mon-Thur 11-9, Fri-Sat 11-10, Sun 11-3. Rooms $60-169, varying by room, season, and day of week. Dinner entrees, $9-22.

Blackfork Inn

THE BLACKFORK INN/LOUDONVILLE—The main house is a stately brick Victorian; the annex is just across the street. Both are impeccably furnished with family heirlooms, freshly cut flowers and an Ohio library. The innkeeper, as a magazine writer and hopeless romantic, can simultaneously pass along a good local tale, squeeze fresh orange juice, sigh over the wilting of a centerpiece and recommend a dozen good Amish locales. The main house has six guest rooms, each with private bath and terry cloth robes, while the annex has two suites. The innkeeper shops Amish country stores for Trail bologna, Amish cheese, Winesburg ham, Amish maple syrup, fresh eggs. If you happen to be in town at dinnertime, plan to eat at Broken Rocks, a downtown restaurant for which the innkeeper's enthusiasm overflows.

303 North Water Street; 419/994-3152; www.blackforkinn.com Pets and children by prior arrangement only. No smoking. Rooms, $75-110; suites $120-150.

ACCESS—This tour starts just west of Holmes County in Loudonville. Take State Routes 39 and 60 east to State Route 514 and turn left/north. At County Road 373 and turn left/north to pottery and clock shop. Afterward return to 39/60 and continue east to Millersburg, the county seat, where you might pick up a county map at the courthouse; to really see Amish Country you should have a map that includes country roads.

AMISH OAK FURNITURE COMPANY/

LOUDONVILLE—Chris Tuttle fetches his merchandise in trucks that wend through back roads, where Amish woodworkers handcraft furniture for this store where every piece is Amish-made. The Amish like to work at home where, by the time children are eight they become involved as gofers, and women do the sanding and finishing. Entrepreneurship for Tuttle is an anomaly. If a customer changes an order he makes a trip to the craftsman's house, because there is no phone. The Old Order won't allow members to put gravel on their drives, so when Tuttle's truck gets stuck a team of horses has to pull him out. The store occupies four old two-story buildings in downtown Loudonville, and they are full of expertly-made, reasonably-priced wooden furniture.

268 West Main Street; 419/994-3721, 800/686-8855; www.amish-oak.com
Open daily and Sat 10-5:30, until 8 on Tue and Thur; Sun noon-5.

HOLMES COUNTY POTTERY/BIG PRAIRIE—Elaine and

Cary Hulin came to Holmes County for the sawmills—not the prime cuts, but the off-cuts. Cary uses this hardwood detritus to fire Ohio's largest wood-burning kiln, which he made and uses three times a year. The kiln, which is tipped on a hillside, looks like an elongated igloo of heat resistant blocks. Almost 30 feet long, it's high enough to walk in and has doors at both ends, not only for loading and unloading but also for creating a draft when firing. Inside it has what look like deep stairs going up into the kiln—they become shelves for ware. Before firing Cary hand turns every piece, using one of his three potter's wheels; it takes him a few months to make enough to fill the kiln. Then it takes ten days to load the kiln, starting in the middle; each load takes two-and-a-half tons of greenware—perhaps 2000 pieces, including bowls, mugs, pitchers, covered jars, lamp bases, plates, planters, steins, vases. Firing takes three days and nights, starting easily, stoking every three to four hours to preheat to 250-300 degrees, to dry both kiln and contents. The last 36 hours, with eight people (including a couple Amish neighbors) taking turns stoking as often as every five minutes, bring temperatures to 2200-2400 degrees, high enough to melt the glaze and even some wood ash. Afterward, while the eight people presumably recover, the kiln cools for four days, and takes two days to unload. Then after the next weekend half the whole batch is gone—sold to customers who drive in, most from cities in the region, and many of whom received post cards advising that a kiln opening was scheduled. The cards are necessary because the three firings a year come at unpredictable times, though the general goal is spring, summer and fall. Merchandise stocks are largest right after a firing. The pieces are beautiful. But Cary works 70-hour weeks (Elaine also works full-time on pottery business), which is one reason wood-fired kilns aren't all that common. When Cary started college at Bradley University in Illinois, he thought he'd be a geologist. Then as a freshman he took a pottery course, and he's never looked back.

8500 County Road 373, accessible from State Route 514 north of Nashville;
330/496-2406. Mon-Sat 9-5.

KEIM VINTAGE WATCHES/BIG PRAIRIE—One of the
people who helps Cary Hulin with firings at Holmes County Pottery, is
neighbor Leander A. Keim, who in 2004 opened a shop for sales and
service of vintage wrist watches and pocket watches, and for servicing
of wall and mantle clocks. One of the most interesting features of this
shop is Leander Keim himself, an Old Order Amishman, who says he
focuses on watch repair because he doesn't get a lot of traffic—his
shop is at the end of a lane through the woods off a county road.
He did apprentice in clocks, and is self-taught in watches, though he's
attended seminars held by the Watchmakers Institute, where he picked
up information on spare parts and techniques. Old Order Amish don't
normally even wear wrist watches, but they do like pocket watches,
though Keim says, "It seems silly to carry a watch when I've all these
clocks," and he waves his hand at all the wall clocks, including one
atomic clock. His favorite of all is one he doesn't have in the shop, the
eighteenth-century tall case, taller than modern grandfather clocks, and
made with unique handmade movements.
*8545 County Road 373; no phone. (Mailing address, Big Prairie, OH 44611.)
Mon-Wed and Fri 9-5, Sat 9-1, closed Sunday and Thursday.*

VICTORIAN HOUSE/HOLMES COUNTY
HISTORICAL SOCIETY/MILLERSBURG—Admirers of
Victorian architecture should stop four blocks north of Millersburg
at the Victorian House. The 28-room house was built in 1902 by
Cleveland industrialist L.H. Brightman, then purchased in 1907 as a
sanitarium. Two years later it was sold to the Lee family, whose last
surviving relative lived alone for many years, using only two rooms.
When the Historical Society bought the house at auction in 1971 the
interior was so blackened by coal soot that they didn't know the floors
were parquet until they were scrubbed six times. Actually, the oily
residue in the soot and lack of use preserved much of the woodwork
and handpainted ceilings, a technique the ladies who scrubbed the floors
say they don't recommend. Today the house is filled with some of Mr.
Brightman's antiques as well as dozens of heirlooms from the area. As
the house marked its centennial in 2002, the Historical Society hired a
professional director, Mark Boley, to assure that the house is well tended
and attended.
*484 Wooster Road/State Route 83; 330/674-0022; www.victorianhouse.org
Daily Tue-Sun 1-4; more hours during Nov-Dec holidays; closed Mon. Adults $7,
seniors $6, 12-18 $3, under 12 free.*

GUGGISBERG CHEESE/NORTH OF CHARM—It's a
short drive east of Millersburg on State Route 39 to State Route 557, the
road to Charm. Turn right. Many years ago, Ohio's Amish population
longed for good cheese. So they sent word to Switzerland where Alfred
Guggisberg had achieved renown as a cheesemaker. He brought his
high standards and secret recipes to this lush valley, and set up a place
that looks like a Swiss chalet. By 1969 he developed the four-pound
Baby Swiss cheese wheels that became well known. Fortunately too, he
trained an apprentice, Raymond Yoder, cheesemaker since Guggisberg's
demise. Yoder oversees production of thousands of Baby Swiss wheels
every day—along with other cheeses. There are some 40 varieties for

sale with cheese flavors varying according to the cows' last meals.
*5060 State Route 557, between State Route 39 and Charm; 330/893-2500;
www.babyswiss.com Summer: Mon-Sat 8-6, winter: 11-4.*

GRANDMA'S HOMESTEAD RESTAURANT/CHARM—

All points in town are measured by how far they are from Grandma's
Homestead. Daily specials include roast beef with real mashed potatoes,
meat loaf, fish, and chicken fried in iron skillets. There are family-style
dinners with reduced rates according to age, and children under three
eat for free. A national review made the restaurant famous for peanut
butter pie, but everything here is delicious. Try the homemade ice
cream, made from a secret recipe.
*4450 State Route 557 at the corner of County Road 70; 330/893-2717; www.
grandmashomestead.com Dinners and specials about $8-$11. Summer: 6:30-7:30;
winter: 6:30-7.*

HERSHBERGER ANTIQUE MALL/NEAR
FARMERSTOWN—In the late 1980s, recalls Roman Hershberger,
he started a little antiques business on his father's farm. Then his own
sons grew up, and when Roman wanted to give up farming, one son was
interested in taking over the farm, while the other, Ben, was interested
in antiques. Ben now runs this business, which since 1992 has been an
antique mall, with plenty of floorspace to accommodate the hundreds
of pieces they found in homes. "Large estates are our specialties," says
Roman. There are a few dealers in the two main buildings they occupy
now, but mostly it's pieces the Hershbergers own, however briefly.
*3245 State Route 557 southeast of Charm; one mile west of Farmerstown (mailing
address is Baltic, Ohio); 330/893-2064; 800/893-3702, ext. 0300). Mon, Tue,
Thur, Sat 8-5, Wed, Fri 8-8; closed Sunday.*

ASIDE It is somewhat misleading to speak of the Amish as a single
people. They come from a common ethnic root—Swiss Anabaptists—
but they are really a galaxy of unaffiliated churches that share a
common theology, differing on how that doctrine should be applied
to this world. Some of the churches have formal names. Other orders
are known only by the names of founding bishops, such as the
Swartzentrubers, who are the most "conservative" of the Old Order
Amish in Ohio, or the Beachys, who are among the more "liberal" of
the New Order Amish. Some New Order congregations have church
buildings or allow members to own automobiles or encyclopedias.
At some point these liberal Amish are more properly described as
Mennonites, the larger Anabaptist tradition of which the Amish are
a sect. Yet even the most liberal Amish or Mennonites would be
considered extremely conservative Protestants in the larger American
society.—John Fleischman

NATURE'S FOOD MARKET/BERLIN—During tourist
season, the main street of Berlin becomes the midway of Amish
Country, so it is a little surprising to find a nice market selling health
products and food in its midst. Nature's Food is the repository for
resale of most area things homemade for eating. Honey, Amish maple
syrup (in pints, quarts and gallons), freshly baked breads, cheeses and
naturally grown local produce are always in stock.
*4860 East Main Street (post office is Millersburg); 330/893-2006; www.
naturesfoodmarket.com Mon-Sat 8-7.*

ACCESS—Just east of Berlin, County Road 77 will take you a short distance north from State Route 39 to the Amish & Mennonite Heritage Center, an interpretive center for visitors. The main feature is the Behalt, a series of paintings presented as a circular mural on the history of the Anabaptist movement. The center also has a bookstore with many offerings on Amish and Mennonite history and culture.
5798 County Road 77; 330/893-3192; www.behalt.com Mon-Sat 9-5, June-Oct Fri-Sat 9-8. 2007 admission charges: adults, $7, 6-12, $3.50.

THE OHIO AMISH LIBRARY/BERLIN—The Ohio Amish Library began as a community project in the mid-1980s—an effort by the eight board members to rescue books on the Anabaptist movement that antique dealers wouldn't handle, and that otherwise might be lost. By now it has 10,000 books, magazines and periodicals. In this specialized area that might make it the world's fifth or sixth largest such collection—the largest is in Amsterdam, Holland, and the second largest is at Goshen College in Indiana. But such comparisons are not the main interest of board member Paul Kline of Kline Lumber and Hardware, which now has a separate building to house the books. Some are bound in leather, some covers are made of wood with rope in the binding. The earliest book in the library is dated 1536. Kline is the willing librarian and holder of the keys, and quite apart from the library he is a knowledgeable source of Amish history. He admits, though, that a 1977 dissertation about the Amish by a Quaker at the University of Chicago was enlightening even to him. It's part of this collection. Researchers, interested individuals and donations are welcome.
4292 State Route 39, east of Berlin (Millersburg post office); 330/893-4011. Open weekdays 7-5, Sat 7:30-11:30.

ACCESS—While in Amish country, buy a one-dollar copy of *The Budget*, the weekly newspaper that's been serving the local and international Amish and Mennonite communities since 1890. *The Budget* is written by country correspondents called scribes, whose news accounts provide a fascinating glimpse into what's important; most stories begin with the weather and go on to church news, gardening, accidents, farming. The newspaper's headquartered in Sugarcreek, is owned by a Jewish family and edited by a Mennonite named Fannie Erb-Miller, who started working here in 1985. Her predecessor was George Smith, a Lutheran, who worked at *The Budget* for over 80 years before he died in 2000.

GERMAN CULTURE MUSEUM/WALNUT CREEK—This museum in downtown Walnut Creek is where to learn who the Amish *really* are and why some speak the local German dialect but don't have beards. They are all related by their common language, but their religions set them apart. There are seven rooms filled with furniture, quilts, textiles, photographs, folk art and documents on the Amish, Amish Mennonite, Mennonite, Brethren, Moravian, Lutheran and Reformed Church members in this area in the 1800s. When the museum is open, a man portraying Jonas Stutzman, the first Amish settler in the area, wanders around town drumming up business.
4876 Old Pump Street, though expecting to move in 2008 to the basement of the new community center across the street; 330/893-2510. Free, donations welcome. June-Oct Thur-Sat 12:30-4; museum hopes to operate year-round after move.

YODER'S AMISH HOME/WALNUT CREEK—Follow State

Route 515 north out of Walnut Creek and watch for signs to the most non-commercial, visitable Amish farm in the area. No one lives here now but it looks lived in, especially the kitchen of the newer home—where a lady in bonnet and plain dress punches a balloon of bread dough for loaves that are made to sell. It's a 116-acre working farm with some unusual accoutrements like gas floor lamps. The newer house has a bathroom, running water, and colorful quilts. The barn is full of affectionate animals, the yard turkeys can be petted and the half-mile buggy ride catches a view of the family hilltop cemetery.
6050 State Route 515, between Walnut Creek and Trail; 330/893-2541; www.yodersamishhome.com April-Oct Mon-Sat 10-5. Two houses, barn, school, and buggy ride: $10, 2-12 $6; homes and barn only, $5, 2-12 $3; buggy $3.50, 2-12 $3; school $3, 2-12 $2.50.

TROYER'S GENUINE TRAIL BOLOGNA/TRAIL—The

most agreeable characteristic of a tour through Holmes County is that one can literally eat one's way through the countryside—thus the bologna in Trail is halfway between the black raspberry pie in Walnut Creek and the finest Winesburg ham. The country store that sells the bologna sits in front of the factory that doesn't allow tours because it wants to guard its secret recipes and not be sued for someone slipping on wet floors. But the visit to the grocery is suitable enough because there is a counter with eight stools and you can order a custom-made Trail bologna sandwich, with or without the cheese of your choice, and a pop. This, for $3. Many customers come in for a sandwich and a take-home pack of 25 pounds. It's $2.79 a pound. Visitors will also like the atmosphere, which is still free.
6552 State Route 515; 330/893-2414. Mon-Fri 7-5, Sat 7-4; Jan-Mar 7-3:30.

WINESBURG MEATS/WINESBURG—The entire Ukrainian

settlement in Holmes County arrived when Walter and Katharina Pacula bought a home and settled in Winesburg in 1959. After a while they started a meat-processing business and attached it to the house. Now their son Marion runs it and the only thing that's changed is the vista from the front picture window: the trees across the street have grown so big. The Paculas specialize in cured, smoked meats with no preservatives and no water added. Their casing wieners are their number one item. By word of mouth, their hams and smoked turkey have become annual Christmas gifts shipped as far as Hawaii. And one year 30 hams went UPS to Alaska. The reviews down the pipeline were outstanding. While they don't make sandwiches they guarantee their meat for a day's trip in an ice chest.
2181 U.S. 62; 330/359-5092. Mon, Tue, Thur 8-5, Fri 8-6, Sat 8-3. Closed Wed and Sun.

MOUNT HOPE HARNESS AND SHOE AND LONE

STAR QUILT SHOP—From Winesburg pick up County Road

160, which just south of town intersects U.S. 62 and will take you east to Mount Hope; turn right at County Road 77 and you'll come to this shop, which in spite of its name sells fewer harnesses nowadays. It does have softballs and gloves, all kinds of work boots, athletic shoes for the whole family, hunting and fishing gear and men's straw hats, among other things. The quilts, made by local women, are in the back, and range in price from $695 to $1395. All the clerks are related to Ervin and Sara Yoder, who founded this shop in 1972. They're still around, too. At one time, Sara Yoder sold a dozen quilts to the governor's mansion; and while her daughters were around and able to help, she also sold quilts that were marketed through Land's End.

7700 County Road 77, off State Route 241 just south of Mount Hope; 330/674-3858 (leave word for call-back).

AUCTIONS—You might catch the cattle auction at Mount Hope on Wednesdays. There's a livestock sale going on somewhere in Amish country practically every day of the week except Sunday: on Mondays at Sugarcreek; Tuesdays at Farmerstown; Thursdays are the biggest sale days at the consignment auction at Kidron; and on Fridays horses are auctioned at Sugarcreek. One auction that's worth a special trip is the Mennonite Relief Sale held every year on the first Saturday in August in Kidron (330/682-4843; www.OhioMccReliefSale.org). Mennonite and Amish congregations participate, and the quilts offered for sale starting Saturday morning are among the finest made today. Collectors bid in four figures; non-collectors come for the food. The eating starts at 7 a.m. with pancakes and sausage drowning in maple syrup, which should hold you until the ladies begin frying apple dumplings and the men get the pig roast underway. By the way, one of the food items advertised as a specialty here is Laotian Egg Rolls.

MOUNT HOPE HARDWARE/LEHMAN BRANCH STORE/MOUNT HOPE—The Lehmans went into the hardware

business in Kidron in 1955 in order to serve the Amish with old-fashioned and non-electric products. To this day, it's the store (newly expanded) where you have to go if you want to live "off-the-grid." This branch store in Mount Hope, opened in 1969, originally was just like the main store, but in recent years it's changed its name to Mount Hope Hardware. Smaller than the Kidron store, this one carries more hardware but fewer housewares and non-electric appliances. But, for example, it does have electric ice-cream machines, as well as the old fashioned hand-crank ice-cream makers. Branch store:

One Lehman Way, Township 634 at State Route 241; 330/828-8828. Mon-Thur 7-5:30, Fri 7-8, Sat 7-5. Main store: 4779 Kidron Road, Kidron; 330/857-5441; www.lehmans.com Mon-Sat 8-5:30, Thur 8-8.

HOMESTEAD FURNITURE/MOUNT HOPE—Amish

furniture, always a significant business, has become even more important than it used to be. One of the relative newcomers is Homestead Furniture, which is doing a land-office business in quality and customized furniture. You can order, say, a Shaker table with the number of leaves you want, the chairs you want, and you can have it in oak, hickory, maple, cherry or quartersawn white oak. (With one leaf the table is $679 in oak, $848 in hickory/maple, $939 in cherry.) Of course, you can find hutches, buffets and chairs to match. Homestead was founded in 1989-90 by Sara Yoder, of Lone Star Quilt, and her daughter, Barbara Hershberger. They contracted with local builders and adapted a former chicken house behind the shoe and quilt shop. Though Barbara Hershberger is still involved in Homestead, Sara Yoder has withdrawn. She is still pleased that she was the one who named the store ("because it was on our homestead," she explains.) Today Homestead has left the chicken coop and graduated to a spacious new building north of Mount Hope. There Junior Yoder, son of Sara and himself a 12-year veteran of the business, explains that Homestead contracts with about a hundred local builders who are in two- to six-man shops, each specializing.

8233 State Route 241, just north of Mount Hope; 866/674-4902; www. homesteadfurnitureonline.com Mon-Sat 8:30-5.

AMISH CULTURE TOURS/BERLIN—Lavonne DeBois began

offering tours of Amish Country in April, 1993. For a while she'd been driving Amish to work and on trips and, she says, "I kept seeing the beautiful back roads. I thought there was more to Amish Country than coming to eat." She began bringing visitors to Amish homes, and to the shops of artisan candle and basket makers. Today meals in homes are increasingly popular. "People like having their own time with a family," DeBois says, speaking of custom tour possibilities. Stays in Amish homes offer an escape from telephones and television. Amish Culture Tours offers standard morning and afternoon tours, daily in season and lasting five to six hours. If eight people sign up, the afternoon tour ($67) includes dinner in an Amish home; morning tours, without the meal, are $49. Tours include artisans, a country store, back roads, tourist attractions. Two-hour tours are also available, starting at $25. DeBois also prearranges tours for people who will drive themselves, sending them vouchers and maps. Some such tours are inexpensive. Private meals in a home are $20.

5568 Rhine Road, Berlin (Millersburg post office); 330/893-3248; www. amishtoursofohio.com Full tour schedule mid-April through October; customized tours year-round.

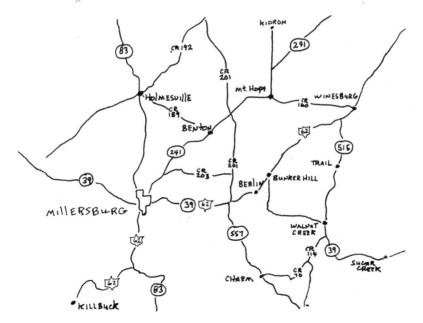

The Breakers

Sandusky

S andusky is a lake town that relies heavily on
patience, its economic prosperity having been
based largely on its ability to wait, first for fish, then
for thickening ice, and now for tourists. It is a pretty
town with an old seaside flavor that's been largely
unnoticed by the millions of visitors who throng
the causeway to Cedar Point. Perhaps this is just as
well, for the original mayor was a Mason who laid
out the streets to resemble a Masonic symbol. Today,
making stops at the resulting five-way and seven-way
intersections is an exercise in automotive cha-cha—
patience becomes not only a virtue but also a savings
on collision insurance.

Sandusky proper, a robust 27,844, was settled
originally by Connecticut Yankees whose homes had
been burned by British soldiers in the Revolutionary
War, entitling them to land here—hence the regional
name Firelands. Their attraction to the spot even
then known as Cedar Point, was for Christmas trees,
timber, and fishing good enough to become the
economic basis for survival. When the pound net
was introduced, local anglers were able to catch up to

15,000 fish a day, creating the need for ice, which E.E.
Upp began harvesting in 1852.

Then the only place on Lake Erie's southern shore
that could be relied upon to freeze, Sandusky once
harvested more ice than any other town this side
of the Hudson River; it supplied 90 percent of
Cleveland's ice. The more ice, the more fish; the more
fish, the more caviar. Around 1883, Sandusky caviar
was being shipped to Europe, given a Russian label,
shipped back to the U.S. and sold as an import for
higher prices. Sandusky saloons drank up the profits.

In one way or another, Sandusky has always tried to
please its visitors. Its pioneers, having left one coast
for another, closely reproduced the lives they left
behind. And perhaps by chance, or by the lay of the
land, Sandusky mimics life on the Atlantic shore. Like
Nantasket and its famous Paragon Park, or Atlantic
City and its Boardwalk, Sandusky has many pleasures
of a seacoast town. You'll come to think every Ohio
town should have a coastline.

WAGNER'S 1844 INN—Close to downtown, this is a pretty
Italianate house in Sandusky's historic district. Wagner's has three air-
conditioned rooms with private baths. Breakfasts are continental but
include some of Barb Wagner's home-made baked goods.
230 East Washington Street; 419/626-1726; www.lrbcg.com/wagnersinn Rooms
are $125 in season, $100 off-season.

FARRELL HOUSE LODGE AT SUNNYBROOK TROUT

CLUB—Farrell House Lodge is a B&B in a wonderful house—a
1941 manse with spacious rooms and fine detailing—in one of the
most beautiful settings of any lodge in Ohio. The extensive lawns have
mature trees and an extraordinary stream fed by underground springs,
so that it's running all year; it permits the trout club. Fishermen here
don't wade, but cast from the bank. Rooms are spacious, with king or
queen beds, private or shared baths and some with fireplaces; several,
in the one-time servants' quarters, are cheaper and smaller and share
a shower room and rest room. Continental breakfast is in the dining
room, which at one end has a rounded bay, where you'll see that the
window glass is curved too.
1104 Fremont Avenue, which is U.S. 6 west of town; 419/625-8353; www.
farrellhouselodge.com Rooms are $159, with special rates for family suites and
servants' rooms.

EAST SIDE CAFÉ—This café "opens when my mom comes
downstairs at seven. If she knows you, she'll let you in. If not, she'll
open at eight." When breakfast is over, Dan Sharp and his sister Candy
take over for Mom. The East Side has a faithful clientele of working
people, including a large portion of the Cedar Point summer work force
who show up on Tuesday night for tacos and eat hundreds of them.
The cafe makes 700-plus hamburgers a week and about 500 pounds of
French fries. Homemade soup is standard; five-pound containers are
available for take home, but bring your own wagon. Red oilcloth covers
the tables, cool breezes blow in the side windows, the tin ceiling has
ceiling fans, and there's room for sixty or so. By 10 a.m., the pool table's
been converted to a salad bar—the Plexiglas health shield lowers from
the ceiling. It was designed by a sailor from the local parasail service.
And the clock here is always seven minutes fast.
*1319 First Street; 419/627-1964. Mon-Fri 7-whenever. Sat 7-6. Closed Sun and
major holidays. Dinners $6-9.*

BERARDI'S FAMILY KITCHEN—This is a third-generation
Italian family restaurant. The surprise is, as Maria Berardi says, "We're
famous for our French fries." They also do homemade pies, soups and
salads, and Italian favorites like lasagna and spaghetti marinara.
*1019 West Perkins just west of State Route 4; 419/626-4592; www.
sanduskyberardis.com Mon-Sat 6 am-8 pm; Sun 7:30-1:30. Sandwiches $5.99-
$7.59; dinners with sides, $8.59-$13.99.*

ZINC BRASSERIE—Opened in May 2007, Zinc Brasserie became
an immediate hit with its French-inspired food—and everybody in
Sandusky had to start learning how to pronounce "brasserie", which
means a café. Owners are Andrea Crawford and Cesare Avallone—he's
the chef, and a Culinary Institute of America graduate—and their last
stop before Sandusky was New York. Their restaurant, which they
describe as "casual, upscale", is small, seating 34 plus 10 at the bar,
under 15-foot ceilings. Food is all from scratch, with seven dinner
entrees on the menu, plus specials; the bouillabaisse has been a hit.
*142 Columbus Avenue; 419/502-9462. Mon-Sat 11-10. Lunch entrees $7-$12;
dinner entrees $16-$24, with some specials up to $34.*

MARGARITAVILLE—In their flour-making heyday, the Heywood
and Venice Mills, five minutes west of downtown Sandusky, were state-
of-the-art operations connected by a one-mile canal. Flour was taken
by horse-drawn cars directly from the Venice mill to a warehouse on
the dock or loaded onto boats for Cleveland or Toledo. All hoisting
or lowering was done by waterpower, fed by a superior spring—The
Blue Hole—just four miles away. Now, a century and a half later, on a
Saturday night Margaritaville is offering 60-gallon barrels of nacho corn
chips. The restaurant has a wall of plate glass facing the historic Venice
Mill Pond and waterfall dropping 1,572 gallons a minute. The restaurant
seats 200, if you like crowds; a quieter time to go is on a hot weekday
afternoon when the sense of a cold and wet rush of water becomes a
fine accompaniment for a chicken, steak or shrimp fajita, chargrilled
with onions and peppers and served on a steaming hot platter.
212 Fremont Avenue (west of downtown U.S. 6 becomes Fremont); 419/627-

8903 or www.margaritavilleonline.com Mon-Sat 11-4. Happy Hour Mon-Fri 4-7. Dinner $7-18. Margaritaville, normally open all year, had a kitchen fire in July 2007. They planned to close for renovations in winter and reopen in May, 2008.

DALY'S PUB AND EATERY—More than half a century ago, there were two bars, side by side. They lived and breathed as Jack's Bar and the Echo Lounge. Then they died and in 1980 a man named Mike Lewis bought the buildings and turned them into Daly's, the Siamese twin, literally joined at the bars. This giant angled horseshoe bar now seats fifty. Seventy more can be seated at tables. It's the local watering hole, a favorite of the Happy Hour crowd and of boaters—two entrances, one on Columbus and one on Water, go right to the piers. Favorite dishes include clam chowder, Lake Erie perch dinners, seafood pasta, and lots of other good options—just no dessert. Music includes bands, djs, karaoke.
104 Columbus Avenue; 419/625-0748. Summer 11 am-2:30 am daily (food until 10); winter 3 pm-2:30 am (food until 9). Sandwiches $5-7, dinner $10-15.

GRIFFING FLYING SERVICE—In the summer, a shuttle makes regular runs back and forth to Cedar Point Amusement Park. Year-round there's scheduled air service to Kelley's Island, Put-in-Bay and Canada's Pelee Island, and there's also charter service to those places or anywhere else you please in the U.S. or Canada.
3115 Cleveland Road: 419/626-5161; www.griffingflyingservice.com Restaurant open seven days, 8-2. Closed Easter, Thanksgiving, Christmas.

FOLLETT HOUSE MUSEUM—It took three years to build the Follett house, even though the stone came from a quarry in Memorial Park right across the street. It's an 1830s Greek Revival that once had twenty rooms and now has only eleven; the last nine removed because the owners thought it would be easier to sell the house. Today owned by the public library, it's filled with the things the library has collected since 1902. Look for the glass cane collection in the basement, exquisite, one-of-a-kind examples of what a local glass blower from the Sandusky Glass Plant made as souvenirs from "end-of-the-day" leftover glass. In the attic is a fine Civil War collection with artifacts from Johnson's Island. Climb the long, angled stairway to the "Captain's Walk" outside, at the top of the house. The view of the island, once the Civil War prisoner-of-war camp, is juxtaposed with the other landmark, Cedar Point Amusement Park, a fortress of a different sort.
404 Wayne Street at East Adams; 419/627-9608; www.sandusky.lib.oh.us April and Oct-Dec, Sat noon-4; Sun 1-4. May and Sept Sat 10-1. June-Aug, Wed and Fri noon-4; Sat 10-1. Closed Jan-Mar. Free.

WENDY KROMER CONFECTIONS—Wendy Kromer returned to her home town, Sandusky, in 2003 and opened a shop that sells small pastries, cookies and, usually, chocolate caramel candy for the drop-in crowd; but the specialty is ordered-ahead wedding cakes. She makes beautiful, imaginative wedding cakes that she promises will taste good too. And she sells them all over—Tuscany, for instance. Kromer came back to Sandusky because the Victorian family house that she loved was available, and for her shop she could hire two cronies from her school days, one as manager, one as baker. Wendy Kromer did have an impressive career while away. The first ten years she was a fashion model in Paris. She moved back to New York in 1992 and, hoping to turn a life-long hobby into a second profession, enrolled in the Institute of Culinary Education. Later, one of her decorated confections—shaped like a girdle—won a prize. Martha Stewart noticed it, and ultimately Kromer became a contributing editor for *Martha Stewart Weddings* magazine, as she still is; her cakes, many with decorations reminiscent of fine fabrics, appear on four covers a year. When Kromer came home to Sandusky, she brought her new husband, Scott Schell, now an economic development specialist for the city. She was ready to settle down, she says, and she *likes* Sandusky. She says, "I'm sinking my teeth in." Just the right metaphor.

137 East Water Street; 419/609-0450; www.wendykromer.com Mon-Fri 8-6.

MERRY-GO-ROUND MUSEUM—What better for what was once the country's only round post office building than a carousel museum? That's what Sandusky has in its 1920s neoclassical post office: a working merry-go-round with a full-time in-house restorer working on it. This is a 1939 Herschell-Spillman carousel rescued through the efforts of Sanduskians whose summer childhood memories can now be multiplied through adulthood and winter. Thirty other carousel animal originals and two chariots are on display, as well as nineteenth-century wood carver Gustave Dentzel's original workshop, purchased from a Florida collector and shipped north tool by tool, his sign included. An elaborately carved M.C. Illions' sleigh, miniature carousels and miniature carousel rides and changing exhibits from Cedar Point all add up to about a half million dollars of inventory. Probably one of the finest collections ever put together by non-collectors, it's a credit to a group who lunged for the brass ring and got it.

301 Jackson (at the corner of Jackson and Washington); 419/626-6111; www. merrygoroundmuseum.org Open year-round, Jan-Feb, Sat 11-5, Sun noon-5; spring and fall, Wed-Sat 11-5, Sun noon-5; Memorial Day-Labor Day, Mon-Sat 10-5, Sun noon-5. Adults $5; children 4-14 $3; seniors $4. Admission includes one carousel ride.

ACCESS—One of the biggest bottlenecks of backed-up traffic occurs throughout the summer on U.S. 250 going into Sandusky as hordes of cars all try to reach the Cedar Point Causeway, a tiny thread of pavement leading to Cedar Point. Try this, instead. Take State Route 101 or State Route 4 into downtown to U.S. 6. Take 6 right/east through town to the causeway. But the prettiest route is from the east. Exit State Route 2 at Rye Beach Road; turn right and then, at the stop light, turn left onto U.S. 6. In a few miles you will come to the Cedar Point Chaussee—the back entrance to the park. This scenic waterfront drive is lined by beautiful beachfront homes.

CEDAR POINT—Founded in 1870, Cedar Point Amusement Park has waxed and waned through the years. In the 1920s it pumped life into the national amusement park trend and inhaled more visitors and exhaled more revenue than most other parks in the country. On one day in 1921, when there were fewer than 20,000 cars registered in the U.S., 3,000 were at Cedar Point. However, the Depression, Prohibition, and World War II gasoline restrictions reversed the tide. Concessions failed, rides fell to ruin until only twenty-three remained. But after World War II, Cedar Point became northern Ohio's most popular attraction. It has 17 roller coasters—more than anyone else—364 acres and, among its 69 rides, three restored carousels. Since it's impossible to encompass all in one day, you have several choices for overnight stays at the park, including the Hotel Breakers, which faces the Cedar Point beach. If you arrive by boat, there are 700-plus slips to choose from. If your time in the park is short, first go to Frontiertown and the Town Hall Museum—a charming microcosm of Cedar Point's past, filled with original games that still take a dime and still work. Second, ride the Magnum roller coaster. It falls 194 feet at 72 mph. One employee has ridden it 500 times, and it's not unusual to see Sandusky's civic leaders flying along on the Magnum. Over 3,000,000 people a year visit Cedar Point.
One Cedar Point Drive; 419/627-2350; www.cedarpoint.com Open May-Labor Day and September weekends from 10; closing varies. Admission for one person age 3-61 and at least four feet tall, $42.95; over 61 and under 48 inches, $12.95; specials available; parking, $10.

WATER PARKS—Kids love water parks because of all the action. Sandusky has three, with different themes. They typically offer resort-level hotel accommodations that come with passes for the water parks. Rides include slides, uphill water coasters, and 1000-gallon buckets that tip every few minutes, as well as options for toddlers and quieter, lazy-river-type rides for more sedate visitors, like moms who are spending the day with the kids while dad is fishing. Sandusky has led the state in water parks; visitors there may stay at one and visit a couple others. But hotels in other areas are adding water parks too, and they aren't cheap. Room rates in Sandusky start at about $140 and escalate quickly past, say, $350, and up to a stratospheric $1500 for a multi-bedroom suite with amenities; look for special packages. Room rates include water park tickets. Here are Sandusky's three biggest:

KALAHARI WATERPARK RESORT—Named for a major
desert in southern Africa, Kalahari Waterpark has an African theme. It
features size: with an indoor water park the size of two football fields,
Kalahari is Ohio's biggest; by December 2007 it expected to be the
nation's biggest. It also has the nation's first uphill accelerating water
roller coaster and a surfing ride.
*7000 Kalahari Drive; 419/433-7200 or 877/525-2427; www.kalahariresorts.
com Park is on U.S. 250 1.5 miles south of State Route 2. A midweek off-season
room that sleeps four and comes with four passes is $149; mid-week in season,
holidays or spring break is $229.*

GREAT WOLF LODGE—Great Wolf's theme is the north woods,
which means lots of logs and knotty pine in the décor and an outdoor
pool named for raccoons. The 42,000 square-foot indoor area has nine
slides, two whirlpools and a feature called a treehouse water fort where
you'll find the 1000-gallon tipping bucket. Great Wolf was Ohio's first
water park.
*4600 Milan Road; 419/609-6000 or 800/779-2327; www.greatwolf.com Park
is on U.S. 250 half a mile north of State Route 2. Room rates are $99-389.*

CASTAWAY BAY—Castaway Bay is Cedar Point's entry in the water
park stakes. The theme is Caribbean, which means slides named for
pineapple and mango.
*2001 Cleveland Road. U.S. 6; 419/627-2106; www.castawaybay.com A room
starts at $179 off season; a walk-in for water park only is $29.*

ASIDE During a seemingly uneventful summer on the shore of Cedar
Point, two young Notre Dame collegians by the names of Gus Dorias
and Knute Rockne learned to toss—and catch—the over-inflated
lump of leather that then passed for a football. The amusement
park was paying them as lifeguards, but in reality, was subsidizing a
revolutionary development in college athletics. The pair took their new
game east to play that Goliath of American football, Army, and with an
unforeseen passing game, pasted the troops, 35-13. That summer at
Cedar Point established both the forward pass, and Notre Dame as a
gridiron power. Said Rockne afterward, "We went out like crusaders;
we were representing the whole aspiring Midwest."

SHORELINE PARK—At the end of Warren Street, three long
finger slips protruding into Sandusky Bay used to be railroad docks.
Sandusky has cleaned them up, built footbridges between the slips,
planted grass and trees, supplied sturdy playground equipment and, in
the end, provided locals and visitors with the very best view to watch
the Wednesday night sailboat races.

SANDUSKY STATE THEATRE—William Seitz, a tailor, spent
$965,000 to give Sandusky what he thought it needed—a movie palace.
But he ran out of money before completion and a family named Schine
finished the job in 1928. So it was Schine that shone from the marquee
and not Seitz. In an area that clung largely to Victorian architecture
and limestone building materials, its Spanish Baroque stood apart
like a costumed foreigner. Outside were arches and turrets; inside,
an abundance of red, gold, teal and amber tiles. The auditorium was
fitted with "mood" lights that changed with the action. After 60 years

as Schine, the theater became Sandusky State and is today the county's largest arts not-for-profit. It shows movies (on Erie County's largest movie screen) and live entertainment.
107 Columbus Street; 877/626-1950; 419/626-1347; www.sanduskystate.com

MARITIME MUSEUM OF SANDUSKY—This museum has

exhibits on Great Lakes maritime history, from the Sandusky point of view. Artifacts, photos and displays tell about historic twentieth-century ferries that served the Lake Erie islands. Another exhibit tells the story of Sandusky's Lyman Boat Works, which made wooden-hulled boats from 1928 to 1972. Lyman was a leader in the 1920s in introducing outboards, but in the 1960s, as fiber glass was taking over, Lyman stayed in wood. The company peaked in the 1950s, when it produced thousands of boats every year and sold them all over America. The museum has a modern replica of a 13-foot Lyman rowboat.
125 Meigs Street across from Battery Park; 419/624-0274; www. sanduskymaritime.org Open all year Fri-Sat 10-4, Sun noon-4. Memorial Day-Labor Day open also Tue-Thur 10-4. Closed holidays. Adults $4, children under 12 and seniors $3, family $7.

BOATS TO THE ISLANDS—There are two options for island-

hopping from Sandusky during the summer season—May through September. The 365-passenger Goodtime I leaves the Jackson Street Pier and makes an excursion to Kelley's Island and Put-in-Bay seven days a week, rain or shine. It leaves at 9:30 for Kelley's Island where it docks for an hour and a half; then it goes to Put-in-Bay on South Bass Island where it docks for three-and-a-half hours, returning to Sandusky by 6:15.
419/625-9692; www.goodtimeboat.com Adults $25; children 4-12 $15, Seniors $23.
Jet Express also operates from the Jackson Street Pier and runs excursions on a regular schedule to both Kelleys Island and Put-in-Bay.
800/245-1538; www.jet-express.com

TOFT DAIRY—Chances are that any ice cream you eat in the

Sandusky area will have been made at Toft Dairy, founded in 1900 and still locally owned. Area residents swear by the ice cream's goodness, though butterfat content is 11 percent—compared to Haagen-Dazs' 20 percent—which some will see as an advantage. All the Dairy Queen–like stores in town sell Toft's soft-serve ice cream, but to get hand-dipped, go to the Dairy Store, part of the factory on Venice Road.
3717 Venice Road; 419/625-5490 or 800-521-4606; www.toftdairy.com Dairy store open daily 8-9, until 11 in summer. A small regular cone is $2.25; waffle cone, $3.10.

FIRELANDS WINERY—The largest winery in Ohio, Firelands

bottles 960,000 bottles a year, many under the gaze of tourists who watch the process from an elevated walkway overlooking the wine cellar, bottling line and champagne rooms. Originally the Mantey Vineyards, the company has been making wine here since 1880; the original wine cellar and the Mantey home are part of the operation. A video gives a good overview of north coast grape growing.
917 Bardshar Road; 419/625-5474 or 800/548-WINE; www.firelandswinery. com Open daily year round, Mon-Sat 9-5 (9-6 in summer), Sun 1-5. Tour any time; tastings, $1.

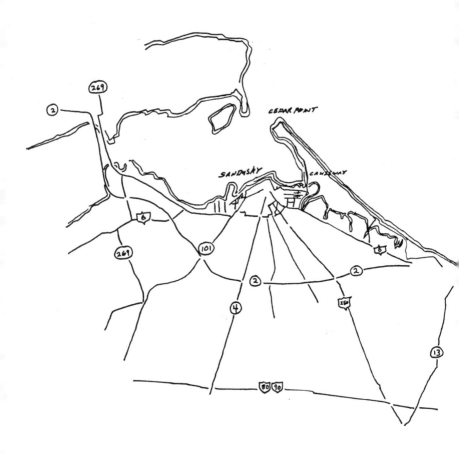

The Old Tavern

Lake Erie Eastern Shore

Summer at the Lake Erie shore was something Ohioans did as a matter of seasonal ritual. Rich people owned their cottages; the rest just rented, by the week or the month. There was a certain protocol involved in these summertime decisions, and your cottage neighbors came to be as familiar as your "back home" neighbors. But vacation styles changed in the Sixties. A polluted Lake Erie was less inviting. Faraway resorts beckoned. Youngsters whined for Disneyland. And so it came to pass that virtually an entire generation—or two—grew up without knowing the sand-on-the-floor, bugs-in-the-bathroom, wet-towels-on-the-furniture thrills of the summer cottage on Lake Erie.

It is for such culturally deprived folks that we propose an updated version of the shoreline vacation that reflects the changes of the last several decades. Much has been lost, but much more has been gained. Most of the cottage communities have disappeared, replaced by bed and breakfasts and the more substantial marina/condominium settlements that now grace the shoreline. Gone too is the sprawl of chemical plants that once crowded the bluffs above

Fairport Harbor. Fortunately the fragile wetlands at Mentor Marsh have been saved, as have the sand dunes next to Headlands Beach State Park. The state has improved many beaches, and some shore towns have embraced tourism eagerly and lured many folks back to the lake. Wineries are flourishing, and with their numbers draw visitors from around the state.

Although the shore area east of Cleveland has been slower to develop its tourist potential than the busy vacation meccas to the west, there is real beauty in the lesser known ports of Lake and Ashtabula counties. In places like Fairport, Grand River and the muted honky-tonk town of Geneva-on-the-Lake, families are re-establishing the Ohio tradition of summers at the shore. A charter-fishing captain who operates in these waters says that his greatest pleasure is showing folks how wonderful it can be when the winds are fresh, the waves are white-capped, and the blue-green lake extends as far as the eye can see. He likes to keep them out late so they can witness that magical moment when the setting sun slips beneath the water. "One sunset on Lake Erie and they are hooked for life," he says.

Indeed. There are some experiences that can happen only on the water.

FITZGERALD'S IRISH BED & BREAKFAST/

PAINESVILLE—Fitzgerald's is a relatively new addition to old downtown Painesville. Debra and Tom Fitzgerald, two Irish-Americans from the west side of Cleveland, bought their handsome 1937 Tudor Revival house in 1998. They have four rooms for guests, all air-conditioned, all with private bathrooms, all very nicely appointed; in fact, these bedrooms are some of the most thoughtfully detailed that you'll find anywhere, especially if you like Kleenex both in the bathroom and next to the bed. The livingroom, available for guests to use, has a huge fireplace and beamed ceiling. Weekdays breakfast is continental-style, but on weekends Tom makes a full hot breakfast—his recipe for scones has had national exposure, having appeared in *USA Today*. You'll probably hear some Irish music in the background downstairs, which is perhaps more Irish than the Irish.
47 Mentor Avenue; 440/639-0845; www.FitzgeraldsBnB.com Children over 13. No smoking except outside. Rates range from $95-150; open year-round.

*Rider's Inn
Bed 'n Breakfast*

RIDER'S INN/PAINESVILLE—Painesville's oldest hostelry—
and Lake County's first bed and breakfast—is a good place to park
your suitcase before heading for the attractions on Lake Erie; it has a
restaurant as well as rooms. The guest rooms, all with private baths, are
spacious and comfortable, and the charming downstairs parlors and
dining room have antique pieces that belonged to the Rider family, who
built the original log stagecoach stop here in 1812. Overnight guests can
have their breakfast served in bed. Most of the dining room's entrees
are based on recipes from the mid-1800s—the recipes turned up in the
attic. The bar is open, though local "dry" forces challenge it periodically;
for now the tradition of liquid hospitality continues. Early travelers
needed their whiskey to dull the pain of the bumpy roads; modern
tourists merely enjoy the peace of the cool, dark tavern.
*792 Mentor Avenue/U.S. 20; 440/354-8200; www.ridersinn.com Lunch Mon-
Sat 11:30-4; dinner Mon-Sat 4:30-9; Sun Stagecoach Breakfast 10-3; Sun supper
5-7. Dinner entrees $16-$22. B&B rooms $87-$105.*

HELLRIEGEL'S INN/PAINESVILLE—Except for the
addition of an outside patio, Hellriegel's, one of Painesville's best-loved
restaurants, has scarcely changed in 40 years—it has the slightly frayed
gentility of an old-fashioned country club. The kitchen's best efforts
continue to be the prime rib, the flaky little dinner rolls made sweet and
gooey with butter, brown sugar and cinnamon, and the banana cream
pie. If the place ever dared to change its ways, all of Lake County would
rise up in protest.
*1840 Mentor Avenue/U.S. 20; 440/354-9530; www.hellriegels.com/ Mon-Thur
11:30-10 and Fri-Sat until 11; Sun noon-9. Closed Christmas and New Year's
Days. Prime rib and seven-course dinner, $23.*

ASIDE Old Painesville reveals its Connecticut heritage in the
orientation of its Main Street (which begins as a long village green) and
in the post-Colonial homes that survive on U.S. 20, the first wilderness
road. One of the early settlers was Jonathan Goldsmith, a carpenter/
builder who fashioned extremely fine homes and made liberal use of
the *American Builder's Companion,* a how-to manual of fashionable
Eastern styles. As a result, Painesville's first families lived quite
elegantly, while the rest of Ohio was still building homes out of logs.
One of the best Goldsmith houses, the 1829 Mathews House, can be
seen on the campus of Lake Erie College on Mentor Avenue/U.S. 20.

ACCESS—Except for some covered bridges, wineries and the Victorian Perambulator Museum in Jefferson, the towns and attractions on this tour are all located north of I-90, which cuts across the northern third of both Lake and Ashtabula counties. To begin the tour, exit I-90 at U.S. 44 and follow it north toward Painesville, Fairport Harbor, Grand River and Mentor. After you have visited those towns, follow U.S. 20 east toward Geneva, and then take State Route 534 north to Geneva-on-the-Lake. From there State Route 531 skirts the Lake Erie shoreline for a truly scenic drive as you go east into Ashtabula and finally Conneaut.

LAKE COUNTY—Some of Ohio's most beautiful lakefront scenery lies in this county, where the Grand River empties into Lake Erie. Here, at Headlands Beach State Park, are two little-known treasures: Ohio's longest natural beach, and Ohio's only state-protected sand dunes. There is also a wonderfully secluded pocket beach, tucked into the protecting embrace of the Grand River break wall, and, as a bonus, two pretty little port towns: Fairport Harbor on the river's east bank, and Grand River on the west. Perhaps because of some industrial sites still in the area, the waterfront assets appear to excite primarily local interest. Residents seem to prefer it that way and are satisfied to keep their beautiful secrets to themselves.

It is difficult to imagine the village of Grand River as it was when Thomas Richmond owned it lock, stock and schoolhouse. It was called Richmond then, and the founder ran it like a lakeside utopia, where wholesome thoughts were encouraged and whiskey was banned (not too successfully when sailors were in port). Richmond was a high-minded fellow with a short fuse. When the canal builders double-crossed him, he tore down everything he had built and quit the place entirely.

The present village, which was renamed Grand River in the 1940s, never approached the size and sophistication of the earlier town. It remained a sleepy fishing village with a population that never rose much beyond 400. Grand River is locally famous for its two good fish restaurants:

Brennan's Fish House, 102 River Street; 440/354-9785; www.ncweb.com/biz/brennans Mar-Oct Mon—Thur 11-8:30, Fri-Sat 11-9:30, Sun 1-8; Nov-Feb Mon-Thur 11-8, Fri-Sat 11-9:30; and **Pickle Bill's**, 101 River Street; 800/352-6343 or 440/352-6343; www.picklebills. com/ Tue-Sat 4-9, Sun 1-8; longer hours and lunch June-Aug. Both run long lines on sunny weekends; Pickle Bill's has outdoor dining. Pickle Bill's faces the river, and Brennan's is across the street. Most of the rest of the river front is controlled by Mary Ann Rutherford, a widow who, as owner of a marina and boat docks, reigns as Grand River's entrepreneurial grande dame. Now in her mid-eighties, she's slowed down a little and no longer owns and runs the five river cruise boats she used to have.

For a long time, Fairport Harbor has been a town of tourist potential. For most of the twentieth century, the village prospered, with plentiful jobs at the Diamond Alkali chemical plants. Then Diamond pulled out in the 1970s, leaving Fairport stunned. Many of the stores and restaurants on High Street are still closed, but the very pretty beach, which lies at the foot of the High Street hill, remains Fairport's ace in the hole; it's one of Ohio's three most popular beaches. It's kept immaculate by a zealous parks department.

With its grid of wide brick streets and well-kept houses, Fairport Harbor is a pleasant town for walking. It wakes up in July for a five-day Mardi Gras celebration that always includes the Fourth. Every year it draws 60,000 or more for Lake County's biggest parade and beach party. You'll find lots of food, including candied apples, corn dogs and sausage sandwiches on the lakefront midway.

The future may be arriving in Fairport Harbor, with a brownfield cleanup where chemical plants used to be, east of town along both sides of State Route 535. Work began in 2002-2003 on an 1100-acre site, which includes over a mile of lakefront on one side and two miles along the Grand River on the other. At least in the planning stages, the Cleveland developers included everything they could think of. That meant a golf course, sports facilities for developing players, a hotel, over 2000 residential units and vacation condos, a trout club, and a 100-acre vineyard with winery and cooking classes. The golf course and first residential community were expected for spring 2009.

FAIRPORT MARINE MUSEUM/FAIRPORT HARBOR—

When mechanization threatened Fairport Harbor's handsome stone lighthouse in 1945, the people saved it and made it into a museum, the first lighthouse museum in the United States. The artifacts they saved—navigation instruments, marine charts, photographs, ship carpenters' tools—are on exhibit in the 1871 keeper's house and form an enduring expression of a lost way of life on the lakes. For a view beyond the breakwater, you can climb the circular steps to the top of the lighthouse, where on a clear day you can see ten miles out. *129 Second Street; 440/354-4825; www.fairportlighthouse.com/ Open Sat before Memorial Day-second weekend in Sept Wed, Sat, Sun and legal holidays 1-6. Adults $3, seniors $2, 6-12 $1.*

ASIDE Ohio's nursery industry was born in the 1850s on Fairport-Nursery Road, where Storrs & Harrison had 300,000 plants growing on 1200 acres of Lake County's superior sandy loam. From this single root sprang dozens of "pocket nurseries," so called because they were started with the seedlings that Storrs & Harrison employees sneaked home in their pockets. Storrs & Harrison is gone, but the county is still a major supplier of nursery stock for the landscape trade, and there are dozens of family-owned fruit farms selling fresh fruit at farm markets and farmers markets. Depending on the season, you can pick your own berries, cherries, apples and grapes. Watch for the roadside signs.

HEADLANDS BEACH STATE PARK/MENTOR—There

is a wonderful contrast between Headlands Beach State Park and Headlands Dunes State Nature Preserve just east of it. The swimming beach, Ohio's longest natural sand beach, is kept up and used. At the dunes, however, nature is allowed to take her course. The beach grasses sink their roots, trapping the wind-blown sand and causing it to drift, and the billowing sand forms lovely hillocks tufted with tall sharp grasses that sigh in the wind.

Headlands Beach is best seen at sunrise, when the enormous, well-treed parking lot is empty, except for the cars of a few fishermen who park here to fish from the break wall. Follow the "fishing access" sign at the east end of the parking lot. The trail takes you into the cool shade of wild cherry and swamp willow trees. Soon the deep sand begins to feel firmer underfoot. You are on the break wall, although the huge stones are not yet visible beneath the wind-blown sand. The water on your right is mirror smooth, no matter how rough the waves at the beach on the windward side of the wall. Timid bathers favor this secluded beach, and boaters drop anchor here when they crave tranquility. Sandpipers and killdeer skitter among the driftwood, looking for breakfast. In spring and fall, birders take up positions on the beach to admire the variety of migrating species traveling the Great Lakes Flyway. You can walk the sweeping curve of the break wall all the way out to the end, on the enormous flat-topped sandstones that have been breaking these waves for almost 200 years. Fairport Harbor, the first working port in the Western Reserve, was also the first to protect its interests with a break wall and lighthouse.

By mid-morning the break wall attracts a few sunbathers. A young painter arrives, carrying sketch pad and charcoal. He sketches the scene: the secluded beach in the foreground, Fairport Harbor in the middle distance, with the lighthouse rising from the top of Lighthouse Hill. From this placid scene he omits the twin towers of the Perry Nuclear Power plant, though they are clearly visible in the distance, preferring to sketch in a few pretty clouds instead.

9601 Headlands Road off the northern terminus of State Route 44; 440/257-1331; Cleveland number 216/881-8141; www.ohiodnr.com Open daily 7:30 am-half hour after sunset.

MENTOR MARSH STATE NATURE PRESERVE/

MENTOR—Follow Headlands Road west from the Headlands Beach State Park, and you'll come to the Zimmerman trail head and the grass-filled lagoons of Mentor Marsh, formed when the Grand River changed its course centuries ago. On the other (south) side of the marsh, the Carol H. Sweet Nature Center, accessible from Lakeshore Boulevard/State Route 283, is run by the Cleveland Museum of Natural History, a co-owner, along with Ohio Department of Natural Resources, of the marsh. If you want to keep your feet dry, an 1100-foot boardwalk called Wake Robin Trail takes you well out onto the marsh, a place of deep silence broken only by bird songs . . . and the ferocious whine of giant mosquitoes.

5185 Corduroy Road; 440/257-0777; www.ohiodnr.com Daily, dawn to dusk; nature center open weekends April-Oct, noon-5 and Nov-March first Sundays, 11-4.

JAMES A. GARFIELD NATIONAL HISTORIC SITE/

MENTOR—Among Lake County's most notable buildings is Lawnfield, the 29-room Victorian manse that was once the home of

James Garfield. Thousands of people came here by train to hear him campaign for the U.S. presidency from the front porch. Now they come to see the family possessions, including Garfield's Congressional desk, his family china, and the waxed funeral wreath Queen Victoria sent after he was assassinated. Lawnfield is also the home of the first presidential library, established here in 1886.
8095 Mentor Avenue (U.S. 20, north of I-90 via State Route 306; turn right/ east); 440/255-8722; www.wrhs.org May-Oct Mon-Sat 10-5, Sun noon-5; Nov-April, Sat-Sun noon-5. Adults, $8, seniors $7, 6-12 $6. Groups should reserve ahead. Children's and behind-the-scenes tours available.

chalet Debonne Vineyards

VINES AND WINES—Thanks to the area's beneficent soil and long growing season (the warmer lake air delays the first frost), more than half of Ohio's grapes are grown in Ashtabula and Lake counties; people say that in the fall, you can drive along State Route 307 between State Routes 528 and 534, and just smell the grapes. The town of Geneva hosts a **Grape JAMboree** *(440/466-JAMB; www.grapejamboree. com)* festival every fall that celebrates the lush fruits of the local vines, and within a 45-minute drive of Geneva-on-the-Lake, there are wineries where you'll find music, meals, tours, lodging and, of course, libations. **Chalet Debonné Vineyards/Madison**—The Debevc family has been making wine for four generations, and now they make enough to qualify as Ohio's largest estate winery—which means, largest that grows its own grapes. You can enjoy their award-winning Chardonnays, Rieslings and Pinot Gris all year and at special events in summer—classic car shows, hot air balloon races, jazz concerts. *7743 Doty Road; 440/466-3485 or 800/424-9463; www.debonne.com* **Buccia Vineyard/Conneaut**—Fred and Joanna Bucci provide the comforts of wine and home with a tasting room, picnic tables under the grape arbors, and four air-conditioned B&B rooms that—along with a hot tub and continental breakfast—accommodate overnight guests year-round. *Rooms are $75-$115. 518 Gore Road; 440/593-5976; www.bucciavineyard.com* **Tarsitano Winery & Café/Conneaut**—Ken Tarsitano is producing 17 varieties of wine on his great-grandfather's farm, where he's also turned chef with a mostly Italian menu that includes in-house-made pasta. *Dinners $14-$21. 4871 Hatches Corner Road; 440/224-2444; www.tarsitanowinery.com*

Markko Vineyard/Conneaut—This small but distinguished winery had the first vinifera wines in Ohio, and you can sip the Chardonnay, Riesling, Cabernet Sauvignon and Pinot Noir with crackers and cheese. *Open Mon-Sat 11-6 but best to make appointment ahead. 4500 South Ridge Road; 440/593-3197; www.markko.com* For maps and detailed information about these and other wineries, contact the **Ohio Wine Producers Association,** *33 Tegam Way, Geneva; 440-466-4417, 800/227-6972; www.ohiowines.org*

WARNER-CONCORD FARMS BED & BREAKFAST/

UNIONVILLE—Kay Herdman's commercial vineyard includes a bed and breakfast located in a remodeled 150-year-old barn with high—up to 35 feet—ceilings and open spaces. Two of the three guest rooms have their own fireplaces and one of those also has a private balcony. Kay makes elaborate gourmet breakfasts, including crème brulee french toast and cornmeal pancakes.
6585 South Ridge Road West/State Route 84 just west of State Route 534; 440/428-4485; www.warner-concordfarms.com/ No children. No smoking. Rates range from $110-160; open year-round.

LAKEHOUSE INN/GENEVA-ON-THE-LAKE—In 2000

the Fagnilli family from Geneva took over this B&B and the adjacent cottages, and transformed and expanded the place. Now everything is new, and all rooms have bathrooms; three are suites with Jacuzzis. The large room where breakfast is served has what seems like a wall of windows overlooking the lake. Lake views continue outside, where the Fagnillis have launched a winery and a restaurant, Crosswinds Grille; porches and terraces with chairs facing the lake seem to be everywhere. There's also a pretty little private beach.
5653 Lake Road; 440/466-8668; www.thelakehouseinn.com Rooms from $80-$120 in season; suites $145-$215. Open all year except January; lower rates off season.

ASIDE The Lakehouse Inn is internationally known because it is the site of the annual Spencerian Saga, a combination calligraphy workshop and history lesson celebrating the life and times of America's foremost penman, Platt Spencer. Spencer was a local teacher, poet and commercial college pioneer who developed the graceful handwriting style that bears his name in the early 1800s. Participants in the Saga come from all over the United States and Canada for a week every fall, to practice their Spencerian loops under the tutelage of The Master's present-day apostles. When they're not working on their penmanship, they can be seen at the Geneva Cemetery making rubbings of their hero's monument, which features a three-foot-high quill pen in bas relief.

BEULAH'S LAKESIDE INN/GENEVA-ON-THE-

LAKE—Nancy Mawhinney is a jolly woman from Pittsburgh who came to Geneva-on-the-Lake as a girl and liked it so much that she's come back now to open a B&B. She bought a big old house on a street off the main drag, stocked the dining room with crystal and china to give breakfasts (the likes of french toast or blueberry pancakes) a touch of class. So far she has four bedrooms with private baths available, and offers air-conditioning and a big porch with lake views. *5013 New Street; 440/466-0012. Rooms $100-$125.*

GENEVA-ON-THE-LAKE—In the beginning, Geneva-on-the-Lake was a popular blue-collar vacation land, attracting families from the steel towns of Youngstown and Pittsburgh who came to swim in the blue waters and stayed in rooming houses and tourist hotels. Today, those families still come to spend a week on the lake at the last of the Lake Erie honky-tonk resorts—while this place has 1500 year-round residents, 30,000 will throng here on a summer weekend. But unlike Cedar Point, which grew huge and corporate and has way vaster crowds, Geneva-on-the-Lake stayed relatively small and funky with a carnival-type midway—The Strip—surrounded by cottages and small motels.

Not everyone appreciates a place like this. One who does, however, calls it "a county fair, without all that wholesome 4-H stuff." By day Geneva-on-the-Lake is quiet. At night, it's all neon and music, as the mile-long Strip along Lake Road/State Route 531 simmers in a haze of carnival smells: cotton candy, hot dogs, and pizza by the slice. Kids cruise; grown-ups do too, some in 1950s Chevies and Thunderbirds, which seem just right in this time-warped resort.

Most of The Strip is owned by the Woodward-Pera family, descendants of the man who built the first casino and dance hall in the early 1900s. The family keeps adding new attractions, and their electronic games arcade, **Woody's World** *(5483 Lake Road; 440/466-8650. May 1-Labor Day, plus two Sept weekends, 11 am-midnight)* is one of the largest in the country. There are several other vintage penny arcades on The Strip, a fine miniature golf course that is said to be the oldest in continual operation in the state, and enough local characters to keep life interesting. One proprietor still talks about the burlesque headliner who was known, for obvious reasons, as "Busty Russell and her B-52s." Each afternoon, before show time, she'd stroll down The Strip in a tight T-shirt with the number "52" on the front, a walking advertisement.

Geneva-on-the-Lake doesn't have a really good beach, but it's so centrally located, you can swim at a different beach every day without driving more than 30 minutes east or west. Only five miles west of The Strip, **Geneva State Park** *(4499 Padanaram Road; 440/466-8400)* has an excellent swimming beach, free boat-launching ramps, a long fishing pier, campgrounds, and fully-equipped cabins on the lakeshore. It also has a twenty-first century hotel—"the first new development in ages," as one amazed woman puts it. **The Lodge and Conference Center at Geneva State Park** *(4888 North Broadway/State Route 534; 800/801-9982 or 440/466-7100; www.thelodgeatgeneva.com)* has rooms for two at $189 in season, but off-season packages offer the same room plus breakfast for $79. Not all rooms have lake views; those that do cost more. For contrast, at the east end of town, there's **Indian Creek RV Resort** *(4710 Lake Road East; 4440/466-8191; www.indiancreekresort.com)* a long-time family operation that finds itself busier every year. For additional information and a list of cottage rentals close to The Strip, contact the **Geneva-on-the-Lake Convention and Visitors Bureau** *(5536 Lake Road; 440/466-8600 or 800/862-9948; www.visitgenevaonthelake.com Open June-Sept, Mon-Sun 11-7; limited hours during the rest of the year.)*

EATING YOUR WAY DOWN THE STRIP/GENEVA-ON-THE-LAKE—At the **Old Firehouse Winery,** grapes are pressed on the premises, and you can sample the award-winning house wines while you relax on the brick patio or its adjacent gazebo. Since the winery is built on a bluff above the lake, the view is splendid, and the food—burgers, steak, barbecued chicken and ribs—is tasty. *5499 Lake Road; 440/466-9300; www.oldfirehousewinery.com/ Open daily in summer; off-season noon-8 Sun-Thur and noon to midnight Fri-Sat. Weekends only Jan-mid April.* **Mary's Kitchen**—A huge lighted sign on The Strip points the way, and there is almost always a line of people waiting to get in. It's tucked in among summer cottages because Mary started out as a cottage vacationer who, while everyone else was off at the beach, cooked for the neighborhood. The place doesn't look like much, but it offers hearty, home-cooked meals—stuffed peppers, lasagna, Swiss steak, cabbage rolls—when you tire of midway fare. In 2007 a new owner took over, but she's been working here for so long that the menu will stay the same. *5023 New Street; 440/466-8606; no web site.* **Eddie's Grill**—Eddie Sezon and his family offer a menu with a famous foot-long hot dog, basic burgers, chili dogs, fried fish sandwiches with better-than-average slaw. The jukebox music is the innocent rock of the Fifties and Sixties, and the grill is a favorite hangout for cottagers... and the nostalgic. *5377 Lake Road; 440/466-8720. Summer only.*

The Old Firehouse Winery

MICHAEL CAHILL BED AND BREAKFAST/ASHTABULA—Built in 1887 on the prettiest street in town, this enormous house is inviting, inside and out. It is painted in its original Victorian colors—handsome shades of olive, chocolate and crimson—and boasts enough lace and antiques to be charming as well as comfortable. The four guest bedrooms are all air-conditioned, and all have baths; owners Pat and Paul Goode provide a full breakfast.

Ashtabula's Walnut Beach, shops and restaurants are only a few
steps away.
*1106 Walnut Boulevard; 440/964-8449; www.cahillbb.com/ Closed Jan-April.
No credit cards. Rooms $70-$95.*

ALESSANDRO'S RISTORANTE/ASHTABULA—In 1999

Alessandro and Tanya Pilumeli bought a former Dairy Queen restaurant
near Ashtabula and started transforming it into a little bit of Italy. It's
a genuine Italian, Italian restaurant, because Alessandro is a native of
Sicily who has always worked in kitchens. He did study agriculture
("Obviously, I know my herbs," he says), but when the time came
to earn a living, he followed his choice and not his degree, and went
to work in a kitchen in Florence. He and Tanya came to America in
1994—she's from Geneva, which explains why they ended up here. The
old Dairy Queen counter is still there in front, only now with a row of
wine bottles on it, and the dining room has eleven tables with green-
and-white check table cloths. Alessandro does all the work himself. He
makes bread ("Thirty loaves last night," he recalls); every other day,
he makes three lasagnas; he does pastas, four sauces, pizzas and salad
dressings. Specials are fish on Fridays, game on Saturdays, pastas during
the week. The veal dishes are way above average. Not surprisingly,
there's almost always a line outside Alessandro's in summer and on
weekends. The chef's favorite time of year is September-December,
after summer crowds let up. One more thing. This may be Ashtabula
County, but the wines are almost all Italian.
*6540 Lake Road West/State Route 531, between Geneva and Ashtabula;
440/964-5766. Tue-Thur 4-8:30, Fri-Sat 4-9:30. No reservations. Closed from
Christmas through Jan, when he and Tanya take the kids to Italy. Pastas $10-$17;
main courses about $14-$23.*

EATING IN ASHTABULA HARBOR—

Hil Mak Seafoods—This is a long-time family operation where you
can enjoy the sit-down restaurant or buy fresh fish around the corner.
You'll find a full line of fresh-catch seafood.
*Store at 1619 West Fifth Street, restaurant at 449 Lake Avenue; 440/964-
3222; www.hilmaks.com Market Mon-Thur 9:30-6, Fri 9:30-7, Sat 9:30-6.
Restaurant Tue-Sat 11:30-2:30, 5-10. Dinners from $10.95 to $42.95
for lobster.*
Doxsie Deli Eatery—This popular spot has a menuful of sandwiches
and hamburgers. It also has a row of tables next to large windows
overlooking the bridge. *1001 Bridge Street; 440/964-8090. Open daily 7-3;
winter 7-2. Lunch $3.75-$8.25.*

ASHTABULA HARBOR—With its busy harbor, beaches and

impressive, gentrified downtown, Ashtabula is a fine place to visit.
It resembles a New England seacoast village with strong Midwest
industrial overtones, for the town was once the busiest coal-shipping
port on the Great Lakes. Ashtabula's harbor area is uncommonly hilly,
which adds to its charm, and Hulbert Street, on both sides of Bridge
Street, is the steepest and bumpiest street of all, its worn old bricks
having pitched and heaved over the years to form a terrain that's roughly
as turbulent as Lake Erie during a storm. Locals say the street can make

you seasick if you drive it too fast. The finest homes are on Walnut Boulevard, a beautiful street where lake captains once lived along a bluff that overlooks the harbor, which the Ashtabula River flows through. That long-polluted river has been in the throes of a $50 million cleanup. Dredging began in 2006 and should finish in 2008, leaving this a sweeter place than it's been in living memory. In recent times most harbor traffic has been pleasure craft and fishing charters, although some freighters still come in to unload stone and pick up coal for power plants in Canada. You'll see that coal comes in by train on the east side of the river and soars over the river on a transporter dubbed the "coal arch" to freighters waiting to be loaded on the west side. There are some shops on Bridge Street, where every 30 minutes throughout the summer, the Bascule Bridge is raised to let boats pass through, even relatively small boats. At the east end of Walnut Boulevard, Point Park is an overlook, the best place for watching boat traffic and the bridge. Regular as clockwork, bells ring and sirens wail, and Bridge Street traffic comes to a halt. The bridge tender releases the 450-ton counterweight. As the stone sinks, the bridge rises. Then the waiting boats scoot through and the bridge descends once more into place. The bridge operates regularly, but everything else seems to run at half speed in Ashtabula Harbor. It is a pace well suited to the needs of sedentary, porch-sitting summer vacationers who are pleased to find themselves in a slow-moving harbor town that has a nautical, New England flavor. www.ashtabulaharbor.org.

THE GREAT LAKES MARINE & U.S. COAST GUARD MEMORIAL MUSEUM/ASHTABULA—The exhibits and photographs here explain the importance of Ashtabula's location—roughly halfway between the coal fields to the south and the iron ore fields to the north—when America's steel industry was the envy of the industrialized world. The museum is both instructive and whimsical; there's a knife "to be used for cutting fog," but there is also a working model of the Hulett unloader (designed by Akron engineer George Hulett), which revolutionized Great Lakes shipping. The first Hulett was built at nearby Conneaut in 1898; it immediately put hundreds of laborers out of work—they used to unload the boats with shovel and wheelbarrow—and made Andrew Carnegie a happy man. Now that most freighters have self unloaders, the Hulett is obsolete in turn. The business end of a Hulett—the vertical beam with the clamshell bucket and the operator's cab just above it—is on display across from the museum at Point Park, where there are old-timers about who will gladly explain how it worked.
1071 Walnut Boulevard; 440/224-0472; www.ashtabulamarinemuseum.org Open Memorial Day-Aug 31 Fri-Sun and holidays, noon-5; Sept Sat-Sun noon-5. Tours for groups year-round by appointment. Adults $4, 6-16 $3.

HUBBARD HOUSE UNDERGROUND RAILROAD MUSEUM—William and Catharine Hubbard, recently arrived from New York State with their six children, built this handsome brick house about 1836. Because the Hubbards were ardent abolitionists, their house soon became a way-station on the pre-Civil War underground railroad—"Mother Hubbard's Cupboard" was one of its code names. Fugitive slaves probably didn't stay in the house, but rather waited a few blocks

away in the Old Yellow Warehouse on the Ashtabula River for a ship to Canada. Though as a museum the house has little structural evidence of hiding slaves, exhibits document the underground railroad in Ashtabula County, Hubbard family history and the Civil War.
Walnut Boulevard and Lake Avenue; 440/964-8168; www.hubbardhouseugrrmuseum.org/ Fri-Sun Memorial Day through Sept, 1-5. Adults $5, seniors $4, 6-16 $3. Call ahead for group tour any time.

HISTORIC BRIDGE STREET/ASHTABULA—The block
between Hulbert Street and the Ashtabula River was "modernized" in 1886, when the old frame buildings were razed to make way for the impressive brick structures. There were nine hotels and 52 saloons, and only the notorious port of Singapore, it is said, had more. The buildings are mostly shops now (the likes of antiques, nautical gifts, American Indian crafts) but you can match the present-day businesses with their Victorian counterparts by consulting the maps and walking tour brochures available through the Ashtabula Area Chamber of Commerce, *4536 Main Avenue; 440/998-6998; www.ashtabulachamber.net Mon-Fri 8-4:30.*

COVERED BRIDGES—Together wineries and covered bridges
have made tourism Ashtabula County's biggest business. The county has more covered bridges than any other county in Ohio—sixteen—and every year during the second weekend of October it celebrates with a Covered Bridge Festival. The main festival activities are located at the county fairgrounds in Jefferson, but the festival will pass out free maps for self-guided tours of bridges at any time. During the festival, van tours go to several bridges, and "step-on" guides are available for bus tours. Most of the county's covered bridges date from just after the Civil War to 1900, but starting in 1983 County Engineer John Smolen, Jr. designed and built four new ones. He also renovated the old ones, so today all but two of the sixteen carry traffic. Before he retired in 2003, Smolen designed a 600-foot covered bridge that will be the longest in the United States. Being built of wood, it will have four 150-foot spans over the Ashtabula River southeast of Ashtabula. Smolen's successor, Tim Martin, who's in charge of construction, expected completion by late summer, 2008.

Ashtabula County Covered Bridges: **Benetka Road**, 1900, renovated in 1985; **Caine Road**, 1986, Ohio's first Pratt truss; **Creek Road**, date unknown, over Conneaut Creek; **Doyle Road**, 1868, over Mill Creek; **Giddings Road**, 1995, one of the new bridges (Netcher was the other) helped by ODOT timber funding; **Graham Road**, rebuilt from parts of a 1913 bridge lost in a flood, now bypassed; **Harpersfield**, 1868, over the Grand River and 228 feet long, longest in Ohio; **Mechanicsville Road**, 1867, Ashtabula County's oldest; **Middle Road**, 1868, over Conneaut Creek; **Netcher Road**, 1999, 110-feet long; **Olin Bridge**, 1873, located on Dewey Road and named for a family; **Riverdale Road**, 1874, over the Grand River, with the lowest clearance—eight feet—of these covered bridges; **Root Road**, 1868, raised a foot and a half during renovation in early 1980s; **South Denmark Road**, 1890, now bypassed; **State Road**, 1983, first of the new bridges; **Windsor Mills**,

1867, named for a locality. All are on county and township roads, so to find them you'll need the map that the festival provides. Phone, write or email through the web site Ashtabula County Covered Bridge Festival Committee, *(25 West Jefferson Street, Jefferson OH 44047); 440/576-3769 or www.coveredbridgefestival.org*

VICTORIAN PERAMBULATOR MUSEUM/

JEFFERSON—At first, independently, twin sisters Janet Pallo and Judith Kaminski each bought an antique baby carriage. Then, once they'd realized just how many different kinds of antique carriages were out there, they began collecting them. One thing came after another, and since 1970 they've operated the world's only perambulator museum. It's in an attractive, nine-room, 4000-square foot addition to Janet's house. Their international collection of more than 200 carriages includes many rare and ornate ones that are works of art in themselves, as well as some constructed in whimsical shapes such as swans, gondolas, cars; most are from the nineteenth century. Their celebrity carriage is an English perambulator that Queen Elizabeth and her sister Margaret rode in as children. The museum also exhibits antique dolls and doll carriages, antique toys and vintage clothing for children and dolls. Every November and December the museum is lavishly decorated for the holidays. There's a store too. It sells miniature gold baby-carriage ornaments for $20.
26 Cedar Street (off State Route 46 south of I-90; 440/576-9588; www.victorianperambulatormuseum.com June-Aug Wed and Sat 11-4; May and Sept-Dec Sat 11-4; rest of year groups of six or more by appointment. Adults $5, children $4.

ASIDE—The northernmost point in Ohio is in far eastern Ashtabula County near the town of Conneaut; its latitude is approximately 41 degrees, 58 minutes.

CONNEAUT—Conneaut is a sometime industrial port with a real jewel next to its vast natural harbor: the incomparable Conneaut Township Park (480 Lake Road; 440/599-7071), which must be one of Ohio's best. It's unusually hilly and wooded, has picnic groves, superb recreational facilities, and one of the longest, finest beaches around. There is also excellent fishing in the deep waters off the harbor—charters are a big business—and Conneaut Creek is renowned for steelhead. A sizable community of devoted summertime fans snap up the spaces in the trailer parks, campgrounds and lakefront rental cottages.
For more information contact the Conneaut Chamber of Commerce (235 Main Street; 440/593-2402; www.conneautchamber.org/ Open Mon-Fri 10-4:30.)

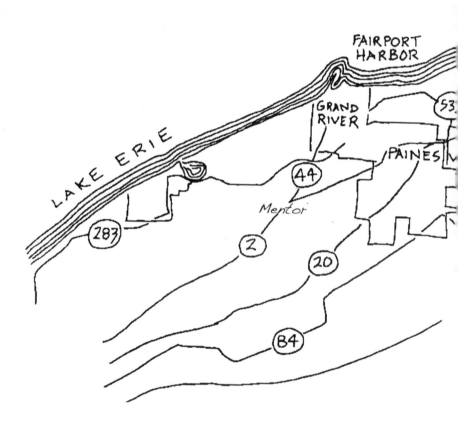

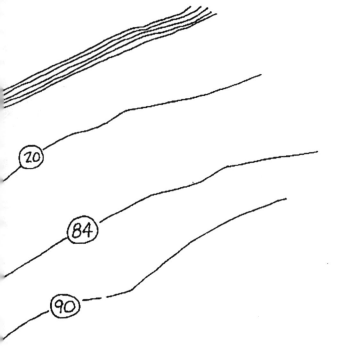

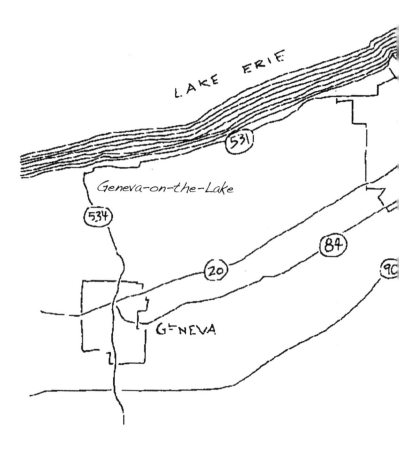

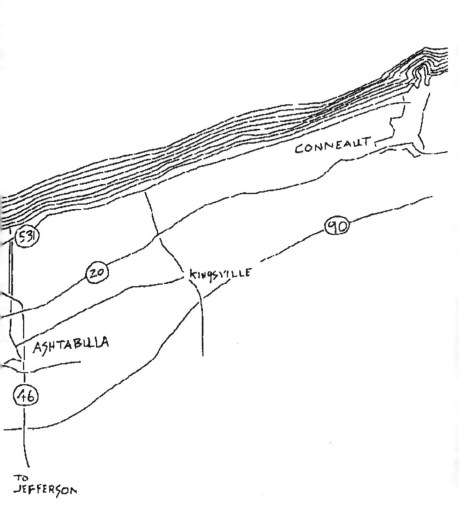

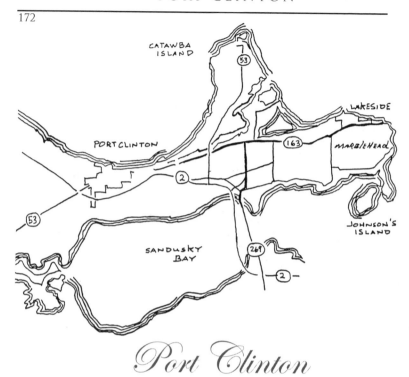

Port Clinton

The self-proclaimed "Walleye Capital of the World," Port Clinton curves around the mouth of the Portage River. Walleye are one reason to visit; another might be the wonderful walk in the park along Port Clinton's lakefront. And there are trips to the islands, the peach and apple bounty of local orchards, the rifle and pistol matches at nearby Camp Perry, duck hunting. Port Clinton was first settled by Scottish immigrants shipwrecked on their way to a small settlement called Chicago. They liked what they saw and in 1828, laid out the town.

Three other worthy settlements dot this peninsula on the north side of Sandusky Bay: Catawba, Lakeside and Marblehead; their only similarity is that they are joined at the land mass. Catawba has a concentration of luxury condominiums. The county map calls Catawba an island, but shows it connected to Port Clinton by a slender strand of land. Out here all the yachts, sailboats and golf courses make the drive picturesque. Owners of prime property usually own prime property elsewhere, too. On the other hand, property owners at Lakeside own their cottages but hold only 99-year leases on the ground under them.

Some cottages are so close together they share the same gutters. In Lakeside, walking and biking are the best means of travel. The *Wall Street Journal* once called it the safest place in America. The police force has two men and the last big crime was on the Fourth of July when some teenagers, at the height of holiday revelry, set off a car alarm. The old Hotel Lakeside guest book goes back so far you can read the signatures of several early twentieth-century presidents and on a sunny day, you can look through a public telescope, see an island in Canadian waters and not even wish you were there.

This leaves us with Marblehead. Famous for winter gales and ocean-sized waves, it has a gentler personality in the summer. Its history was dug out of the huge limestone quarry, a place so big that the National Guard has used it to practice war games. From the single road skirting the easternmost point is a panoramic view of Lake Erie like no other, for here, Ohio ends abruptly at a rockbound shore.

PHIL'S INN/PORT CLINTON—The one gastronomical custom that must be upheld upon visiting Port Clinton is to try the spaghetti at Phil's. The sauce, from a recipe that's over a century old, is such a well-guarded secret that the owners still add the final spices—at 10 a.m. and at 8 p.m. each day—while no one else is around. It takes 120 gallons of sauce, 1000 meatballs and 70 employees to keep the summer ritual flowing smoothly on a daily basis. If you like, you may buy a quart of the sauce, fresh from the kettle, to take home. The booths and tables seat 130, plenty of room in a normal restaurant but here, with the lake breeze from across the street wafting the aroma of Phil's sweet Italian sauce down East Perry Street and into the nostrils of unsuspecting travelers, plan to wait in line on weekends.
1708 East Perry Street; 419/734-9023; www.philsinn.com Daily 11-9 weekdays; until 10 weekends; 11-8 off-season. Closed by Dec; reopen March. Dinners with sides, $9.75-14.95.

THE GARDEN AT THE LIGHTHOUSE/PORT

CLINTON—Don't look for a lighthouse; it went when trade fell to one ship a day. Do look for a real adventure in fine dining because these people take pride in freshness, saying that most in-season produce is as near as the closest farm. Meals begin with a tray of crackers and liver pate, a meal in itself. Very recommendable is the "Fish Market," a marvelous blend of shrimp, melon, grapes, oranges, pineapple, and strawberries on a bed of fresh lettuce, topped with a poppy seed dressing. Only the heartiest can eat it all and still have room for a main

course like lobster tail, breast of chicken and Swiss cheese, all wrapped up in a heavenly puff pastry. There's a nice outdoor dining area.
226 East Perry at Adams; 419/732-2151; www.gardenrestaurant.com Dinner in season Sun-Thur 4:30-9:30 and until 10:30 Fri-Sat. Open year-round; check hours off season. Dinner $15-$25.

THE JET EXPRESS/PORT CLINTON—You can feel the rush of the twenty-first century when, through a glass-encased window of the second-floor captain's bridge, you see the captain wielding a joystick of sorts; he is driving the boat. Well-trained in the art of steering and propelling a three-and-a-half-million-dollar catamaran, he is Jet Express's "old salt," though he has nary a gray hair. Meantime, traveling at up to 42 miles an hour, propelled by two diesels with water jets that spew 1000 gallons per second, you're almost to Put-in-Bay, where on a busy summer week-end, 380 passengers are waiting to come aboard. Jet Express has trips from Sandusky also.

North Monroe Street and Perry; from State Route 2, exit Port Clinton Route 163 and follow signs to the foot of Monroe. 800/245-1538; 419/732-2800; www. jet-express.com Service from May through Oct; weekends only at beginning and end of season. Departures every 45 minutes in peak season. Adults $24 round trip; 6-12 $4.

MCKENNA'S INN BED AND BREAKFAST/CATAWBA ISLAND—McKenna's Inn will introduce you to Little Pittsburgh, a private community of houses with big front yards facing a land that ends at a dock and beach. On this easternmost part of Pittsburgh Street, McKenna's driveway is the first on the right, with two big stone pillars to mark it. Proprietors Joseph and Rebecca Jessen (her maiden name was McKenna; her father ran this B&B before they arrived) have a three-story house with four guest bedrooms, all with private baths, queen beds and fridges; some have fireplaces. Three are on the third floor, one on the second. Downstairs there is a diningroom for the Continental breakfast, but on mild days the wrap-around screen porch is perfect.

5714 East Pittsburgh Street (Port Clinton post office); 419/797-6148 or 877/417-5733; www.mckennasinn.com Rooms are $149 or $179 in season on weekends, $107 weekdays. Rates lower off season. Weekends only in winter.

MON AMI RESTAURANT AND HISTORIC WINERY/ CATAWBA ISLAND—Owner John Kronberg likes to brag that Mon Ami is more of a state restaurant than a local one—and since they serve 1000 dinners on Friday night in summer, they're clearly doing something right. Housed in an 1870 winery building with stone walls and a fireplace, Mon Ami has two diningrooms, one a chalet and bar, the other a large room that seats 300. Visitors can also tour the cavernous limestone cellars where, they say, some wines have been lolling around for 130 years. On Friday and Saturday nights there are bands; jazz on Sunday. Some things at Mon Ami never change, like the excellent steaks and seafood that some people drive all day to get, and the servers who offer wine samples to help you choose.

3845 East Wine Cellar Road, off West Catawba Road (Port Clinton post office); 419/797-4445 or 800/777-4266; www.monamiwinery.com Restaurant opens 11:30 Mon-Sat, 10:30 on Sunday; dinner until 9, 10 on weekends; bar until crowd wanes in wee hours. Same menu all day, $9-$35.

LAKESIDE—Lakeside never really changes; it just gets better and richer. Cottages still have the old, comfy feel but are trimmer and more freshly painted. There's all the small town charm one could want. And Lakeside is not just a summer event now—the theater is open on weekends all year. A century ago, Lakeside was Cedar Point's biggest competition for the summer tourist trade. However, this Methodist theme park of sorts closed on Sundays, leaving tourists to pay at one end and pray at the other. While visitors at Cedar Point were throwing down Ohio wine, the campers at Lakeside were flinging their jewelry to the ground, ridding themselves of material possessions. Dozens of cottages, designed to mimic the Gothic architecture on Martha's Vineyard, sprang up; the grounds were landscaped; docks were built; famous speakers like Amelia Earhart, Billy Sunday, and Lowell Thomas arrived; and the hinged walls of the huge auditorium were raised to create more room. Originally, no smoking, intoxicating beverages or dancing was allowed. Today, it's no open containers on Lakeside property. Some of the cottages became bed and breakfasts. The Hotel Lakeside, which dates from the late nineteenth century, has been restored, and the 700-foot dock with jetties provides safe swimming. Restaurants in the village are dry but the prices and the entertainment packages still draw crowds. Thousands of visitors return every summer, and 600 people make it their year round home. If you imagine Lakeside as the way you think life was in the good old days, that's only because it is.

Lakeside Association, 236 Walnut Avenue: 419/798-4461 or 1/866/952-5374; www.lakesideohio.com Daily entry rates in season (2007) are $15 per person and $6 per car or $4 for three hours. No skateboarding allowed, but shuffleboard, volleyball, tennis, and miniature golf have serious competitions.

Hotel Lakeside

HOTEL LAKESIDE—Like the rest of the village, this rambling hotel is on the National Register of Historic Places. Once the focal point for Methodist camp meetings, this wonderful 1870s hotel offers 76 rooms recently restored and filled with antiques, three meals daily, an authentic Victorian ambiance throughout, as well as a wrap-around screened veranda with a sea of rocking chairs facing a most scenic view of Lake Erie. Lakefront rooms enjoy natural breezes; others have air conditioners.

236 Walnut Avenue; 419/798-4461 or 1/866/952-5374. Memorial Day through Labor Day. Rooms $45-$215.

STONE'S THROW COTTAGE/LAKESIDE—A historic landmark (since 1890) with a deep welcoming front porch overlooking the lake, Stone's Throw opened in 2001 right across the lane from the Hotel Lakeside. Restored in 2000-2001, it offers four very attractive king and queen rooms with private baths. The bridal suite features a Jacuzzi and two rooms have an alcove for a third guest. A full breakfast is included, with favorites like Blueberry French Toast or Strata. *221 Park Row; 419/798-1711; www.stonesthrowcottage.com For those 13 and older. Open June through Sept. Rooms $239-$289.*

IDLEWYLD BED & BREAKFAST/LAKESIDE—Before he retired, Daniel Barris was in the produce business in Cleveland; he's kept up his contacts, so that Idlewyld's guests can indulge in eating from the largest fruit bowl on the shoreline. Usually there will be 40 people for breakfast, which takes a considerable fruit bowl. The 14 bedrooms, each individually decorated and some with private baths, have had such rave reviews that guests have returned for a second stay within a week. Reservations here should be made well in advance. Daniel, who owns Idlewyld with his wife Jean, is also doing the baking now—he makes bread and coffee cakes, and an occasional bacon and Swiss quiche. *350 Walnut Street; 419/798-4198 or 216/970-4552 (year-round); www. idlewyldbb.com May to Sept, $65-$95.*

ABIGAIL TEA ROOM/LAKESIDE—The Martin family has owned Abigail since 1933 and though they didn't give it its name, they gave it a grand reputation. Now that his brother Ladd has retired, Sheldon Martin is in charge, the third generation to use his grandmother's fresh rhubarb pie recipe, the most requested dessert. Alternating apple, peach, and red raspberry, he bakes a total of 15-20 pies before lunch, assessing the damages afterward and restocking the ovens for dinner. The rest of the menu changes daily—lamb stew, scalloped chicken, hamloaf—because there is never much left over. Fried perch and walleye are a staple. Over 75 years, the ambiance is about the same. The two cottages, joined at the seams and gutters and encased in a porch shrouded with vines, seat 140. The tables get a fresh coat of red or green paint every year before the season begins. The ceiling fans work hard to circulate the air. Eating at Abigail is a Lakeside tradition. Praise the pie. *104 West Third Street; 419/798-5561. Open mid-June-Labor Day. Breakfast 8-10. Lunch 11:30-1:30. Dinner 5-7:30. Closed on Monday. Dinners with trimmings (2006), $7-$9. No credit cards; personal checks OK.*

KIDS ON THIRD STREET/LAKESIDE—If you are looking for those wonderful old-fashioned wooden toys that are not extensions of somebody's marketing campaign, this shop will be a real find. The owners, Sarah and Ryan Hamilton, have two small children who often are in the shop and at play. Some things are pricey, but the indulgent grandma we know consoled herself with the thought that quality is never cheap. *217 West Third Street; 866/668-4473 or 419/798-5321; www. kidsonthirdstreet.com June-Aug Mon-Sat 10-7. Reduced hours May and Sept.*

SOUTH BEACH RESORT AND MARINA/
MARBLEHEAD—Since 1993, this has been a family-owned and operated resort with a wide variety of accommodations. The 55-room hotel has Jacuzzis in every room. Cottages have hand-painted landscapes outside and real lake views. The property extends over eight acres, includes a private sand beach, three fishing piers, and a 38-slip marina. Restaurant closed in 2006.
8620 East Bayshore Road; 419/798-4900; www.sbresort.com Hotel open all year; cottages close after peak season.

U.S. COAST GUARD STATION/MARBLEHEAD—There
always are a few die-hard fishermen who ignore the warnings and risk being carried away—and some are. And it's the alert Coast Guard team at this four-frequency operational panel who call out crewmates to man whatever is needed to rescue those wayward souls in trouble on the water. They average, annually, nearly a thousand calls for assistance here in one of Lake Erie's busiest stations, where in quiet moments courteous guides let you board a vessel, explain the peacetime duties of "America's oldest continuous sea-going service"—afloat since 1790—and take you for a walk-through of their watch room, training room, dining area. There's also a display of old photos and a 1926 wooden rescue boat that the crews are restoring when they have any time.
606 Prairie Street at the harbor; 419/798-4445. Open daily, but call first to make sure it's a convenient time.

MARBLEHEAD LIGHTHOUSE/MARBLEHEAD—The
oldest lighthouse in Ohio, as well as the oldest still operational in the Great Lakes, has a beacon that, since 1821, has gone from whale-oil candles to kerosene to electricity. Manpower (and twice in the nineteenth century, womanpower) was exchanged for an electric eye in the 1950s. But its perch, on what has been termed "the roughest point on Lake Erie since navigation of the Great Lakes began," continues to lure photographers in search of the right angle and anglers in search of the winning lure. On a clear day, one can see Cedar Point and Kelley's Island. The Ohio Department of Natural Resources acquired the lighthouse in 1998, and it became a state park. The 1895 keeper's house holds a museum (see the next entry).
On Lighthouse Drive off State Route 163, at the eastern end of town, just past the Byzantine Church; 419/732-1166; www.ohiodnr.com/parks Open for free tours during the summer Mon-Fri 1-4:45 and second Saturdays. Group tours can be arranged ahead any time.

THE BENAJAH WOLCOTT HOUSE/MARBLEHEAD—
Benajah Wolcott was the first keeper at Marblehead Lighthouse. William Kelly, who built the lighthouse in the fall of 1821, built this house the next spring, 1822, of the same local limestone. The oldest permanent structure in Ottawa County, the house has a hall, parlor, two bedrooms, hallway and pantry. The Ottawa County Historical Society bought it in 1989 and two years later began still ongoing restorations. Manned by volunteers, improved as the money comes in, the house is two-and-a-half miles west of the lighthouse.
9999 East Bayshore Road, on the south side of the peninsula; 419/798-9339; www.thekeepershouse.org/ Open June 1-Aug 31, Mon-Fri 1-5 and second Saturdays in summer 1-5. Donation requested.

Benajoh Wolcott House

JOHNSON'S ISLAND—By the end of the Civil War, almost 10,000 Confederate prisoners had passed through the prison on this tiny 275-acre island in Sandusky Bay, just off the peninsula that faces Cedar Point. According to historian Harlan Hatcher, the camp was a rather grim village, especially in mid-winter when the temperatures sometimes dipped under 20 below zero. A worse fate was the monotony of the place. The prisoners were guarded inside and out, inside by, among others, the famous "Gray Beard Brigade," a Federal unit that contained octogenarians (one had 15 sons in the Union army) and outside by a gunboat. When the prison closed in 1865, 206 Confederate soldiers were left, buried in that lonely spot. Most of them had died of pneumonia. For a long while, the island—and the soldiers—were forgotten. Then the people of Sandusky, wartime passions cooled, put marble headstones on the graves and installed a statue of a soldier pointing his Confederate flag toward the homeland. None of the prison buildings still stands; the last remaining part of the fort was burned before World War II. The only warring today is against real estate developers.
www.johnsonsislandmemorial.homestead.com

OTTAWA NATIONAL WILDLIFE REFUGE/OAK HARBOR—For the birds of passage, this is Ohio's rest stop of choice. Thousands of birds of multiple family lineages use this marsh, woodlands and grassland during their journey along the Mississippi fly-way. In February, the place is thick with swans arriving from the Arctic for the summer. The thousand resident Canada geese swell to 8,000 during migration, and, in March, the place is reed-to-reed ducks. It is probably the finest place in Ohio to watch migratory birds when, during the peak season in October, one can see as many as a hundred different kinds of birds on a single morning. The ONWR wraps around Crane Creek State Park where birders (and others) can swim and picnic. There's a mile-long boardwalk in the adjacent Magee Marsh Wildlife

Area and, altogether, over nine miles of pathways plus an observation deck. There's also a new visitor center, opened in May 2007.
14000 West State Route 2, about 12 miles west of Port Clinton; 419/898-0014; www.fws.gov/midwest/ottawa/ Office hours are Mon–Sat 9-4; park accessible dawn to dusk every day.

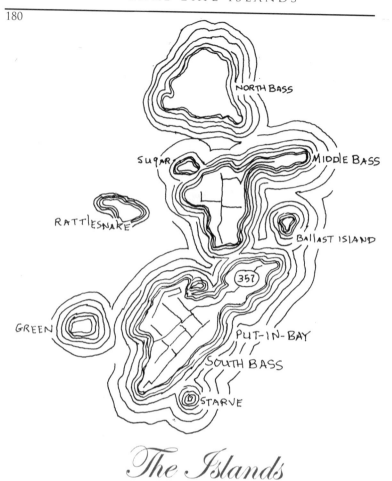

The Islands

SOUTH BASS ISLAND—Today, you'll find that virtually everything in Put-in-Bay looks shiny and well-kept, while keeping its old-timey, low-rise appearance; there's plenty to do, and visitors feel welcome. That's likely why 1.2 million of them arrive every year, though only about 400 stay through the winter. The summer shores are so crowded you can go around the island by stepping from boat to boat. Those who come by ferry are notoriously short-sighted about transportation on the island. All the cottages, motels and B&Bs fill to overflowing on weekends, but the general welcome doesn't extend to tourists sacking out on people's front lawns. Nor can visitors sleep in their cars—the ferry won't let you take your car on a weekend, unless you have proof of accommodations. But for those willing to deal with the logistics and see over the heads in the crowd, the sunset from South Bass is well worth the trip.

MIDDLE BASS ISLAND—When Gloria Wolf's labor began, late on a November night in 1969, the island doctor was summoned from Kelleys to Middle Bass. The islanders heard the news on their party lines. They formed a little convoy, escorting Gloria and her husband, Bud, to the grass landing strip to wait for the doctor's plane, arranging their autos so the headlights would illuminate the unlighted runway. As Gloria clambered aboard for the flight to the mainland hospital, headlights flashed in cheery Morse code. Although Middle Bass is filled with generous inhabitants, it is late to the modern world as we know it. A commercial district barely exists, and while Fox Road traverses the length of the island, it looks like the country lane it is. Only lately has Middle Bass added street signs and some street lights, and introduced golf carts for getting around; until now the main attraction here has been the quiet. Lately the Ohio Department of Natural Resources has had its eye on Middle Bass. It bought 123 acres here in 2001, and its marina was closing for renovations in 2008. It's scheduled to reopen in 2009 with a proper sewer system and about 150 new boat slips. In 2003 ODNR also bought 465 of North Bass Island's 677 acres, previously mostly vineyards, and plans to use it for primitive camping by permit.

KELLEYS ISLAND—When Datus Kelley, the island patriarch, bought the island in 1833, he chased off outlaws and offered a cash bonus to anyone who would abstain from hard liquor. Kelley made a fortune with his quarries, wineries, sawmills and boat docks, but he himself lived simply and shared his wealth. He built the islanders a school and a town hall and supported a local newspaper that was praised on the mainland as a marvel of erudition. During the 30-plus years of Kelley's influence not a single felony was recorded. The police chief had little to do but play checkers at the general store where the brotherhood was known as the Independent Order of Island loafers. There's little time for checkers today as the island bustles, in its quiet fashion, with a steady influx of cottagers, fishermen, campers and day-trippers who come to see the America's biggest Lake Erie island and its sights, the glacial grooves, the mysterious Indian-carved pictographs on Inscription Rock, and the nature trails.

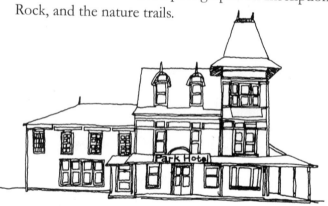

PARK HOTEL/PUT-IN-BAY—Three floors of vintage preservation add a dose of nostalgia to the heart of this harbor town. You'll find a Victorian ambience intact in the first floor lobby, with its period furnishings and Bavarian etched glass windows. On the upper two guest floors, you'll also find Victorian ambience, with rooms sparsely furnished but comfortable, and communal bathrooms at the end of the hall, one set to each floor. It's what lodging used to be back in the 1800s, when excursionists steamed into this summer playground by the thousands and wanted a place to stay in the heart of all the action. They still do, and it still is. There is one modern amenity: air conditioning.

234 Delaware Avenue, at the harbor; 419/285-3581; www.parkhotelpib.com/ May 1-Halloween; weekends only May and October. Rates range from $67 on weekdays, and up to $180 on weekends.

THE VINEYARD/SOUTH BASS—East Point is the quiet end of the island, and the Vineyard B&B maintains its seclusion, an 800-foot beach and a long list of returning guests. The six-acre vineyard next door is over one hundred years old and still provides enough Catawba grapes for the local winery and jellies for a full breakfast. Three bedrooms are filled with antiques, many original to the three and four generations that have owned the house. Owners today are Barbi and Mark Barnhill. *910 Columbus Avenue, one mile from Put-in-Bay; 419/285-6181; www.vineyardohio.homestead.com Weekends only, two-night minimum. In season rooms are $135 and $150 per night. No smoking, no children, no pets.*

OTHER BED & BREAKFASTS—South Bass has dozens and dozens of places to stay. Here are three B&Bs that are just a block up Catawba from downtown Put-in-Bay: one is Victorian and spacious, one a 1917 brick and stucco bungalow, and the third is new. Built in 1863, **Ashley's Island House** has never stopped hosting tourists; it qualifies as South Bass's oldest and, with 13 bedrooms, largest B&B. Wicker chairs line the front porch. Four rooms have private baths, the rest share; breakfast is large. *Peak season rates range from $70 midweek to $175 on weekends. 557 Catawba Avenue; 419/285-2844; www.ashleysislandhouse.com* In retirement Joey Wolf and her husband, Kit Minielier, moved from Denver to South Bass Island, where she grew up; then they bought a 1917 bungalow and launched **Anchor Inn**. They have three bedrooms with a bath and a half in the house, a two-bedroom cottage in the yard; a gourmet breakfast. *Rates go from $99 to $149; open year round, rates lower off season. 500 Catawba Avenue; 419/285-5055; www.anchorinn.info* **The Ahoy** was built in 2004 and opened in 2005, so everything is spiffy. It has four bedrooms, all with baths; those in front have a deck too. *Breakfast is serve-yourself continental; rates are $99 in season weekdays; higher weekends; lower off-season. Open all year, complimentary bicycles.* Co-owner manager Nick Michael started out in England, arrived in Put-in-Bay a few years ago as a single man, a lifeguard; and now he's married to Samona, managing this business, and wheeling their baby out on walks. *361 Doller Avenue; 419/285-2469; www.ahoypib.com*

Crescent Tavern

THE CRESCENT TAVERN/PUT-IN-BAY—Islanders George and June Stoiber reclaimed an old hotel building, kept the pressed tin ceilings and the Gay Nineties frivolity and added a frilly gazebo for outdoor dining. The Crescent Tavern menu goes beyond deep-fried. Try the charcoal grilled tuna or the barbecued pork for lunch. Outside there's a gazebo bar and grill; inside look for the Tap Room bar and dining room.

198 Delaware Avenue, past the harbor; 419/285-4211; www.crescenttavern.com Serving lunch and dinner 11-10. Sandwiches $7-13, entrees, $14-28. Mother's Day through Sept.

BEER BARREL SALOON/PUT-IN-BAY—On the outside, the Beer Barrel Saloon could pass for a supermarket, while on the inside, it's a superbar, 405 feet 10 inches of serpentine counter with 165 bar stools. It's the world's longest, as attested by *Guinness World Records*; and if anyone builds a longer bar, the Beer Barrel will extend theirs until it's even longer. This is not the place for an intimate tete-a-tete. There are no napkins, no blenders, drinks are served in plastic, and the beer comes in 16-ounce cans. In season, when the tables and bar are both filled (capacity 1200), it takes a semi-trailer to bring in enough beer for a week. The world's longest bar producing perhaps the world's longest hangovers also has the island's liveliest island balladeer, Pat Dailey. His shows, on Saturdays from 7 to 9, draw the most enthusiastic audience participation on the island.

324 Delaware Avenue at Catawba; 419/285-2337; www.beerbarrelpib.com 11 am-2 am daily in summer. Two bands on weekdays, three on weekends, at 2, 7 and 9. Pizzas average $10.

FROSTY'S BAR/PUT-IN-BAY—Everyone who has ever set foot on this island has a nodding acquaintance with Frosty's Bar. It's known for pizza and frosty mugs of beer; the pizza for its thin and crispy crust with just the right amount of cheese, and the beer comes draft or bottled.

240 Delaware Avenue; 419/285-4741; www.frostys.com Open daily 7 am-1 am May-Sept; weekends only in April and October. Full service family-style breakfast, $7-8, 7 am-11 am

ROUND HOUSE BAR/PUT-IN-BAY—Another landmark watering hole is the Round House, a perfectly round restaurant-turned-saloon built in 1873 by "Round House" Smith, who also constructed the Park Hotel next door, a logical place to sleep it off. The story goes that the Round House was actually fabricated in Toledo, then shipped in by boat. It's known for dancing when there's a live band, though often it's really too crowded for dancing.

60 Delaware Avenue, at the harbor; 419/285-2323; www.theroundhousebar.com Open noon-1 am, daily, May-Sept, weekends April and Oct.

AXEL & HARRY'S WATERFRONT GRILLE/PUT-IN-BAY—It's hard to get closer to the shoreline than Axel & Harry's has; they're right on the harbor, with lake views from windows and from the terrace. Or at least, views of all the boats anchored out there. On the menu here the Admiral Perry is what used to be called a club sandwich;

dinner offerings ($19.95-$54; surf and turf fetches highest price)
include rack of lamb and pasta alfredo; bar and wine list.
*227 Bayview Avenue; 419/285-2572; www.axelandharrys.com Summer hours 7
am-10 pm*

THE SKYWAY/SOUTH BASS—The planes are pulled up to
the front door, sometimes twenty or thirty at a time, tied like horses
to a hitching post. Pilots climb out, stretch their legs and head for
the swinging door of Skyway Restaurant. Tourists in the summer,
ice fishermen in the winter, islanders year round—they come for
homemade soups, burgers, hand-cut steaks, fresh perch and walleye,
homemade pastas. The windows in front overlook the runway; the
windows in the back overlook the lake.
*1248 Trimotor Drive; 419/285-4321; www.put-in-bayskyway.com/ Open daily
11 am-2:30 am. Closed Thanksgiving and Christmas. Dinner entrees $10-24.*

SUMMER FOOD FINDS/DOWNTOWN PUT-IN-
BAY—Fried perch at the **Boat House** *(419/285-5665; 11 am-1 am
daily)*; Jumbo shrimp at **Book's Seafood on the Boardwalk** *(419/285-
3695; 11-10 daily);* homemade Grand Marnier fudge at the **Candy Bar**
(419/285-2920; 9-9 daily).

HEINEMAN WINERY/SOUTH BASS—When Gustav
Heineman planted a grape arbor four generations ago, it was with the
idea of becoming a vintner. He succeeded. When he dug a well nine
years later, it was with the idea of hitting water. He hit crystal. A lot
of it. So much, in fact, that this winery offers a dual "trip." Take the
underground tour first, where steady footing winds 40 feet below in
the world's largest—and only—walk-in geode. Topside, you'll find a
flowered wine garden, a warm and woody drinking room, a gift shop
and 21 varieties of wine, by the glass or bottle.
*978 Catawba Avenue at Thompson Road; 419/285-2811; www.heinemanswinery.
com Sales year round; drinking room and outdoor garden 10-8 daily, Memorial
Day-Labor Day. Winery and cave tours, 11-5; $6, 6-11 $3.*

PERRY'S CAVE—Fifty-two feet below ground, the cave has been
here since long before Commodore Oliver Hazard Perry allegedly
discovered it in 1813. What's new are all the other things to do. There's a
miniature golf course, a butterfly house, a maze and, for kids, gemstone
panning and a climbing wall. In the antique car barn there are always
ten to fifteen antiques; on Sundays at 2, they join Put-in-Bay's classic-
car parade. Perry's Cave as you see it was the brainchild of the late Skip
Duggan, a great man for ideas. He bought the cave in 2001, tapping
into history, for in 1870 this was the island's first paid attraction. Now
50,000 people a year are paying for the 20-minute trip down into the
cave, to see the lake at the bottom. Dianne Duggan, Skip's daughter, has
been running the butterfly house, where 60 different kinds of colorful
creatures, which arrived from Costa Rica and Malaysia in the chrysalis
stage, flit around a tropical garden.
*979 Catawba Avenue; 419/285-2405; www.perryscave.com Daily to cave
every half hour from 10:15-6 May-Oct; 11-5 spring and fall; $7 for cave, golf
or butterflies; 6-12 $4; combo, three attractions for $16, adults; 6-12 $10. The
antique cars are free.*

STONEHENGE/SOUTH BASS—Stonehenge is a restored 1855 stone farm house and wine press cottage, also stone—wine making was the business of this farm, so the cottage and was built before the house. An ongoing restoration has been in the hands of the Benjamin family, who moved to South Bass in 1980. They bought the old farm house intending to live there, so first they installed an up-to-date kitchen. Fixing up the rest of the house—which meant removing paint from almost everything, including a brass lamp—went on for years; but the result is a wonderful restoration. The only anomaly is the kitchen, which they just haven't had the nerve to take out. Before the Benjamins began offering house tours, they opened a gift shop which has won awards for its eclectic collection of clothing, models, ornaments.
808 Langram Road; 419/285-6134; www.stonehenge-put-in-bay.com Self-guided tours use cassettes; average circuit takes twenty minutes. Daily 11-5 Memorial Day-Sept; tour is $7 for adults, 6-15 $4. Money goes for upkeep. Call for free shuttle to and from ferry, winery or caves.

DE RIVERA PARK/PUT-IN-BAY—Here, with music from the nearby carrousel as background, is a shady grove of serenity amid island madness when boats choke the harbor and tourists swarm the waterfront shops. The fountain sparkles invitingly and the lake breeze is generally cool. The park is named for the wealthy Puerto Rican who bought the island in the 1850s and established the first vineyards. De Rivera made a fortune and lost it all, due to his son's wild living. The park has a handsome and splendid comfort room, which shows just how thoughtfully run Put-in-Bay is as a tourist attraction.

SOUTH BASS ISLAND STATE PARK—On the west edge of the island you can rent a campsite and swim—no lifeguards—from a pebble beach. The famous 1892 Hotel Victory was on this spot until it burned in 1919. Ten full-service hookup sites ($30 weekdays) and 125 primitive non-electric sites ($25) are available for reservation.
1523 Catawba Avenue; 419/797-4530 (main office); 866/644-6727 (reservations); www.ohiostateparks.org

PERRY'S VICTORY AND INTERNATIONAL PEACE MEMORIAL/SOUTH BASS—The largest Doric column in the world honors a 28-year-old naval officer who, with a brother less than half his age as his aide, led a three-hour battle followed by almost 200 years of political harmony between Canada and the U.S. The 317-foot high observation platform affords a panoramic seascape of Perry's battle site and a gull's eye view of these clustered islands and Canada. It's a great place for historical imagery and zoom lenses. A public sand/stone beach is next to the Memorial. No lifeguards.
93 Delaware Avenue, State Route 357; 419/285-2184; www.nps.gov/pevi Open daily mid-April through Oct; 10-8 in summer, reduced hours spring and fall. $3 charge for adults to go up monument; children and seniors free.

LAKE ERIE ISLANDS HISTORICAL SOCIETY MUSEUM/PUT-IN-BAY—In 1998 the Historical Society Museum graduated from an old-photo exhibit in a former bottling

works to a new, 6000-square-foot museum. It has exhibits on hotels, Native Americans and schools; and it has 80 models of boats that have served the islands, starting with a canoe. They also have photos from the days when the Bass Islands were known as the Wine Islands, and the hotel keepers claimed there were absolutely no mosquitoes.
25 Town Hall Place; 419/285-2804; www.leihs.org Open daily in summer, 10-6; 11-5 in spring and fall; closed after Oct. Adults, $2; seniors $1.50, 12-18 $1; families $5 for all.

ACCESS—By Air—Griffing Flying Service offers scheduled service to Put-in-Bay year-round from Griffing-Sandusky Airport in Sandusky, and from Port Clinton. It also offers service to Middle Bass, North Bass and Kelleys Islands. *$42 for an adult one-way to Put-in-Bay. 419/626-5161; www.griffingflyingservice.com* By Boat—Miller Boat Lines runs a ferry service, an 18-minute ride, from Catawba Point to Lime Kiln Dock on the south side of South Bass Island. *Adults $12 round trip; children $1.50; cars $28. The dock-to-dock downtown bus costs $2. 419/285-2421; www.millerferry.com April-Oct; June-Aug departures every half hour 6 am-midnight.* Put-in-Bay Boat Line runs from downtown Port Clinton to downtown Put-in-Bay, a 22-minute ride on the Jet Express, a hydro jet catamaran, one of the fastest in the country. *Roundtrip fares $24 adults, $4 6-12; no cars. Every 45 minutes May-Oct. 800/245-1538; www.jet-express.com/* On-Island Travel—Bikes and golf carts (carts about $15/hour) are available for rent at both docks, at the Depot, 148 Delaware, and at Bayview and Hartford Avenue. Taxis average $3 per person. An island tour tram ($10) leaves from the Depot. For winter travel Joe Kostura offers a $50 round-trip from Catawba to Put-in-Bay on his airboat, by reservation only. *419/285-3106; www.hardwatercharters.com*

LOCAL CUSTOMS—Skip Duggan was the only graduate in the Put-in-Bay class of 1958. His grandfather was the lighthouse keeper on the island. Duggan, who died early in 2007, owned multiple properties on South Bass, though the only one not mortgaged, he used to say, was his lot in the cemetery. But if you ride the tram, rent bicycles or golf carts, ride the bus, visit Perry's Cave or lease a shop, you can thank Skip Duggan. He used to own Jet Express, which he founded in 1989 to bring more people out to his island properties, and then sold out a few years before his death. When Duggan launched the Jet Express, it was the fastest passenger ferry boat in North America. It travels at over 40 mph while propelling 1000 gallons of water a second out both of its jet nozzles. At the turn-of-this century Joe Kostura, who runs fishing charters, began ferrying winter-time passengers on an airboat that was custom made for him in Florida. Kostura's airboat is propelled by a motor on top and, with a tough polymer bottom for protection, it travels on any surface, including the parking lot, a gravel beach, ice and water. It holds six people in its heated cabin, costs less than flying, takes five to twelve minutes. By 2006, Joe said there were eight to ten airboats on South Bass using his design.

ASIDE—Gibraltar Island, a lump of six acres of solid limestone that can be seen from Put-in-Bay harbor, was where posted lookouts first spotted Oliver Perry's battered squadron emerging from the cannon smoke a few miles to the west. Today it's an Ohio State University research center, where summer school students spot squadrons of tourists emerging from the smoke of their charcoal grills. South Bass year-rounders have grown accustomed to the mainlanders, though they've always been mindful of the distinction. Once, a Put-in-Bay school teacher assigned her pupils to write an essay about Julius Caesar. One fifth grader began: "First of all, Julius Caesar was an off-islander."

ASIDE — The showy Lonz Winery castle is still standing on Middle Bass Island, and the Lonz label endures on wine bottles. But the winery hasn't been open to the public since May 2000. Then, on a fine day when lots of people were here drinking wine, a concrete terrace collapsed, killing one man and sending 76 to hospitals. As it happened, this was only six weeks after ODNR had bought the building and 123 acres for a state park (to be developed in 2008). Originally winemaker George Lonz put up this colorful building in 1934 to celebrate the end of Prohibition. Tourists came by the thousands to revel in his liquid hospitality. He opened a dancing pavilion and often entertained by playing his violin. As weekends got wilder, a well-meaning acquaintance tried to put a stop to it by appealing to Lonz's monetary sense. "Your guests are no longer confining their intimate activities to the bushes," he said. "Isn't the spectacle of them cavorting on the lawns bad for business?" "You're absolutely right," replied Lonz. "We'll have to plant more bushes."

THE MIDDLE BASS CEMETERY

—Directly behind the schoolhouse on Runkel Road is the cemetery that's served the island for over a hundred years. The elaborate Gothic mausoleum belongs to German vintner and island pioneer William Rehberg. George and Fannie Lonz are here too. Having lived for their wine, they died with their passions. George buried Fanny with her telephone and took his violin with him.

THE VIEWS

—At least so far, Middle Bass has been a quiet place. That means that one of the best views is at night, when it's so dark you can see only the lights on Perry's monument on South Bass, imagine all the tourists swarming over it, and hear nothing. Too, in an area close to the dock, there's a rocky parapet just out beyond the land. Stand on the cliffs and watch the sailboats.

ACCESS

—**Sonny Schneider** is a great-great grandson of William Rehberg, pioneering vintner on Middle Bass Island. He's keeping up his island connections with his passenger ferry boat, which holds 70 people and runs back and forth on the 12-minute trip between Put-in-Bay and Middle Bass dock. Daily service June-Labor Day, some weekends May and Sept. Boats leave on the hour from Put-in-Bay and return at quarter past from 11 am-midnight in peak season. Adults $10 roundtrip. *419/285-8774; www.sonny-s.com*

Miller Boat Lines offers a car (by reservation only) and passenger service to Middle Bass from Catawba. The trip takes 45 minutes; daily service in season, infrequent service in April and Nov. One-way fares, *adults $8.50; cars $18. 419/285-2421; www.millerferry.com*

GET ME TO CHURCH ON TIME—Come Sunday morning, you'll find two church services at Middle Bass's Town Hall. One is nondenominational, at 10; and at 12:20 there's a Catholic mass. It has to be twenty past because at noon, the priest is in Put-in-Bay boarding the on-the-hour ferry, and after he arrives he has to walk up the hill to Town Hall.

CAMPBELL COTTAGE BED & BREAKFAST/KELLEYS
ISLAND—This bed and breakfast is one of the nicest you'll find anywhere. June and Bill Campbell have three bedrooms for guests, all with bathrooms and two with lake views. (There's a $10 break in the price for the room with the backyard view.) The house's front porch is lined with rockers facing the lake; the big yard is for the use of guests, as is a bench across the street at the beach. There are complimentary bicycles; a book of menus from local restaurants; a slate with tomorrow's breakfast menu; a weather forecast every morning; a fridge for the use of guests; and homemade chocolate chip cookies every day. Besides, June knows almost everything there is to know about Kelley's Island, including details like when bugs may be a problem on a nature trail.
932 West Lakeshore Drive; 877/746-2740, 419/746-2740; www. campbellcottage.com Well-behaved children 12 and over. Rooms are $140 and $150 every day; May 1 to late October; TV's by request.

THE CASINO/KELLEYS ISLAND—Summer weekends bring on the music at a waterfront picnic-table bistro that's about as alive as things get on this quiet island. They're known for seafood stew at lunch, steaks and, on Saturdays, barbecued ribs and chicken. After Labor Day there are clam bakes.
104 Division Street, 419/746-2773; www.kelleysislandcasino.com Daily 11 am- "if people are here I'll stay open". May 1 through Oct.

THE VILLAGE PUMP—It may not be much to look at from the outside; inside its main virtue is that it has two big adjacent rooms, each with a bar. But locally the Village Pump is the hands down favorite place to eat. It's famous for perch dinners, which are sold by the pound. The fried perch also comes in dinners and sandwiches, if your appetite is less than whale-sized. The Village Pump is also famous for potent Brandy Alexanders, the island equivalent of milkshakes, which are sold by the pitcher. This bar and restaurant has been in the same family since the late 1940s.
103 West Lakeshore Drive; 419/746-2281; www.villagepump.com Daily 11-11 March 15-Dec 15.

ISLAND HOUSE—Mr. Trieschman the butcher built this place in 1876. He kept adding rooms as more babies arrived; because he had a big family this white tablecloth restaurant has lots of little nooks for intimate dining. Today's menu offers fine dining: Italian Piedmontese beef, pastas, fresh vegetable specialties.
131 Division Street; 419/746-2600; www.kelleysislandhouse.com Summer Tue-Thur 4-1 am; Fri-Sun noon-1 am; May and Sept-Oct, Thur-Fri 5-11; Sat-Sun 2-10. Dinners $15-$33.

GLACIAL GROOVES—When Kelleys Island quarrymen uncovered the glacial grooves in the 1830s, they had no idea what they'd unearthed—only that they were deep, sinuous furrows, twisted and polished to a fine sheen. Visiting scientists marveled at these intricacies, considered to be the most spectacular anywhere in the world. But the quarry owner was more pragmatic. After he exhausted the island's other limestone deposits, the grooves themselves seemed too valuable to ignore. So he hired a photographer to record them, then proceeded to quarry the rocks. In the end, he left intact a short section, which was deeded to the state in 1932. In 1971 the Ohio Historical Society excavated another long stretch—some 400 feet long, 34 feet wide, and 15 feet deep. Now, protected as a State Memorial, the Kelleys Island Glacial Grooves are the world's best example of rock gouging by glaciers.
At the north end of Division Street.

KELLEYS ISLAND STATE PARK—This park has the best natural sand swimming beach in the islands—a hundred feet long. It also has six miles of hiking trails and 129 campsites, including 84 with electricity; two premium yurts (canvas cabins) with kitchens and showers; and two rent-a-cabins.
920 Division Street; 419/797-4530; www.ohiostateparks.org

NATURE TRAILS—The Kelleys Island Audubon Club is an active group that not only does a monthly bird census, but also puts out brochures on island nature trails. East Quarry, North Pond (which has a mile of boardwalk) and North Shore Loop trails are all in the State Park. So is The Alvar, which is part of the North Shore Loop. This is Ohio's most intact alvar community and one of the world's most southernmost, with unique, stunted vegetation on rocks subject to extreme weathering. In the northeast corner of the island, the Cleveland Museum of Natural History manages Scheele Preserve, which has several kinds of habitat and examples of the rare rock elm; none are labeled. *Brochures on nature trails are available at the Audubon table in the Chamber of Commerce on Division Street; or call 419/746-2258; or www. kelleysislandnature.com and click on natural areas.*

ACCESS—**The Kelleys Island Ferry** has service all year from Marblehead to Kelleys Island. Summer departures are every half hour. *419/798-9763; www.kelleysislandferry.com Round-trip fares are $14 for adults, $7 for children 6-11, $26 for cars.* **Griffing Flying Service** in Sandusky has scheduled flights year-round. *419/626-5161; www.griffingflyingservice.com $42 one way.*

ASIDE—June Campbell grew up in Sandusky, but every summer she came back to Kelleys Island, where her mother had been born. She can point out the house where she stayed as a girl, and where the farm across the road used to be; every morning she was sent over for fresh milk. She can pull out facts on, say, churches: at one time Kelleys Island had five, while now there are just two, one Catholic, one Methodist. When she sees stone walls, she explains how farmers culled those stones from their fields so they could plow. She points out that a third of this 2800-acre island is owned by the state park

(900 acres) and the Cleveland Museum of Natural History (100) and will always be preserved. She talks about the Kelley Mansion, surely the island's most conspicuous built landmark, at Addison Road and East Lakeshore Drive. This large limestone house was built for Datus Kelley's son Addison in 1861-65. (It took a long time to build because the stoneworkers left to fight in the Civil War.) In 1932 some Cleveland sportsmen bought the house; in turn they sold it to a convent which ran a girls' camp here. The only alterations the convent made were to add a bathroom and a dining hall, in an addition to the east. Today, it's a private house, under renovation and unoccupied.

INSCRIPTION ROCK/KELLEYS ISLAND—Right on the shoreline at Lakeshore Drive and Addison Road is the famous rock, now dimly inscribed in pictographs by the carvings of long-ago Indians.

KELLEYS ISLAND WINE COMPANY—In the late 1980s the Zettler family brought wine-making back to the island and within two years their Chardonnays and Rieslings were winning awards. This wine company started out with its own vineyards, but now they're buying grapes from growers in northeastern Ohio. A pleasant wine garden is outside in the yard; inside there's a deli and bistro.
418 Woodford Road about one-half mile east of the water tower; 419/746-2678; www.kelleysislandwine.com Summer hours are 11-9 daily. Closed Nov-April.

ASIDE—One of Ohio's greatest air shows is actually a rather unheralded event that takes place here every fall; millions of Monarch butterflies rest at an early stage in their 2,500-mile migration to their ancestral homes in Mexico, Florida or the Caribbean islands. Their fly-by of the islands is a lovely, compelling sight. The Monarchs return in late spring, but their numbers then are lower and the sight is not so spectacular. A Butterfly Trail starts behind the Kelleys Island Historical Association church building on Division Street. During a season, the trail offers a chance to see as many as 25 butterfly species and 16 kinds of dragonfly.

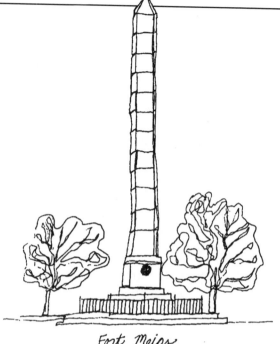

Fort Meigs

Maumee River Valley

Local historians like to say that the Maumee River was the first Ohio Turnpike. A short portage from the southward-flowing river across the divide, it carried the Indians, the French, the British and, finally, the Americans through that big sponge called the Black Swamp to Lake Erie and the St. Lawrence. It was a hotly-contested piece of real estate, a 150-mile freeway for our frontier forebears that the Americans finally won from the Indians and the British. If it weren't for the local battles, the Treaty of Greenville would never have been signed and there would be no Rocky Mountain high or California dreamin'. Americans would be crammed on top of one another east from here to the Atlantic Coast and we'd have a national anthem that wouldn't rhyme. But we won it for ourselves, made a canal and built bridges, drained the land, cut down the trees, built railroads and highways. Then, because we weren't really careful what we'd wished for, the river lost its usefulness, grew older, was ignored and would have liked to have retired to Florida, which it tried several times by way of Grand Rapids. Lately, though, the river has noticed signs of appreciation. While travel agents aren't flying tourists into Toledo Express Airport for Maumee River vacations, natives know a good thing when they see it, even when it's up to their waists. Water doesn't need to be useful. Sometimes it just needs to be.

The Maumee River snakes from Fort Wayne, Indiana, to Defiance, where it fattens—there the Tiffin River flows in from the north, and the Auglaize from the south—and then takes an honest course to Toledo and Lake Erie. Its small-town flavor is carried upstream, at its midsection, from Perrysburg to Defiance.

ASIDE Travelers arriving from the south on I-75 should watch for the minarets. Not only do they guide you to Perrysburg, but these towers beckon Muslims to the Islamic Center of Greater Toledo, the first traditional Islamic mosque west of the nation's capital and a breathtaking sight rising out of the cornfields. If you'd like to join a tour of the inside you may, but you need to make arrangements ahead of time (call 419/874-3500). You will come away from a tour better educated and, having just exited the crowded highways you may reflect, as one Ohio writer did, that, "We are all one … fellow travelers in the human condition, rushing through the landscape of the moment, bound for a common end."

PERRYSBURG—Before Bowling Green became the seat of Wood County, Perrysburg was it, from 1822-1870. Having thus been an early scene of action, Perrysburg has lots of fine old houses and several historic districts, but for a long time it languished. Now, says resident Sydney Rogers, "Perrysburg is coming alive!" She's not the only one who thinks the place has become busier and more lively, though it's also more suburban than the other towns on this tour. That may account for the posh dress shops you'll find here.

THE GUESTHOUSE/PERRYSBURG—Sydney Rogers and her sister Diane, a chef, used to run a restaurant. Today Diane has moved out of retail and into Incredible Foods, a wholesale-only producer of dips, dressing and marinades; and Syd is running the Guesthouse, a B&B in an 1860 house. She has three bedrooms there, but only one-and-a-half bathrooms; and since she's reluctant to ask different parties to share the bathroom, she usually takes only one tenant at a time—or one family group. She has an eye for keeping room decor simple and very attractive. She describes the breakfasts as "hearty". Because she accommodates only one party at a time, Syd has encouraged two neighbors to join her in the B&B business; one is Tina Mather Bothe of the Santa Fe listed below.
122 West Indiana Avenue; 419/874-9223; www.sydanddianes.com Rates are $95 for one person, $115 for two.

PETIT FOURS PATISSERIE/PERRYSBURG—After

years pursuing a business career, Karen Lucas decided on a different objective: bringing a little bit of Paris to downtown Perrysburg. She opened her shop in March 2006, and brought a distinctive presence to Louisiana Avenue. As she says, "We do something unique." Patisseries are her specialty, a cream puff for $3, or a tiny, boxy petit four, a little cake frosted on top and on four sides, for $1.75, or a little scone for 60 cents. That's just for starters. The shop serves breakfast and lunch, and everything is made from scratch on the premises. Drinks range from coffees and teas to fruit smoothies; an extra dollop of whipped cream is 50 cents. Breakfast offerings include a sandwich with eggs and meat, and several granola variations. Lunch offerings include soups (the house staple is tomato basil), salads and sandwiches, including the French croque monsieur, a grilled ham and smoked mozzarella. *219 Louisiana Avenue; 419/872-8510; www.petitfourspastries.com Tue-Fri 7-2; Sat 9-11.*

OTHER RESTAURANTS—Perrysburg has lots of places to

eat. Here are two that pass the popularity test. **Lamplight Café & Bakery**—Six days a week, Kevin Haas follows in his father Jim's footsteps and begins making two- and three-egg breakfast omelets at 7 a.m. Around 11:30 the lunch crowd arrives. Hot sandwiches like turkey, cheese, sauerkraut and horseradish on a croissant, served with chips or potato salad, feed up to 75 people at a sitting. Kevin's sister, Deanna Montion, runs the bakery, producing cookies, brownies, pies, cheesecake and, only on Fridays, the Lamplight's famous cinnamon rolls. *121 West Indiana Avenue in Perry's Landing; 419/874-0125. Open at 7 Mon-Sat; close at 2:30 weekdays, 2 on Sat. Closed Sun and major holidays. Breakfast or lunch, $5-8. No credit cards.* **Stella's** has two levels, with the bar downstairs and tables up, and serves lunch and dinner. Dinner entrees include several beef options, cumin-scented lamb chops and baby beef liver, an uncommon find. *104 Louisiana Avenue; 419/873-8360; www. stellasrestaurantandbar.com Mon-Sat opens at 11. Dinner $13 to $26. (Liver is relatively cheap too.)*

RIBBONRY/PERRYSBURG—Camela Nitschke travels to France

once a year to study seventeenth- and eighteenth-century ribbons at the Bibliothèque Nationale. She picks her favorites from copies made at a factory in St. Etienne where jacquard looms weave ribbons that sell in downtown Perrysburg for $7-$65 a yard. Customers from across the United States arrive or place orders and buy these authentic reproductions to adorn wedding dresses, dolls and historical costumes. Some people just collect them. Jackie Onassis bought ribbons from Camela after they met at the Louvre. Ribbonry also sells ribbon-decorated hats, priced from $65-$350; or it will decorate customers' hats. It also caters happily to locals who come for beautiful hair bows and headbands. *You can also buy a kit to make a ribbon flower, $20-45. 119 Louisiana Avenue; 419/872-0073; www.ribbonry.com Mon-Sat 10-5.*

SANTA FE WAY/PERRYSBURG—Tina Mather Bothe sells

folk art from New Mexico. She also has prints by artist Michael Ives, who works in Tucson depicting folk art memories of his Perrysburg

childhood. But mostly, in spite of her shop name, Bothe is region-impartial as she gathers up merchandise, including some unusual handmade jewelry, Appalachian folk art, clothing for the fuller figure, and art-painted furniture—hand-painted pine trasteros. Tina also runs a one-room B&B with folk art decorations; it's called the Little Purple House and is on West Indiana; shop phone number.
121 Louisiana Avenue; 419/874-0707. Mon-Wed and Sat 10-6, Thur 10-8, Fri 10-7. Shorter hours in winter.

577 FOUNDATION/PERRYSBURG—In the late 1980s, Toledo heiress Virginia Secor Stranahan found herself nearly 80 and living alone on her 12-acre riverside estate, which sloped gently down to the Maumee River. After watching neighboring estates disappear as they were divided into home lots, she decided on a singular course of action. She formed and endowed a non-profit corporation, which permitted her to remain in the house until her death (she was 81 at the time), while the rest of the property would be open to the public for educational, environmental or experimental purposes. So it was. People came to develop organic community gardens, experimental compost heaps, bee hives, a 22-foot high geodesic dome, and a used bookstore. Until her death at 90 in 1997, Stranahan cruised around on her golf cart, watching as a river hiking trail passed through orchards and as a cottage was adapted for Yoga, painting and bird-feeder-building classes. Today the house is used for meetings and retreats; foundation headquarters occupy a 1916 riding stable.
577 East Front Street; 419/872-0305; www.577foundation.org Daily 9-5. Free. Group tours by appointment.

FORT MEIGS STATE MEMORIAL/PERRYSBURG—Built on the edge of the great Black Swamp by William Henry Harrison, the commander of the Northwestern Army, this fort and its signal battles in 1813 helped repel Harrison's worthy Indian adversary, Tecumseh. On the first of May, the British and their Indian allies, set up across the Maumee, established three batteries and three mortar positions, and opened fire on the outmanned and outgunned Americans. Harrison, short on ammunition, offered a gill of whiskey—a quarter of a pint—for every British cannonball that fit his swivels, and his men crawled off into the night looking for them. By the time the siege was over, Harrison owed his men over sixty gallons. Tecumseh, impatient with the white man's ability at digging in and waiting, called Harrison a "groundhog" and asked him and his men to come out and meet his braves, hand-to-hand. The general declined, and the attack was staved off as much by prudence as by valor. (Later that year Harrison's men killed Tecumseh in the war's final battle of consequence, the Battle of the Thames; Harrison went on to become president, but Tecumseh became a legend.) The fort, with its seven blockhouses and stockade wall, was carefully reconstructed—and recently that 1970s reconstruction was renovated. On summer weekends, re-enactment groups camp here, lending some air of authenticity but barely compensating for the encroachment of housing developments almost resting on the fort's walls. Fort Meigs is an Ohio Historical Society site.
29100 West River Road/State Route 65, west of intersection with State Route 25;

419/874-4121; www.ohiohistory.org/places/ftmeigs/ Fort open April-October; Museum, year-round. Wed-Sat 9:30-5; Sun and holidays noon-5. Adults $7, students $3, children 5 and under free. Rates lower in winter.

WALL-TO-WALL WALLEYE—From mid-March to mid-May, up to 12,000 fishermen collect in a four-or-five-mile stretch of the river. In 2006 the harvest was 34,533 walleye captured by anglers from 30 states and Canada. One of the best places to get a view of this phenomenon is Schroeder Farm's Campground, about two miles west of Perrysburg, where Tom Steinwand sells lures and presides over a campground. Here, among the frenzied human species, you can ponder millions of frenzied walleye swimming madly upriver to spawn. In the end the fishermen get what they came for (four-a-day limit) and so do most of the walleye. *26997 West River Road; 419/833-9411. March 20-May 1; 5:30 a.m. to dark. Fishing parking $5; camping $15; boat launch $3. Viewing free.*

ACCESS—From Perrysburg to Waterville to Grand Rapids, the scenic choice is State Route 65 along the south side of the Maumee; en route to Napoleon 65 turns south and you'll follow State Route 110.

ROCHE DE BOEUF (BUFFALO ROCK)/WATERVILLE—

Waterville's famous old Columbian House, a three-story yellow frame building at 3 River Road, has been transformed from a restaurant into a private home. No such options apply to a rock. On this rock Indians gathered for tribal councils. Here, according to the records left by a French settler, a young Indian chief pushed his wife off the precipice for the accidental drowning of their son. And here lie the remnants of the Lima and Toledo Traction Co.'s longest steel-reinforced railroad bridge in the world. People are still angry at the builder, who blasted away a third of Roche de Boeuf. It's a rock with papers, on the National Register of Historic Places. It's also celebrated with a festival in Waterville every year on the fourth Saturday in September—food, crafts, carnival, parade.
For festival information: 419/878-5188. Waterville's River Road, which runs along the river, has a pull-off opposite the rock. From State Route 65 take the bridge (State Route 64) across to Waterville; turn left on River Road; drive about three quarters of a mile to turn-off.

OTSEGO PARK SHELTER/OTSEGO—Voted the handsomest roadside stop along the Maumee, this piece of handiwork, the stately 1938 stone shelterhouse and popular picnic and reunion spot, is near an overlook with a sweeping view of the Maumee. There's a stairway down the bluff to the river. Nice restrooms, too.
20000 West River Road/State Route 65.

NAZARETH HALL/GRAND RAPIDS—Be careful. Sloooow down. First-time travelers on State Route 65 can wrench their necks wondering what lies there. From 1928 Nazareth Hall was a piece of God's Kingdom, the Catholic part, and served as a nationally-known military school run by Ursuline nuns. In 1982 it closed down and remained empty until ten years later, when Bob and Barb Bettinger, from Perrysburg, paid the nuns $35,000 for the building and 37 acres.

Stealing from nuns, you say? Nah. The Bettingers ended up spending ten times the purchase price on new systems and interior designs; then they opened the hall for weddings, receptions and events. This rent-a-palace has a second-floor chapel with stained glass windows and oak pews that can seat 200. The stained glass windows, chandeliers and terrazzo floor in the original dining room now ornament a reception hall. The nun's lunchroom is a ladies' room. And so on. For an outdoor ceremony the grotto has a replica of the grotto in Lourdes, France. And the staff chefs are known for delicious meals. Rentals should be booked well in advance.

21211 West River Road/State Route 65; 419/832-2900; www.nazarethhall.com Office hours Mon-Fri 9-5. Rental fees: chapel or grotto $500; either reception room $1200; rehearsal dinners and receptions, per person.

GRAND RAPIDS AND THE RIVER—Grand Rapids is an

entirely agreeable destination. The main reason is that the town isn't very high, so it's close to the river, which is fully visible all along the bank. (Alas, that's rare otherwise—for much of this route it's hard to see the river.) Grand Rapids also has a walk along the river, with intermittent benches and swings where you can sit and watch the sunset. And Grand Rapids has things to do and see, including a pretty street full of shops. The town is perched between two parks: Mary Jane Thurston State Park just to the west and Providence, a Toledo Metropark, is just across the river and offers canal boat rides in summer. Nice as it is to wander through Grand Rapids on a fine summer day, keep in mind the price of being so near to the great Maumee. That is, the occasional possibility of too much river, for this charming business district has been underwater more than once. Area resident Steve Parsons once said, "Our determination to live here is equal to the force of that river." Must be. Over the years merchants notched the high water marks in their stores, cleaned up and carried on. Buildings might have a notch or two or three. In the pharmacy, the door frame to the little museum room was cut at the level of the 1913 flood. You have to stand on your tiptoes to reach the notch-level of that same flood in the Olde Gilead County Store. At LaRoe's restaurant there's a plaque on the bar, waist high, commemorating the level of the 1959 flood, and another, knee high, marking 1982. If you want to get the whole picture in one place, there's a display board at one end of Front Street next to Shambles, a British tearoom and gift shop. Other towns use similar boards to measure campaign money for the YMCA. In Grand Rapids it records the high water level of each flood.

The Mill House

THE MILL HOUSE BED & BREAKFAST/GRAND
RAPIDS—Once among the working, steam-driven flour mills on
the Maumee, this B&B is the most charming place to stay during a
trip along the river. Four well-appointed, air-conditioned, comfortable
downstairs bedrooms with private baths serve the guest. Proprietors
Ron and Kathy Munk live upstairs, and in the mornings Kathy cooks
a full breakfast on weekends, and a continental style version with a hot
dish on weekdays. The breakfast room and deck overlook the Gilead
Side-Cut Canal, Bluebell Island and the Maumee: a wonderful view on
a sunny morning. Walk down to tiny Bluebell Island, which has two
benches and a peony; you can reach it by a tiny pedestrian bridge.
*24070 Front Street; 419/832-6455; www.themillhouse.com No smoking, no pets,
no children under 8. Room rates: $80-140. Lower during week. Special discounts
for pastors of any denomination.*

LaRoe's of Grand Rapids

LAROE'S RESTAURANT/GRAND RAPIDS—Dave LaRoe
is the unofficial ambassador of Grand Rapids. He arrived in town as a
wet-behind-the-ears college graduate who meshed well with a wet-up-
to-your knees kind of town. With the help of friends, he renovated a
building and opened an ice cream shop, lived in the apartment behind
it, through which he dragged the store's daily trash, and began a life.
Youth and energy inspired him to move on from ice cream and buy
a tavern across the street. Another nice Victorian renovation later, he
took a second-floor apartment for himself and launched a restaurant
that now serves 100 people downstairs and has banquet facilities for
150 on the second floor. The husky, bearded brother, Tom LaRoe, is the
unofficial chef of Grand Rapids. He bakes the great country chicken
and cooks the BBQ country ribs, steak and seafood that tour buses stop
for. The homemade cream pies have their own reputation, especially the
chocolate mousse which is often seen wandering home through town,
but in Styrofoam containers.
*24138 Front Street; 419/832-3082; www.grandrapidsohio.com Mon-Fri 11-2;
Mon-Thur 5-9; Fri 5-10; Sat 11-10; Sun 9-8. Dinners $10-16.*

ASIDE LaRoe's Restaurant is the repository for a completely
distinctive art gallery: the private collection of Grand Rapids artist,

Bill Kuhlman. Kuhlman worked as a commercial artist, but for his own pleasure began doing charcoal portraits of the local citizens from memory and photographs. Dave LaRoe began hanging the portraits in the main dining room in 1981. There about 50 local citizens, mostly deceased, are perpetually hanging about. Kuhlman was urged to do a self-portrait but hesitated because it brought to mind his own mortality; ultimately, he agreed. But some local mortals still eating and breathing, like ex-mayor Jim Carter, are holding out. He explains that he wants a wall of his own.

SHOPPING/GRAND RAPIDS—With 1006 citizens, Grand Rapids has 20 antique and specialty shops and you can have it all to yourself off-season. Stores include: **Dandy's Lane** *(24164 Front Street; 419/832-6425; www.dandyslane.com)* sells clothing, collectibles, and superb homemade fudge, 50 flavors, which the owner makes in the second-floor kitchen. **Olde Gilead Country Store** *(24139 Front Street, 419/832-7651)* is an upscale general store with an old-fashioned candy counter (over 100 kinds of candy). The second floor has toys that don't need batteries and a sea of greeting cards. A few years ago **Fernando's, a Mexican restaurant,** *(24129 Front Street; 419/832-1503)* took over the premises that used to be the Old Fashioned Ice Cream Shoppe. So now Fernando's serves Mexican food AND ice cream from Archbold. **Village Apothecary,** *(24187 Front Street, 419/832-4615; www.myhometownpharmacy.com)* has a little museum in the back, with the original owner's apothecary bottles, paperwork and pharmaceuticals on display. The bestseller is the antiseptic "Bag Balm", a soothing ointment for cow's udders and baby's bottoms.
The drugstore is closed Sundays; others here are open seven days, including Sun noon-5.

THE TOWN HALL/GRAND RAPIDS—In 1898 Grand Rapids, in existence for only 65 years (and called Gilead for the first 35) spent its wisest $6959 ever. They purchased land near the end of Front Street and built a Romanesque Town Hall that's been in use ever since. The second floor provides a mini-opera house. It's complete with a slanted stage and a trap door, dressing rooms under the stage, balcony seating and footlights. Historically plays, graduations, recitals, reunions, and even medicine shows were held here. The bell in the tower still rings and has been used to announce meetings, to warn of floods and, more recently, when it's time for the canning of apple butter at the annual Applebutter Fest in October. The village council meets downstairs, where the arts council and the sheriff's satellite office are.

ASIDE Approximately 15 percent of Grand Rapids's population belongs to the local Historical Society. That hefty percentage should make other Ohio towns weep. A visionary mayor, Jimmy Carter, now a Wood County commissioner, encouraged the formation of the Historical Society in 1976. During Rapids Rally, the second weekend in July, the society sponsors a play, usually a musical, in the Town Hall auditorium, where the big windows are thrown open and actors compete with crickets in the night air. The shows at Town Hall and the Applebutter Festival, which is the second Sunday in October, have made the Society the richest non-profit organization in town, and it plows the money back into the village on a regular basis.

The Kerr House

KERR HOUSE/GRAND RAPIDS—And speaking of riches,
what's that black limousine doing driving through town? Well, there
really is another place for guests to stay overnight in Grand Rapids. It's
just that, well, it'll cost ya. Laurie Hostetler has welcomed hundreds
of guests to her world-renowned holistic health retreat just two blocks
up from Front Street. Since 1980, the immaculately restored 35-room
Victorian has been accommodating six to eight guests who would like
breakfast in bed, mind-body exercises, massages, facials, manicures,
pedicures, hand and foot waxings, reflexology, elegant candlelit dinners
and peace and quiet all for $2950. (That's for five nights in a private
room. Take off $400 for a double.) Clients include a Dutchman who's
built bridges all over the world, Saudi Arabians, ranchers from Montana,
and famous folk who wish to remain nameless, at least here. And
because it's the way it should be, weary moms show up too. Some from
Texas, for the day. Others from Chicago, for the weekend. Doesn't
matter. Laurie and her staff of 30 housekeepers and specialists pamper
men and women alike and do it so very well that most come back for
more.

*17777 Beaver Street; 419/832-1733; www.TheKerrHouse.com Reservations
are often booked a year in advance. Weekend rates (two nights) $850 single, $750
double; three nights $1575 single, $1375 double; five nights $2950 single, $2550
double.*

PROVIDENCE METROPARK/GRAND RAPIDS—In
Providence Park you'll find a trailhead for the wonderful long **Towpath
Hiking Trail,** which goes downriver to Farnsworth Metropark at
Waterville. The trail's choice destination is in between, **Bend View
Metropark,** six miles from Grand Rapids and two miles from
Waterville—for the shorter walk, just start from Waterville. Bend
View is a beautiful river overlook, not accessible by car. Even so, the
park is installing a parking lot and restrooms. How's that again? It
will stay inaccessible because the facilities (except for a shelter house
already there) will be a mile away. *Toledo Metroparks, 419/265-2920; www.
metroparkstoledo.com A car entrance to Providence is at 13200 U.S. 24, half a
mile east of State Route 578, the bridge to Grand Rapids. Farnsworth is upriver*

from Waterville (two miles from that bridge) at 8505 South River Road/U.S. 24.
Canal Boat Ride—In warm weather at Providence Metropark you can
take a canal boat ride. A team of mules, Molly and Sally, pull your boat
along a mile-long restored section of the Miami & Erie Canal; you'll
even go through a lock. The steel-hulled boat is 60 feet long and 14
feet wide, an authentic freight boat design with two small cabins and
an open deck; it holds up to 65 people. On the way back to where you
started, if you wish the boat will let you off at the Isaac Ludwig Mill,
which offers saw- and grist-milling demonstrations. Rides take about
45 minutes. (For a quieter ride, go when schools are out; the ride is very
popular for school groups.) *In May, September and October, rides are on the
hour Wed-Fri 10-2, weekends noon-4. From Memorial Day to Labor Day, Wed-
Fri 11-4, weekends noon-4. Adults $6, seniors $5, 3-12 $3.*

ACCESS—West from Grand Rapids take State Route 65 to 110, which
follows the river to Napoleon. West from Napoleon to Defiance, take
State Route 424, which hugs the river's north bank most of the way.
It's a scenic route. In fact Harley Davidson Inc. names it one of the
ten best touring roads in the U.S. Before leaving Napoleon, 424 passes
Riverview Frosty Boy, an old-fashioned sandwich and ice cream drive-in
with picnic tables. Try the barbecue beef. *Riverview Frosty Boy, 1000 West
Riverview Avenue, Napoleon; 419/599-3830.*

HENRY COUNTY COURTHOUSE/NAPOLEON—The
white tower of the Henry County Courthouse looms over Napoleon:
a promise of the promised land. In 1879 a downtown fire destroyed
the courthouse and 21 buildings. In 1882, a new one of brick and
sandstone, crowned with a 160-foot white clock tower, was built. Atop
the tower a 15-foot Goddess of Justice stood, an elegantly bedecked,
buxom Victorian madam rising magnificently overhead. The people of
Henry County are proud of their courthouse; they passed a $4 million
levy for its restoration, which was completed in 1998. The courthouse
was the first building in the county on the National Register of Historic
Places, and even today it is just one of four, all in Napoleon (a paucity
not due to a lack of architectural merit in other nearby localities.) One
is the Sheriff's Residence and Jail, at 123 East Washington. The other
two are churches: St. Augustine Catholic Church at 221 East Clinton at
Monroe, in High Victorian Gothic, and the First Presbyterian Church,
303 West Washington, an Arts and Crafts confection in a gorgeous
variegated red sandstone.
*Courthouse, 660 North Perry at Washington; tours may be arranged through the
Chamber, 419/592-1786.*

ASIDE One of the attractions of State Route 424 between Napoleon
and Defiance, is the rural character of the area. But the road does
pass through a place called Florida, which in 2000 had a population
of 246. A few miles east of Florida, you'll pass (but may not be
able to see) Girty's Island, named for Simon Girty and his ruthless
brothers, who supposedly had been raised by Indians after their
parents were killed in a raid. In the late eighteenth century brother
James Girty had a trading post on the north bank, and for a while
Simon took refuge on the island. Simon's ruthlessness fighting with
the Indians and British against the Americans inspired an outdoor
drama, "The White Savage", which is performed on the other side of

Ohio, at Schoenbrunn Amphitheatre, New Philadelphia, every summer *(330/339-1132; www.trumpetintheland.com)* After the Battle of Fallen Timbers in 1794 Girty moved to Canada, where the British rewarded him with a farm. The island that bears his name (or his brother's) was home to an amusement park at the turn of the last century, and then to a dance hall.

INN ON THIRD STREET/DEFIANCE—Stephanie and Terry
Newman own a pretty 1858 house at Third and Jefferson. Downstairs has a living room and kitchen which guests may use. Upstairs under the eaves are two nicely furnished bedrooms, one with a queen bed and one with two twin beds, and a bathroom to share. The other half of the house is separate and complete unto itself, kitchen and all, and that's where the Newmans live. Breakfast is continental during the week; cooked on weekends.
325 Third Street; 419/438-8053. Rooms are $70. Wireless internet.

CHARLIE'S DOWN UNDER/DEFIANCE—Old Defiance
College coeds will remember Charlie's Down Under as the Black Lantern, a dressy dinner spot and the place they were taken to if their date had any money left after buying beer. Today Charlie's serves a more responsible crowd, the employed, and it's up-to-date in business casual rather than dressy garb. It opened in 1951, in the basement as the name implies. Just two families have been in charge, the current proprietor being Peter Lundberg, who used to man the grill, a post that Chef Arron Weible has taken over. Charlie's is known for "halves", a successful psychological dining tool allowing customers to buy half of many menu items, and thus end up going home with half the guilt.
200 Clinton Street; 419/782-2283; www.charliesdownunder.net Mon-Fri 11-2 and 5-9; Sat 5-9; closed Sun. Lunch $6; dinner $18.

KISSNER'S RESTAURANT/DEFIANCE—Kissner's is the
informal place where Defiance eats, the place where you might see race driver Sam Hornish Jr., the place where the mayor meets with citizens every Wednesday morning for breakfast. The building dates from 1888, and the high, ornate cherry and mahogany bar is a splendid memento from 1901. The restaurant has been called Kissner's since 1928. Food is good and modestly priced, with grilled cheese at lunch for $1.55, and dinners from $7 to $20. If you come to meet the mayor (or any other morning) you can order the breakfast Grand Slam, with fries, onions, peppers, cheese, sausage gravy and two eggs for $5.45.
524 Clinton Street; 419/782-1116. Mon-Sat 5:30 a.m. to 1 a.m. Closed Sun.

FORT DEFIANCE/DEFIANCE—At least a dozen Indian tribes
once united into one huge village at "The Glaize" (now Defiance) and their fields of corn stretched as far as the eye could see. Their 1792 Grand Council held here included chiefs from nearly all the tribes east of the Mississippi and from Canada. Two years later General "Mad" Anthony Wayne arrived, and built Fort Defiance. Said to be the strongest fort built during the Indian campaign, it inspired Wayne's words, "I defy the English, Indians, and all the devils to take it." His colleague, General Charles Scott, responded with, "Then call it Fort

Defiance!" And they did. Abandoned in 1796, it was succeeded a
century later by an exact replica with 533 donated logs. Vandals ruined it
so it was later torn down. In 1904 Carnegie funds built another fortress
on the spot, the handsome red sandstone Defiance Public Library. The
most respected historical building in town, the library has a wonderful
reading room with stained glass windows and a view of the river.
Outside, in the surrounding Fort Defiance City Park, a granite boulder
marks the location of the original fort's flagstaff, the surveying point for
all land northward to Canada. It was from here that Wayne marched off
to do battle at Fallen Timbers. The view of the confluence is wonderful.
Library: 320 Fort Street; 419/782-1456; www.defiancelibrary.org

LOCAL HERO—Sam Hornish, Jr., who grew up in Defiance
and lives in Napoleon, won the Indianapolis 500 in 2006. Defiance
celebrated with a parade that, in this town of 16,000, drew 10,000
people on a rainy day. There's also a triangular granite moment in
Pontiac Park, near the entrance from Clinton Street. It has a likeness of
Hornish and a checkered background, like the flag at Indy.
For Pontiac Park, go north across the Clinton Street bridge and turn right.

ASIDE Architecture buffs and many others will be dismayed at the
sight of the Defiance County Courthouse's third floor. In the 1950s
the top of the beautiful Victorian courthouse, including the tall clock
tower, was lopped off and a floor was added. In November 2006
voters agreed not to tear down the old courthouse; perhaps that will
be followed by plans to restore it.
221 Clinton Street

DEFIANCE COLLEGE—It's been heard that at least some high-
school seniors choose Defiance College for its name. Founded in 1850,
this four-year liberal arts college has 1000 students, mostly from Ohio,
with a strong minority from Michigan. The rest, from 14 other states
and two foreign countries, come to study and brave the landscape.
The campus is flat, prone to mud from driving spring rains and to ice
from windy winter storms. Two handsome, original buildings burned
down, giving rise to a campus dominated by 1950ish flat-roofed boxy
structures—a notable exception is the striking modern Pilgrim Library,
which was new in 1992. What the campus lacks aesthetically is made up
for by personal attention to students. It's a one-on-one sort of school
with faculty and administration available, practically, on 24-hour call.
They deal with the worries and war whoops as well as offer classes in
41 major areas of study with a well-established program in education.
In recent years Defiance has launched service and civic engagement
programs that have garnered national recognition.
701 North Clinton Street; 419/784-4010; www.defiance.edu

LOCAL HEROINES/DEFIANCE—The book, *The Prize Winner
of Defiance, Ohio: How My Mother Raised 10 Kids on 25 Words or Less* came
out in 2001. The author was Terry Ryan, sixth of the ten children. She
told the story of how her mother, Evelyn Ryan, had enabled the family
to get through the 1950s and 1960s by writing jingles that won contests,
while her alcoholic father drank up his earnings. The idea for the book
came after Evelyn Ryan's death in 1998, when all ten children gathered

in Defiance and found memorabilia of the prize-winning years. By 2005 the book that Terry Ryan wrote became a movie starring Julianne Moore and Woody Harrelson—a movie that was filmed, alas, not in Defiance but in Canada. Even so, it's a rare honor for a town to have its name and state in the title of a successful book and movie, which accounts for the movie costumes on exhibit at the **Greater Defiance Area Tourism and Visitor's Bureau** *(301 South Clinton Street; 419/782-0739; 10-4 weekdays.)* The tourist office also has a flyer on the *Prize Winner*, listing, along with a map, local sites associated with the story, including the house where the Ryans lived, at 801 Washington Avenue. The book itself is on sale locally at **Bookland**, which carries paperback editions in two sizes *(1500 North Clinton in Defiance Northtowne Mall; 419/782-8293)*. When the book first came out, Defiance College learned that as a young woman, Evelyn Ryan had hoped to attend the college but the partial scholarship she was offered wasn't enough; in 2001 the college awarded her a posthumous honorary degree. Then when the movie came out, Terry Ryan and her siblings endowed a scholarship in their mother's name for students interested in writing. But as the movie came out Terry Ryan knew she had cancer; she died in May, 2007. Mourners were urged to make memorial contributions to the Evelyn Ryan Endowment at Defiance College.

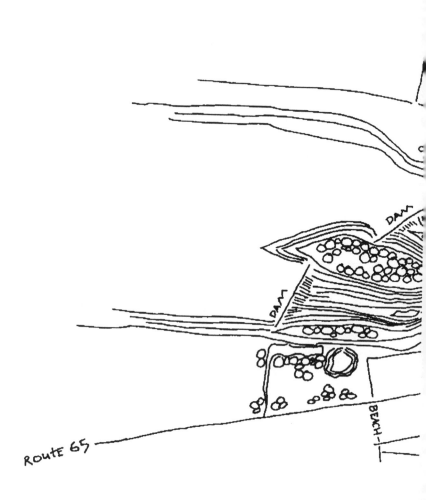

ROUTE 65

DAM

DAM

BEACH

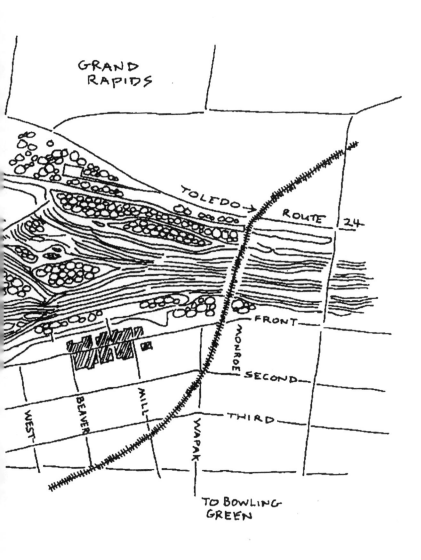

Index

A
577 Foundation, 195
Abigail Tea Room, 176
Adams County, 54-67
Adams County Courthouse, 54
Adams County Heritage Center, 57
Adams Lake Prairie State Nature Preserve, 64
Adams Lake State Park, 64
Ahoy, The, 183
Aladdin, The, 97
Alcove, The, 111
Alessandro's Ristorante, 164
Ambassador's Antiques, 86
Amish & Mennonite Heritage Center, 140
Amish Country, 132-143
Amish Culture Tours, 143
Amish in Adams County, 59
Amish in Holmes County, 132-143
Amish Oak Furniture Company, 137
Anchor Inn, 183
Antioch College Campus, 73
Antioch Review, 75
Apple Butter Inn, 122
Applebutter Festival, 199
Arthur Morgan House, 70
Ash Cave, 46, 48-49
Ashley's Island House, 183
Ashtabula, 163-166
Ashtabula Harbor, 164-165
Athens, 30-39
Athens County Courthouse, 35
Athens Cycle Path Bicycle Shop, 34-35
Auctions in Amish Country, 142
Aunt Bee's Quilts & More, 113
Austyn's, 21
Axel & Harry's Waterfront Grille, 184-185

B
B Hammond Interiors, 97
Bead Therapy Bead Shop, 113
Bear Run Inn: Cabins & Cottages, 42
Beer Barrel Saloon, 184

C

About the Editor

A regional writer since moving to Ohio is 1980, Jane Ware was a history major, a Columbus Museum of Art docent, and a lifelong architectural hobbyist. Ware spent the last two years revisiting the particular places in this volume and finding new particular places, as well, providing her finely tuned opinions about where one should spend their valuable and often limited vacation time.

Ware spent eight years driving around Ohio collecting good buildings for the previous two-volume *Building Ohio* series, the state's first ever architectural guides.

Jane received the 2002 Ohio Historic Preservation Award for Public Education and Awareness for *Building Ohio: A Traveler's Guide to Ohio's Urban Architecture* and the 2003 Ohio Historic Preservation Award for Public Education and Awareness for *Building Ohio: A Traveler's Guide to Ohio's Rural Architecture.*